广西大学立项项目　高级实用英语系列教材

2021年度广西高等教育本科教学改革工程项目成果

LEGAL ENGLISH

Cases and Practice

梁　卿 ◎ 主　编

董银秀 ◎ 副主编

李　珊
韦乔钟 ◎ 编　委
王　婷

法律英语

案例与实践

世界图书出版公司
广州 · 上海 · 西安 · 北京

图书在版编目（CIP）数据

法律英语案例与实践 / 梁卿主编；董银秀副主编 . -- 广州：世界图书出版广东有限公司，2023.1
ISBN 978-7-5232-0063-6

Ⅰ . ①法… Ⅱ . ①梁… ②董… Ⅲ . ①法律—英语 Ⅳ . ① D9

中国国家版本馆 CIP 数据核字（2023）第 005946 号

法律英语案例与实践
FALÜ YINGYU ANLI YU SHIJIAN

主　　编：梁　卿
副 主 编：董银秀
责任编辑：程　静
责任技编：刘上锦
装帧设计：苏　婷
出版发行：世界图书出版有限公司　世界图书出版广东有限公司
地　　址：广州市海珠区新港西路大江冲 25 号
邮　　编：510300
电　　话：020-84184026 84453623
网　　址：http://www.gdst.com.cn/
邮　　箱：wpc_gdst@163.com
经　　销：新华书店
印　　刷：佛山市浩文彩色印刷有限公司
开　　本：787 mm × 1 092 mm　1/16
印　　张：15.75
字　　数：411 千字
版　　次：2023 年 1 月第 1 版　2023 年 1 月第 1 次印刷
国际书号：ISBN 978-7-5232-0063-6
定　　价：68.00 元

前言

《法律英语案例与实践》是针对全球化、法治化时代背景下国家为促进中西法律文化交流、讲好中国立法故事、培育通晓国内外法律知识的“法律＋英语”复合型应用型人才之重要需求而设计编写的高级实用法律类英语系列教程之一。本教程紧扣学习者生产生活环境中的热点问题和典型场景，以丰富、翔实的国内外法律英语报刊和官方网站阅读材料为内容依托，以案释法、法条学法、法条学语、法条学译、普法海报阅读等为促成手段，全方位、多视角英汉双语呈现国内外众多关于民生的法务事宜。通过本教材的学习，学习者的法律知识、法律英语阅读能力、法条汉英互译能力、知法守法用法意识和英汉跨文化交际能力等能够得以提升，进而切实服务于法治社会法治文明。

鉴于目前适合学习的法律英语材料较为匮乏，特编写此书，以满足广大学习者的需求。

一、教程编写原则

1. 紧扣区域特色，展现不同国家的法文化和法律语言

本教材甄选域外和国内具有特色的真实案例和典型场景，提供足量英汉双语阅读材料，基于全球化视野呈现、例释、探讨关乎民生的众多法务事宜。主要选取中国、英国、美国、澳大利亚、新西兰、新加坡、马来西亚等国的法文化资料，既让学习者了解国外与民众安全相关的法律法规，又让学习者熟知国内民法典所倡导的众多益于社会和谐生活幸福的法律原则。力求助力学习者了解相关立法精神，增强知法守法意识和维权能力，还能在此基础上掌握比较纯正的法律英语知识。

2. 以案释法、法条学法、法条学语、法条学译并举，多模态增强法条的理解和翻译能力

在法律英语学习中，法条阅读是绝佳素材。本教程三大篇选材新颖，内容丰富，安排有序，各篇各小节包含大量案释、法条学法、法条学语、法条学译，以阅读、翻译、图释为主要学习途径，多模态增强学习者法条的理解和翻译能力。

3. 普法海报教学成果展示，践行学以致用

本教材第三篇最后一节展示主题各异、多姿多彩、内涵深刻的普法海报教学成果，图文并茂、生动形象地呈现学习者对法律知识的有效多维认知和高阶思维能力，呈现同学们学以致用的成果产出和法宣行动。

二、教程内容简介

本教程的所有选篇、背景知识、法条和练习都围绕“加强法治教育、普及法律知识、弘扬法律精神、习得法律语言”理念建构，旨在提升法制、普法、法宣力度和汉英双语精准法律语言表述能力。全教程由三大篇组成。

第一篇《域外安全案例》关注国外法律热点，案例囊括社区安全、校园安全、食品安全、旅行安全、网络安全和交易安全六个小节情景。每个小节自导读引入，精选三篇域外英语法律案例类阅读文章，提供相关背景知识和重点词汇辅助理解，设置多选、简答、英译汉、正误判断、选词填空等课后练习巩固知识；深度讨论是适度的拓展和延伸，敦促学习者深入思考和探究各小节主题法制内容；各小节罗列枚举的国内外法条，方便学习者精准理解相关法律法规，增长法律知识和法律语言；图文并茂的域外普法海报为学习者提供更生动直观的法制生活情景，便于掌握原汁原味的普法语言。全篇旨在引领学习者认识和增强其社区、校园、食品、旅行、网络和交易不同生产生活情景方面的安全意识和风险防范意识。

第二篇《民法典案例》聚焦《中华人民共和国民法典》六大基本原则，包括平等原则、自愿原则、公平原则、诚信原则、守法和公序良俗原则、绿色原则六个小节。每个小节通过典型案例解读基本原则及其法律适用。各小节罗列枚举的商标法、民法典、婚姻法、消费者权益保护法、著作权法等相关法条速览及形式多样的产出性任务，帮助学习者精准理解民法典法律规定，增长法律知识。全篇旨在讲好中国立法故事，传递法治好声音。

第三篇《法律英语实践》着眼各种类型的法条翻译和普法海报作品展示，由六个小节组成，阐释标准法律表达术语、法条翻译技巧和规范、法律语言语法特色，设置汉英翻译练习操练巩固相关内容，引领和帮助学习者习得严谨、标准、规范的英汉双语法律表述能力。普法海报习作专栏体现有效及时的学以致用和有益有趣的法制宣讲。全篇旨在展现学习者不断增强的法律意识和法律参与感、获得感和认同感。

三、教程使用说明

1. 本教程有三篇共 18 个小节，建议第一篇、第二篇每个小节用 2 个课时，共计 24 学时；第三篇每个小节用 1 个学时完成，共计 6 学时。老师可课前安排学生预习、课后复习，课内教师对阅读、练习、法条难点进行讲解。

2. 案例阅读是本教程的特色和重点，为确保学习者切实精准理解案例深入思考领悟，教师可以布置学生课前精细阅读，以翻转课堂形式梳理、讨论、检查、点评、拓展，同时给予重点内容面授和详解。法条学译是本教程的难点，老师需指导和教授学生进行精准的英汉互译实践，习得法律翻译的严谨性和准确性。

3. 依据第一篇、第二篇各小节的内容，布置学生制作创意普法海报、普法微视频，巩固复习所学法律知识，剖析中西法律语言异同，为普法宣传尽绵薄之力，着力提升民众法治意识，引领民众为法治社会、法治文明贡献力量。

本教材在策划和编写过程中得到广西团校党委副书记李珊老师的专业指导，此外，参加本书素材收集整理及编译工作的还有贾春缘、江曦昀、罗漫粤、罗宇曦、潘红美、吴懿等，在此一并表示衷心的感谢！

由于编者水平和经验有限，本教程难免存在疏漏与不足，敬请专家、广大教师和学习者批评指正，以便修正和提高。

补充说明：为教学目的，本教程在合理的范围内对案例中包含的个人信息进行去标识化和匿名化处理，如有雷同，纯属巧合，望谅解！

编　者

2022 年 6 月 15 日

目录 Contents

第一篇 域外安全案例

第一章 社区安全案例

第二章 校园安全案例

第三章 食品安全案例

第四章 旅行安全案例

第五章 网络安全案例

第六章 交易安全案例

第二篇 民法典案例

第七章 平等原则案例

第八章　自愿原则案例

第九章　公平原则案例

第十章　诚信原则案例

第十一章　守法和公序良俗原则案例

第一篇

域外安全案例

导读

社区是城市治理的基础单元，同时也是人们日常生活的重要载体。社区内的安全隐患，时刻威胁着居民的人身财产安全。如何建设安全社区，营造和谐家园？本章美国的安珀警报、新加坡的鞭刑等案例告诉我们：社区是个家，安全靠大家！

案例阅读

Passage 1

A Teenager Was Charged with Kidnapping and Attempted Murder

青少年被控绑架和谋杀未遂

ALTON, Ill. – A 15-year-old is facing **kidnapping** and **attempted murder charges** after stealing a van while a 3-month-old was still inside the vehicle, promptly authorities in Alton to issue an **AMBER Alert**.

According to Alton Police Chief Marcos Pulido, the kidnapping occurred Friday, March 26 just before 7:30 p.m. in the 700 block of Spring Street.

A woman told police she had parked her gold 2001 Chevy Venture and briefly went inside a residence on Spring Street. Her 3-month-old baby was still inside the vehicle. When the woman left the residence, her van and infant son were missing.

Alton Police contacted surrounding **law enforcement agencies** and an AMBER Alert was issued over the child's disappearance. ①

Police located the stolen van a short time later near the intersection of Wescott Street and Central Avenue. However, the infant was not in the vehicle.

Just before 11:40 p.m. that same evening, Chief Pulido said a concerned citizen found the baby near Common and Elliott streets. Officers learned this concerned citizen saw the AMBER Alert and began driving around to look for the stolen van and missing child. They were in the area of Common and Elliott when they heard the sounds of a crying child and then found the infant laying in a ditch.

Paramedics arrived at the scene and the 3-month-old baby was taken to a local hospital. The baby did not suffer any severe injuries.

Detectives continued working over the weekend to identify a **suspect**, Pulido said. Investigators identified the suspect as a 15-year-old boy and located him on March 30 at about 4:10 p.m., driving in the 1st block of W. Delmar Avenue. The suspect attempted to run away on foot but was taken into **custody**.

Pulido said the suspect will not be named since he is a **juvenile**, only that the teenager lives in Alton and is believed to have acted alone in stealing the vehicle.

The Madison County State's Attorney's Office charged the 15-year-old attempted **murder**, kidnapping, and other **offenses** related to **motor vehicle theft**.

(**Source:** https://fox2now.com/news/illinois/charges-filed-in-alton-amber-alert-case/)

Background Information

AMBER Alert System

安珀警报系统

安珀警报（AMBER Alert）是“America's Missing: Broadcasting Emergency Response”的缩写，即“美国失踪人口：广播紧急回应”。该系统由执法机构、广播电视、无线通信、网络公司、交通运输机构合作组成。当确认发生儿童绑架案后，政府部门会通过各种媒体向公众发布“安珀警告”，如通过电视、广播、手机、电子邮件、路边电子告示牌等现代讯息传播方法，立即告知整个社区绑架案的详细信息，发动民众协助提供破案线索，使民众成为破案的眼睛和耳朵，让搜寻的范围与力度大幅加大，可以帮助父母早日找回孩子。

这套系统的名称来自 1996 年在美国德州阿灵顿被绑架并杀害的九岁女童安珀·海格曼（Amber Hagerman）。正是她的悲剧，才促成了今日美国这套完善的广播警报系统。

美国的这套系统也为其他国家所借鉴。英国就在 2002 年从萨塞克斯郡开始试行类似的“儿童救援警报系统”（Child Rescue Alert System），欧洲不少国家的安珀警报已经实现了跨国协同。

What are Amber Alerts?

The AMBER Alert System began in 1996 when Dallas–Fort Worth broadcasters teamed up with local police to develop an early warning system to help find **abducted** children. AMBER stands for America's Missing: Broadcast Emergency Response and was created as a legacy to 9–year–old Amber Hagerman (安珀 · 海格曼) who was kidnapped while riding her bicycle in Arlington, TX, and then brutally murdered. Other states and communities soon set up their own AMBER plans as the idea was adopted across the nation.

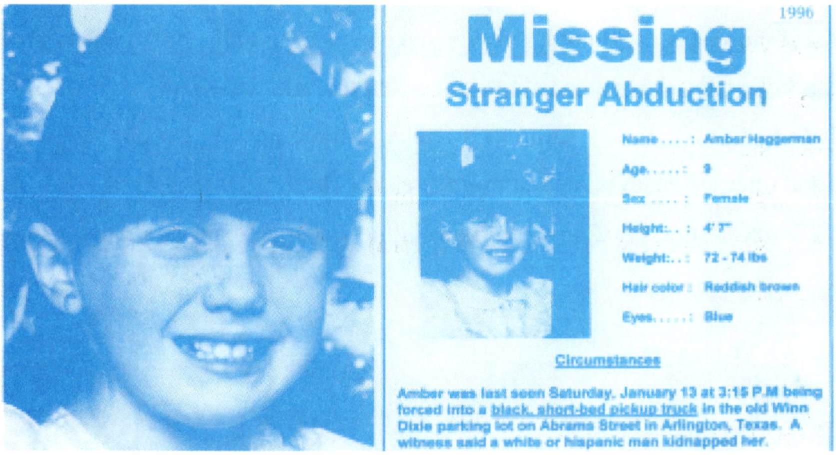

How does it work?

Once law enforcement has determined that a child has been abducted and the abduction meets AMBER Alert criteria, law enforcement notifies broadcasters and state transportation officials. ② AMBER Alerts interrupt regular programming and are broadcast on radio and television and DOT highway signs. AMBER Alerts can also be re-disseminated through lottery, digital billboards, Internet Ad exchanges, Internet Service Providers, Internet search engines, as well as wireless devices such as mobile phones.

What are the criteria for issuing AMBER Alerts?

Each state AMBER Alert plan includes its own criteria for issuing AMBER Alerts. The **PROTECT Act**, passed in 2003, which established the role of AMBER Alert **Coordinator** within the Department of Justice, calls for the Department of Justice to issue minimum standards or guidelines for AMBER Alerts that states can adopt voluntarily. ③ The Department's Guidance on Criteria for Issuing AMBER Alerts is as follows:

- There is reasonable belief by law enforcement that an abduction has occurred.

- The law enforcement agency believes that the child is in imminent danger of serious bodily injury or death.
- There is enough descriptive information about the victim and the abduction for law enforcement to issue an AMBER Alert to assist in the recovery of the child.
- The abduction is of a child aged 17 years or younger.
- The child's name and other critical data elements, including the Child Abduction flag, have been entered into the **National Crime Information Center (NCIC)** system.

How effective has it been?

As of December 2020 there have been 1,029 children successfully recovered through the AMBER Alert system.

AMBER Alerts also serve as **deterrents** to those who would prey upon our children. AMBER Alert cases have shown that some **perpetrators** release the abducted child after hearing the AMBER Alert.

Comprehension Check

PART I Multiple Choice Questions

Directions: *There are five sentences in this part. Beneath each sentence there are four options mark A, B, C and D. Choose the ONE that best completes the sentence or answers the question.*

1. AMBER Alert is an Alert that is communicated to the ________ through various media when a child abduction case is confirmed.

A. police

B. child's parent

C. public

D. offender

2. According to the introduction of AMBER Alert system, we can know that ________.

A. AMBER stands for America's Missing: Broadcast Emergency Response

B. AMBER Alert was created as a legacy to a girl named Amber Heard

C. As soon as someone goes missing, Amber alert will be issued

D. The AMBER Alert System began in 1996. It is an early warning system to help find abducted children established only by the local police

3. Yesterday evening, when Anna was playing on her mobile phone, a message of emergency alert popped up. Who of these four kinds of people may be the victim (s)?

A. Lily, a girl is fresh out of the college working as a nurse in the hospital.

B. Mike, a newborn baby.

C. Paul, who is in his earliest young manhood.

D. Mr. and Mrs. Smith, a couple whose golden wedding anniversary was celebrating with a toast last Monday.

PART II Short Answer Questions

Directions: *There are two short questions based on Passage 1. Please consider and answer them.*

1. What are the criteria for issuing AMBER Alerts?

Answer:

2. What to do if you receive an AMBER Alert?

Answer:

Vocabulary and Key Notes

1. **ALTON, Ill** 伊利诺伊州奥尔顿

2. **kidnapping** *n.* the unlawful act of capturing and carrying away a person against their will and holding them in false imprisonment 绑架；诱拐

3. **attempted murder charges** 谋杀未遂罪名

4. **law enforcement agency** an agency responsible for insuring obedience to the laws 执法机构

5. **paramedic** *n.* a person whose job is to help people who are sick or injured, but who is not a doctor or a nurse 护理人员；医务辅助人员

6. **detective** *n.* a person, especially a police officer, whose job is to examine crimes and catch criminals 侦探；警探

7. **suspect** *n.* a person who is suspected of a crime or of having done sth. wrong 嫌疑人；可疑对象

8. **custody** *n.* the state of being in prison, especially while waiting for trial（尤指在候审时的）拘留，拘押，羁押

9. **juvenile** *n.* a young person who is not yet an adult 青少年

10. **murder** *n.* the crime of killing sb. deliberately 谋杀；谋杀罪

11. **offense** *n.* breaking of a rule or law; illegal act; crime 犯罪；违法行为；罪行

12. **motor vehicle theft** also called "car theft" 机动车盗窃；偷车

13. **abduct** *v.* to take sb. away illegally, especially using force 诱拐；绑架

14. **PROTECT Act** 《保护法》

15. **coordinator** someone whose task is to see that work goes harmoniously 协调员

16. **National Crime Information Center (NCIC)** 国家犯罪信息中心

17. **deterrent** *n.* a thing that makes sb. less likely to do sth. 威慑因素；遏制力

18. **perpetrator** *n.* a person who commits a crime or does sth. that is wrong or evil 行凶者；作恶者；犯罪者

Translation

Directions: *Translate the following sentences from Passage 1 into Chinese.*

1. Alton Police contacted surrounding law enforcement agencies and an AMBER Alert was issued over the child's disappearance.

2. Once law enforcement has determined that a child has been abducted and the abduction meets AMBER Alert criteria, law enforcement notifies broadcasters and state transportation officials.

3. The PROTECT Act, passed in 2003, which established the role of AMBER Alert Coordinator within the Department of Justice, calls for the Department of Justice to issue minimum standards or guidelines for AMBER Alerts that states can adopt voluntarily.

Passage 2

A British Drug Trafficker Has Been Caned 24 Times at a Go in Singapore Jail

英国毒贩在新加坡樟宜监狱被处以鞭刑 24 下

A London-born British drug trafficker has reportedly been caned 24 times at a go in Singapore jail for a slew of **drugs offences**, according to British tabloid Daily Mail who spoke with the inmate's family after the punishment.

The inmate, Yuen Ye Ming, 31, was reportedly caned on Aug. 19 in Changi Prison.

Mothership.sg has reached out to Singapore prison for confirmation that the **caning** has been carried out and that 24 strokes were administered. The full **Ministry of Home Affairs** statement is found at the end.

Yuen was first arrested in August 2016, which marked the start of his problems with the law here.

He was eventually sentenced to 20 years' jail and 24 strokes of the cane.

Emotive reporting

The highly emotive reporting included details of Yuen's upbringing, such as him being academically brilliant, as well as his falling into bad company as **justifications** for his crimes in Singapore.

The article also highlighted sibling Elysia Yuen's repeated **bafflement** at Singapore's tough laws against drugs and the justifications for her brother's crimes here.

Daily Mail reported that Yuen's drugs crimes would have resulted in no more than a 12-month jail term in Britain.

Yuen was caught a second time for **possessing, consuming and trafficking drugs** while out on **bail.** ①

Yuen's brushes with the law

The article highlighted yuen's brushes with the law from a young age.

Before leaving for Singapore at age 17, Yuen got into trouble over an alleged scam involving **forged** driving licenses, which he reportedly sold to other pupils to buy alcohol and cigarettes. ②

He then moved to Singapore to live with his mother's family, a fact that was tracked down by a newspaper in the UK.

This was also after Yuen's father was made bankrupt following a bad investment and lost everything.

But Daily Mail did not report if Yuen was punished for his unlawful conduct as a juvenile in the UK, as he stayed on in Singapore after arriving here as a teenager.

Yuen's father passed away due to Covid-19 in March, Daily Mail added.

Attempt to bring him back to UK

With the caning now over, Daily Mail said the family is fighting for Yuen to be transferred to a British prison.

The report also failed to mention that, ironically, caning in Singapore is a legacy of British colonial rule.

Calls for leniency

Calls for **leniency** were made on Yuen's behalf by **Home Secretary** Priti Patel and former foreign secretary Jeremy Hunt previously.

Daily Mail said that the British **High Commission** in Singapore issued a statement in response to the caning: "The UK strongly opposes **corporal punishment** in all circumstances and condemns its use in this case."

A spokesman for the Singapore High Commission in London previously told Daily Mail: "Singapore deals with the drug problem comprehensively with the strictest enforcement coupled with the severest of penalties to protect the welfare of the public and our collective aspiration to live and raise our children in a safe oasis. ③"

(**Source:** https://mothership.sg/2020/08/daily-mail-caning-dj/)

Background Information

Caning in Singapore

新加坡鞭刑

新加坡鞭刑受英国法的传统和穆斯林习惯法双重影响。鞭刑制度在新加坡的历史可追溯至 1826 年，虽然英国早在 1948 年就废除了本国的鞭刑，却没有废除新加坡和马来西亚等殖民地的鞭刑，直到新加坡独立建国，英国的鞭刑制度在新加坡实施了近 140 年，其间从未中断。1968 年颁布的《穆斯林法实施法令》，就规定如何处理穆斯林法律在新加坡的适用，而鞭刑恰是穆斯林刑罚体系中的传统刑罚。

在新加坡，鞭刑在《刑法典》和多数单行法律中作为附加刑，表述为“caning”，以“必并科”“或并科”“选科”三种方式为主，辅以“加重”“缓刑”“替代”三种裁量方式对违法行为进行适用，可处罚重罪（如强奸、抢劫、贩毒等）、轻罪（如非法入境、出售烟花爆竹、非法金融交易等）、违纪行为（如违反军纪等）以及治安行为（如涂鸦、携带特定禁物参与游行集会等），规制范围涵盖既遂行为、未遂行为和预备行为（如企图实施抢劫）；在《监狱法》中，鞭刑表述为“corporal punishment”，作为惩罚违反狱规行为的体罚措施。新加坡《刑事诉讼法典》对鞭刑的执行程序进行明确规定，规定了“鞭刑判决的执行安排”“鞭刑的执行时间、地点”“鞭刑的执行方式”。另外，限定单一判决对成年人所判处的鞭刑不得超过 24 鞭，对未成年人的判决不得超过 12 鞭；不得对妇女、判处死刑之人、50 岁以上男性、身体健康不允许者适用鞭刑。除此之外，还有严格的“狱医在场制度”，明确规定医生不在场不得执行鞭刑，要求医生确定犯罪人的健康状况是否适合执行鞭刑，在执行过程中对受刑人给予及时救治，并赋予医生根据犯罪人健康状况中止或终止鞭刑的权力。同时辅以“鞭刑替代制度”，对不适合执行鞭刑的人予以改判 12 个月以下的有期徒刑。以及“刑后疗伤制度”由狱医跟踪治疗鞭伤，直至康复。

如今，除《刑法典》和《刑事诉讼法典》外，还有至少 19 部新加坡法律规定着鞭刑的适用，且至少有 95 种犯罪行为或情节被法定施以鞭刑。

Caning is a practice that the Singaporeans picked up from the British during the 19th century while under colonial rule. At the time, Britain itself was using this method as an accepted and legal form of punishment for criminal offenses. Well, caning had been **outlawed** throughout the entire United Kingdom itself by the turn of the 21st century. However, on the **Malay Peninsula** (including Singapore), this practice has not only remained on the books but the number of offences under which a person can receive a caning has been steadily increasing. Simultaneously the number of caning which the judicial system hands out has been increasing also.

Offences for which one can be caned in Singapore

Traditionally speaking, one could be caned for serious offences such as **rape**, robbery and other, less-violent forms of stealing (theft, **burglary**). And as time progressed most of the crimes which have been added to this list, such as kidnapping and drug trafficking, are also what would be defined as major offences.

But there are also many relatively-minor **infractions** – such as selling fireworks, **vandalism,** unlicensed **moneylending** or even being addicted to drugs – for which a person can be caned. And at the end of the day, looking at the length of the list of offences for which caning is applied implies that the best option, to avoid falling victim to such, is simply not to get into any issues with the law in Singapore which can result in imprisonment. That is to say that judicial caning is not carried out as a singular punitive measure. Rather they are a **de facto** component of receiving a jail sentence in and of itself.

Who can be caned in Singapore

However, in these cases, it isn't as simple as a person breaking the law and then finding himself on the caning block. Rather there are certain **stipulations** and even **exemptions**. For instance, only males can be caned. Moreover said males, generally speaking, have to be between 18 and 50 years old, and also they must also be deemed healthy enough to receive the punishment (at the actual time of the caning) by a medical professional. If the criminal is under 18, the cane can only reach a certain prescribed level of thickness. And if he is under 16, he can only be sentenced to receive this punishment by Singapore's highest courts. Moreover if a prisoner is on **death row**, he cannot be caned.

How the caning occurs

These caning occurs behind closed doors (i.e. in the prisons themselves). And they are actually administered by designated caning officers – individuals carefully selected and even trained to perform this task. However, this isn't necessarily for the benefit of the victim, although such training does decrease the officers' likelihood of landing a blow outside of the designated target area (the buttocks). Rather such individuals are instructed on how to use the cane as effectively as possible, as in doling out the maximum amount of pressure (i.e. pain) per blow. Moreover the caning officers in and of themselves tend to be muscular, and many of them are also trained in martial arts.

The recipients of judicial lashings are notified of the exact time upon which they are to receive their punishment, albeit only a single day in advance. This is perhaps to maximize their anxiety, as they are said to be quite distressed upon receiving such notification. And indeed, they know that a harrowing experience lies ahead.

The Steps

First of all, they are stripped totally naked. Then they are bent over and strapped onto an apparatus referred to as a "British dual-purpose prison flogging frame". In addition to the caning officers, as aforementioned, being trained professionals, additional safety measures are taken in that padding is placed around the offenders' lower spine and kidneys, just in case a stroke goes off target and hits one of those sensitive areas. Or looked at alternatively, there is the potential for permanent damage to be inflicted. And in some cases, the punished still sustain long-term wounding to their kidneys despite the protective measures taken.

And for those who are to receive numerous strokes, they are only given about 30 seconds between each lash. Moreover, the maximum amount of strokes which an individual can be sentenced to is 24. But regardless of the number, he must receive all of them in a single session.

Institutions where caning is allowed in Singapore

In addition to prisons, other Singaporean institutions in which caning is allowed include the following:

- The military
- Schools
- Children's homes
- Private residences

In the latter three cases it is of course used as a means of disciplining children, and accordingly there is no apparatus or what have you involved. Moreover military caning is conducted in a much more-humane manner than in prisons.

(**Source**: https://www.sweetsingapore.com/caning-in-singapore/)

Comprehension Check

PART I True or False

Directions: *Tell whether each of the following statements is true or false according to the information in the text.*

1. Singapore deals with the drug problem comprehensively with the strictest enforcement coupled with the severest of penalties.

2. Normally for those who are to receive numerous strokes, they can receive all of them in separated sessions.

3. Caning in Singapore is a legacy of British colonial rule during the 19th century. Nowadays, Britain itself still uses this method as an accepted and legal form of punishment for

criminal offenses.

4. Before a sentence of caning is carried out, the official medical workers will examine offenders' fitness and the caning will be carried out by trained officers.

5. Offences for which one can be caned in Singapore not only include some serious offences, but also many relatively-minor infractions.

PART II Fill in the Blank

Direction: *There are five sentences based on Passage 2. Fill in the blank with the RIGHT WORD(S) in the space provided.*

1. Yuen was caught a second time for ____________, __________ and ____________drugs while out on bail.

2. A rattan cane no more than ____________ in diameter and about ____________ in length is used for judicial and prison canings.

3. Judicial caning is not carried out as a ______________. Rather they are a de facto component of receiving a ____________ in and of itself.

4. Conditions that must be met by the person being caned: ____________________, ______________________, ______________________, ______________________.

5. The maximum amount of strokes which an individual can be sentenced to is ______________.

Vocabulary and Key Notes

1. **drugs offences** 贩卖毒品罪
2. **caning** *n.* as a form of legally sanctioned corporal punishment for convicted criminals 鞭刑
3. **Ministry of Homc Affair (MIIA)** 民政事务部；内政部
4. **bafflement** *n.* confusion resulting from failure to understand 阻碍；迷惑
5. **possessing, consuming, trafficking drugs** 持有、吸食、贩卖毒品
6. **allege** *v.* to state sth. as a fact but without giving proof 涉嫌；指控
7. **forged** *adj.* reproduced fraudulently 伪造的；锻造的
8. **leniency** *n.* mercifulness as a consequence of being lenient or tolerant 宽大处理；仁慈
9. **Home Secretary** the British government minister in charge of the Home Office（英国）内政大臣

10. **High Commission** the office and the staff of an embassy that represents the interests of one Commonwealth country in another （英联邦国家相互派驻的）高级专员公署

11. **corporal punishment** the physical punishment of people, especially by hitting them 体罚；肉刑

12. **outlawe** *v.* to make sth. illegal 宣布……不合法；禁止

13. **Malay Peninsula** 马来半岛

14. **rape** *n.* the crime of forcing sb. to have sex with you, especially using violence 强奸罪; 强奸案

15. **burglary** *n.* the crime of entering a building illegally and stealing things from it 入室偷盗罪

16. **infraction** *n.* an act of breaking a rule or law 犯规；违法行为

17. **moneylending** *n.* the act or occupation of lending money at interest 放款；金钱借贷

18. **de facto** existing as a fact although it may not be legally accepted as existing 实际上存在的（不一定合法）

19. **stipulation** *n.* a condition, demand, or promise in an agreement or contract 规定；条款

20. **exemption** *n.* official permission not to do sth. or pay sth. that you would normally have to do or pay 免除；豁免

21. **death row** the cells in a prison for prisoners who are waiting to be killed as punishment for a serious crime 死囚牢房；死囚区

Translation

Directions: *Translate the following sentences from Passage 2 into Chinese.*

1. Yuen was caught a second time for possessing, consuming and trafficking drugs while out on bail.

2. Before leaving for Singapore at age 17, Yuen got into trouble over an alleged scam involving forged driving licenses, which he reportedly sold to other pupils to buy alcohol and cigarettes.

3. Singapore deals with the drug problem comprehensively with the strictest enforcement coupled with the severest of penalties to protect the welfare of the public and our collective aspiration to live and raise our children in a safe oasis.

Supplementary Reading

Crime Prevention

犯罪预防

Singapore enjoys a low crime rate. This is the result of the close co-operation between the Police and the community in crime prevention.

What is Crime Prevention?

- Crime can happen anywhere, and anytime to anyone. You and your loved ones in the family can be victims of crime too. But you can minimize the risk of being victims by adopting some simple crime prevention measures in enhancing security.
- Preventing crime is a primary responsibility of the Police but success in crime prevention also depends on public support and participation. Crime Prevention is NOT a sole responsibility of the Police. Crime prevention is EVERYBODY'S RESPONSIBILITY. You need to look after yourself and your valuables.
- Police are fully aware that without public support and participation, they cannot effectively fight crime.
- The Police therefore introduce and promote crime prevention with the aim to encourage the community to practice crime prevention measures to protect themselves and safe keep their belongings.
- Police also seek to promote and strengthen Police rapport with the population to encourage public involvement in crime prevention.

Definition of Crime Prevention

Crime Prevention is the technique of elimination of opportunities for the commission of crime. While you are warned to keep away from crimes, gangs and drugs, do not become a victim of crime yourself.

Crime Prevention Habits

Please remember the following:

- Most criminals are opportunists.
- Do not offer criminals any opportunity to strike and suffer the consequences of being a victim.

- Look after yourself and safeguard your belongings.
- Be crime prevention conscious.

Principles of Crime Prevention

Many crimes are opportunistic in nature and are committed through the negligence of the victims. Crime prevention measures should be taken to eliminate opportunities for crime.

People must be made aware that they are personally responsible for their own safety and security of their belongings and it is in their interest to adopt means of protection. Crime prevention measures should be taken to protect oneself and one's belongings.

***Common Crimes (Methods, Preventive Measures and Penalties*)**

Let's now look at some common crimes committed in Singapore. Most of the crimes involve properties and innocent people like you. The crimes include: Housebreaking, Robbery, Snatch Theft, Motor Vehicle Theft and Outrage of Modesty. These five types of crimes can be prevented to a large extent if you practice preventive measures to enhance security and minimize the risk of being a victim.

Actually, Crime Prevention plays an important role in every country. Crime prevention cannot be separated from the active participation of social forces. It is necessary to construct and perfect relevant prevention and control measures.

(**Source:** www.ncpc.gov.sg)

Further Discussion

1. Amber alert systems are now in use in several countries around the world. There's no arguing that AMBER Alerts save lives and reunite hundreds of children with their families. China also has established such system called "China's Child Safety Emergency Response (CCSER). What do you think about the advantages and disadvantages of this kind of emergency alert?

2. After reading the text, we can learn that the primary goal of a caning is to inflict as much pain on the receiver as possible without killing or permanently incapacitating the offenders. Such an experience of course leaves permanent scarring on both the body and the mind of the recipient. But why does Singapore still have such penalties? What do you think?

小语说语：Bail

n. a security such as cash, a bond, or property; esp., security required by a court for the release of a criminal defendant who must appear in court at a future time 保释金；保释

v. to obtain the release of (oneself or another) by providing security for a future appearance in court 保释

- **原文**

Yuen was caught a second time for possessing, consuming and trafficking drugs while out **on bail**.

Yuen 在保释期间因持有、吸食和贩卖毒品的罪名再次被捕。

- **短语**

go bail for 为……做保释人；为……缴保释金

set bail at $1000 保释金定为 1000 美元

on bail 保释；保释中

bail sb. out 把某人保释出来

bail bond 保释保证书；保释保证金

- **例句**

例 1：Excessive **bail** shall not be required, nor excessive fines imposed, nor cruel and unusual punishments inflicted.

不得要求过重的保释金，不得处分过高的罚款，不得施予残酷的、反常的刑罚。

例 2：He was **bailed** to appear in court on 15 March.

他获得保释，定于 3 月 15 日到庭应诉。

例 3：She jumped/skipped bail (= did not appear at her trial).

她弃保潜逃（未如期到庭受审）。

- **国内外法条学习**

例 1：**A bail bond** is a document whereby the defendant agrees that while at liberty after being released on bail, he or she will appear at all subsequent proceedings as required and comply with all the conditions of the bail bond.

保释保证书是一份凭证，在保释后获得自由时，被告同意按要求出席随后的所有诉讼，并遵守保释保证书的所有条件。（《美国宾夕法尼亚州法典》第 525 条）

例 2：**The bail bond surety**, its agents taking possession of collateral, or both, will hold said collateral as a fiduciary until such time as ownership of the collateral passes to the bail bond surety.

保释金担保人及其持有抵押品的代理人其中一方或双方将作为受托人持有上述抵押品，直至抵押品的所有权转移至保释金担保人。(《美国犹他州行政法典》第 R590–196–5 条）

例 3：Where the decision on penalty of administrative detention is withdrawn, or the penalty of administrative detention begins to be executed, the **bail** collected by the public security organ shall be returned to the payer without delay.

行政拘留的处罚决定被撤销，或者行政拘留处罚开始执行的，公安机关收取的**保证金**应当及时退还交纳人。（《中华人民共和国治安管理处罚法》第一百一十一条）

Poster /Flyer/ Brochure Reading

INTRODUCTION 简介

Elderly persons are easy victims of crime because criminals prey on their trusting nature and concern for loved ones. It is important that they are aware of measures to protect themselves against crime.

乐龄人士比较容易受骗。这是因为歹徒利用乐龄人士轻易相信别人的本质来欺凌他们。希望下列的讯息能协助乐龄人士提高警戒，以免成为下一个受害者。

INDOORS 在家中

- Keep your grille gates locked at all times to prevent strangers from entering the house.

  时时刻刻锁上铁栅门与大门，防止不速之客进入您家中。

- Never let a stranger into your house. To identify a stranger, use the door viewer. When talking to the stranger, keep the chain-latch of the door fastened without opening the door to him/her.

  别随意开门让陌生人进入您屋内。从门眼察看来访者。若要开门与陌生的来访者交谈，应先扣上门链然后才开门。

- Keep your valuables and money at the bank.

  别把贵重物品与现金存放在家里。尽可能把财物存放于银行保险箱中。

- Check the identity of the stranger by calling the organisation concerned or with your family members of any such appointment. Call the Police at '999' if in doubt.

  如有陌生人自称为某机构的员工或与您家人有约，先拨电向该机构或您的家人查证是否属实。若有任何疑虑，请拨打'999'报警。

- Do not give any strangers money when he/she asks for cash payments for any bills, goods or services. Check with your family members or call the Police at '999' if in doubt.

  如有陌生人要求您以现款付还您家人所拖欠的帐单，货物或服务费，请先拨电向您的家人查证。若有任何疑虑，请拨打'999'报警。

- Do not open the door to strangers when he/she insists on passing you a gift or item which you did not order. Check with your family members or call the Police at '999' if in doubt.

  如有陌生人坚持要进入您的家中递送您没购买的礼物或赠品，先拨电向您的家人查证。若有任何疑虑，请拨打'999'报警。

OUTDOORS 在户外

- To prevent snatch theft, hold your handbag under your arm and walk facing oncoming traffic.

  在行人道步行时，将手提袋紧夹在您手臂下，并且面向迎面而来的车辆方向行走，以避免被匪徒从您后面掠夺您的手提袋。

- Avoid wearing expensive jewellery or carrying large amounts of cash when going out alone.

  单独出门时，避免穿戴贵重首饰或携带巨款。

- Do not walk alone along dark and deserted streets. Walk in pairs or groups in well-lit areas.

  别单独步行在少人行走的街道或偏僻的地点。

- Carry a whistle or shrill alarm for use during emergency to attract attention of passers-by.

  携带一个警笛或警报器以备紧急所需。

- Be wary of scams. Do not fall for anything that sounds too good to be true, such as fortune telling, magical talismans or objects like 'magic stone' that can cure illnesses, or any schemes that require cash deposits before-hand. Check with your family members or call '999' if in doubt.

  别相信谎言：如算命，神符，治病的魔术石，或能快速致富的投资等。若有任何疑虑，请拨打'999'报警。

- Do not enter the lift with strangers if you are not comfortable with. Use the other lift or wait for the next one.

  别与陌生人共乘同一架电梯。请使用另一架电梯。

- Be wary of strangers who are overly friendly.

  留意对您太友善的陌生人。

Explain and create awareness of the crime prevention measures to elderly members in your family as they could be victims of tricksters and criminals. Together, we can ensure that senior citizens continue to enjoy the golden years.

请向您家中的乐龄人士讲解及灌输罪案防范措施，使他们不会成为罪犯或骗子的下一个目标。只要大家同心协力，我们的乐龄人士肯定能欢享黄金年华。

2008

CRIME PREVENTION FOR ELDERLY
防范罪案 安享晚年

tote board

Visit our websites for more information:
www.spf.gov.sg www.ncpc.gov.sg

第二章 校园安全案例

导读

目前，中国的海外留学人数逐年增长。而随着留学生数量的不断增加，留学生人身安全、留学生法律意识等问题备受关注。与此同时，留学生失踪、遇害等事件也在持续增加。我们在谴责凶手的同时，到底应该从哪些方面帮助留学生防患于未然？如何引导他们做好自我保护？希望下文的案例和建议会为海外学子们撑起法律的保护伞。

案例阅读

Passage 1

Student Alcohol Policy in Stanford University

斯坦福大学学生饮酒守则

I. Preamble

The university **is committed to** the health, safety and well-being of each member of the Stanford community. In order to further student learning and development, and to promote the university's academic mission, Stanford fosters an environment of **personal and collective responsibility** and respectful citizenship. ① This means that all members of the university community— students, faculty and staff— have a role in safeguarding a healthy living and learning environment free of alcohol and other drugs **misuse.** The university also strives to create a culture that supports students who do not use alcohol, and students who are of legal age to use alcohol in a safe and responsible manner.

Throughout this policy "student group" includes all registered student organizations, sports teams, and student-led dorm communities. This policy applies across all Stanford University campuses and **premises** where the activities of the university are conducted, including all off-campus university **sanctioned** or **funded programs and events.** ②

II. Policy Statement

A. Alcohol

Members of the Stanford community are required to **abide by** all applicable laws and university policies, including those governing alcohol consumption, distribution and possession. Under California law and university policy, it is illegal for anyone under the age of 21 to purchase, possess, or consume alcohol in any public or private space on campus. ③ It is also illegal and a violation of university policy to furnish alcohol to an individual under the age of 21. **Violation**s of university policies, state law, and federal law also **constitute violations** of the Fundamental Standard. Relevant specific laws and policy provisions governing the use of alcohol are listed below:

- Hard Alcohol — Distilled liquor/spirits/hard alcohol (alcohol by volume 20% and above, i.e. 40 proof). "Hard Alcohol" bottles, containers, etc. 750 mL and above, in undergraduate student residences (rooms, common spaces, etc.), or in the possession of undergraduate students in university public spaces, is prohibited. Hard Alcohol in bottles, containers, etc. smaller than 750 mL that are allowed under this policy, for people 21 years of age or older, must be contained and stored in the original bottle, container, etc. in which it was purchased from a licensed establishment. All Hard Alcohol, regardless of container size, is prohibited at all categories of undergraduate parties.

- Parties — Parties must be registered with the university **in accordance with** the party planning guidelines coordinated by Student Affairs. Individual parties or social gatherings cannot be registered at the residential level. Beer, wine and packaged pre-mixed alcoholic beverages (e.g. wine coolers, pre-mixed cocktail or seltzer drinks under 20% alcohol by volume, etc.) are the only alcoholic beverages that can be present at on-campus undergraduate student parties. Any student group or residence that includes undergraduate members is subject to this policy restriction. ④ Student groups and residences that are 100% graduate students in membership are **exempt** and may have hard alcohol in the form of mixed drinks at registered "Members" parties. Shots of hard alcohol are prohibited at all parties.

- Drinking Games — Games and activities that promote high-risk drinking or rapid alcohol consumption are not allowed on campus.

- University Funds and the Purchase of Alcohol or Drugs — No university funds or funds collected by the university may be used in a way that violates this policy. In undergraduate student residences, house dues or student group funds may not be used to buy alcohol or drugs.

Requiring or pressuring students to contribute to the purchase of alcohol or drugs is prohibited.

- Dining Halls — Alcoholic beverages are prohibited and cannot be **possessed** or consumed in R & DE dining halls, outside seating areas, or patios, unless allowed as a special exception as approved by R & DE. R & DE staff can deny admission, access or meal service to anyone who **is deemed to** be overly **intoxicated** by the Dining management staff.

…

- Admit Weekend — Stanford students are prohibited from providing, serving, or in any way making alcohol available to any prospective **frosh** ("ProFro"). All undergraduate student groups and residences may host only alcohol-free parties or events during Admit Weekend. This specifically means that no alcohol is to be present, served or consumed at any undergraduate student group and/or residence function during Admit Weekend.
- New Student Orientation (NSO) Period — Stanford students are prohibited from providing, serving, or in any way making alcohol available to any new, incoming undergraduate student (freshman or transfer). All undergraduate student groups and residences will host only alcohol-free parties or events during New Student Orientation. This specifically means that no alcohol is to be present, served, or consumed at any undergraduate student group and/or residence function for the duration of NSO programming.

(**Source:** Student Affairs (stanford.edu))

Comprehension Check

Directions: *Tell whether each of the following statements is true or false according to the information from Passage 1.*

1. Only faculty and staff have responsibility to guard a healthy living and learning environment free of alcohol and other drugs misuse.
2. Students who are of legal age to use alcohol can drink without university regulations.
3. In policy, "student group" includes all registered student organizations, sports teams, outside volunteer group and student-led dorm communities.
4. Violations of university policies, state law, and federal law also constitute violations of the Fundamental Standard.
5. "Hard Alcohol" bottles, containers, etc.350-750 mL, in undergraduate student residences (rooms, common spaces, etc.), or in the possession of undergraduate students in university public spaces, is prohibited.

6. “Hard Alcohol” under 750ml isn’t prohibited at several categories of undergraduate parties.

7. Anyone requiring or pressuring students to contribute to the purchase of alcohol or drugs will be punished.

8. Staff in university dining hall have no right to deny admission, access or meal service to anyone who is deemed to be overly intoxicated by the Dining management staff.

9. Stanford students are prohibited from providing, serving alcohol to any prospective frosh (“ProFro”) at school time.

10. Undergraduate student groups and graduate student residences will host only alcohol-free parties or events during New Student Orientation.

Background Information

California State Law

美国加州饮酒相关法律

美国颁布了《禁止未成年人饮酒法》，防止未成年人饮酒。在美国，为了减少年轻人接触酒精及减少饮酒机会，各州把饮酒最低年龄提高到 21 岁，此外，各州规定 21 岁以下的驾驶人，其血中酒精浓度不得超过 0.00% 或 0.02%，以减少肇事率。而且在商店买烟酒之类的商品，必需出示身份证明，证明你的年龄超过标准。更严格的是，作为成年人，如果帮未成年人买酒是犯罪行为。

1. Distilled liquor/spirits/hard alcohol (alcohol by volume 20% and above, i.e. 40 proof) 国际公认，烈性酒、蒸馏酒是指酒精含量 20% 及以上，即 40 度以上的酒精饮品。2012 年出版的《美国酒类标签法规》一书中，亦有关于酒精饮料的健康警示内容，以规范烈性酒饮用。

2. Beer, wine and packaged pre-mixed alcoholic beverages (e.g. wine coolers, pre-mixed cocktail or seltzer drinks under 20% alcohol by volume, etc.) 在国外，饮酒是成年学生之间常用的社交方式。美国校园本土学生及留学生聚会多采用如啤酒、葡萄酒及包装的预混合酒精饮料（例如“冷酒器”酒、预混合鸡尾酒或含酒精量低于 20% 的苏打水饮料等）。

3. California State Law 美国加州饮酒相关法律：

a. It is illegal for persons under the age of 21 to possess an alcoholic beverage in any public place or any place open to the public (CA Business and Professions Code 25662).

b. Any person who furnishes, gives, or sells any alcoholic beverage to someone under the age of 21 is guilty of a **misdemeanor** (CA Business and Professions Code 25658(a)).

c. Any person under the age of 21 who attempts to purchase an alcoholic beverage is guilty of an **infraction** (CA Business and Professions Code 25658.5).

d. It is a misdemeanor to ride a bicycle under the influence of alcohol, drugs or both (CA Vehicle Code Section 21200.5).

Vocabulary and Key Notes

1. **preamble** *n.* An introductory statement in a constitution, statute, or other document explaining the document's basis and objective; esp., a statutory recital of the inconveniences for which the statute is designed to provide a remedy 序文；导言

2. **be committed to** 致力于

3. **misuse** *v.* 误用，滥用；虐待 n. 误用，滥用；虐待

4. **personal and collective responsibility** 个人和集体责任

5. **premises** *n.* a house or building along with its grounds; esp., the buildings and land that a shop, restaurant, company, etc. uses 房屋；经营场所

6. **fund programs and events** 基金计划及活动

7. **abide by** 遵守；信守；承担……的后果（法）

8. **violation** *n.* 违反；妨碍，侵害；违背

constitute violations 构成违反

9. **prohibit** *v.* 禁止

10. **sanction** *n.* 制裁，处罚 *vt.* 制裁，处罚（法）

11. **in accordance with** 依照；与……一致

10. **exempt** *adj.* 被免除（责任或义务）的，获豁免的 *v.* 免除，豁免

11. **possess** *vt.* 控制；使掌握；持有；迷住；拥有，具备

12. **be deemed to** 被认为

13. **intoxicated** *adj.* 喝醉的；极度兴奋的 *v.* 沉醉；中毒（intoxicate 的过去分词）

14. **frosh** *n.* a freshman 大学或中学一年级生

15. **misdemeanor** *n.* 轻罪；品行不端（法）

16. **infraction** *n.* 犯规，违法行为；（对法律、协定的）违背，违犯

Translation

Directions: *Translate the following sentences from Passage 1 into Chinese.*

1. In order to further student learning and development, and to promote the university's academic mission, Stanford fosters an environment of personal and collective responsibility and respectful citizenship.

2. This policy applies across all Stanford University campuses and premises where the activities of the university are conducted, including all off-campus university sanctioned or funded programs and events.

3. Under California law and university policy, it is illegal for anyone under the age of 21 to purchase, possess, or consume alcohol in any public or private space on campus.

4. Any student group or residence that includes undergraduate members is subject to this policy restriction.

Passage 2

A Father's Plea to a Killer: Tell Us Where Our Daughter's Remains Are

"告诉我们女儿的遗体在哪里"——来自一位父亲的请求

At a courthouse thousands of miles from his home in China, a father pleaded with a killer to tell him where his daughter's body was last placed.

The defendant C, 30, was **sentenced** Thursday to life in prison for the kidnapping and killing two years ago of 26-year-old Z, a Chinese student at the **University of Illinois** Urbana Champaign's department of Natural Resources and Environmental Sciences.

Her remains were never found.

"Now that the trial is over, and the jury has made its decision, we ask the defendant to unconditionally tell us what he knows about Z's location," her father said in Chinese, according to a translator. "If you have any humanity left in your soul, please help end our **torment**. Please let us bring Z home."

Man found guilty of killing a Chinese student at the University of Illinois.

The jury could not reach a **unanimous verdict** on the **death penalty**, so a judge **imposed** the **life sentence.** ①

"We respect the decision of the jury," John M, United States Attorney for the Central District of Illinois, said.

The verdict in June came as no surprise, after defendant C's attorney said in opening statements of the trial that his client killed Z.

But imposing a life sentence over a death sentence has proved **controversial** in Z's native China, where social media users argued that ending the killer's life was "the best and only justice in this case."

The case was among the top trending topics on popular Chinese social media site Weibo on Friday.

"This shows how the injustice in the American legal system. We should condemn them," social media user X said on his Weibo account.

Z went missing in June 2017, when she was on her way to **sign an apartment lease.** She was last seen getting into C's car at a bus stop, according to court documents.

She was one of more than 300,000 Chinese students and scholars attending a US university in 2017. During her time in the US, she had regularly reassured her parents about her safety through FaceTime chats.

Her disappearance triggered widespread concern in China, with groups set up on the messaging app WeChat to share information about her case. ②

Her aunt said in 2017 that Z had dreamed of being a university professor and studying environmental science.

When she vanished, Z's family made the journey from China to the US in search of answers about their daughter's disappearance. They offered up to $40,000 to anyone who was able to offer information which would lead to an arrest in the case of their daughter's disappearance.

Her family attended **the trial and the penalty phase**.

"While we do not agree with the result, ... we accept that he will spend the rest of his life in prison, which still reflects our loss in a meaningful way," her father said. "We hope that every day he spends in prison he feels the pain and suffering that we feel for the loss of Z."

M said the search for her remains continues.

"We have missed Z tremendously in the past two years," Z's family said at his **conviction**. "Our wish has always been to find Z and bring her home, we'll not give up."

(**Source**: https://edition.cnn.com/2019/07/18/us/brendt-christensen-chinese-student-death-sentence/index.html)

Comprehension Check

Directions: *Use an appropriate word or phrase from the box with their proper forms to complete each sentence. Each word or phrase can be used once only.*

be sentenced to	unconditionally	defendant	impose
condemn	attorney	penalty	tremendously
trail	reassure		

1. Whoever commits the crime shall be ____________ to ten years in prison.
2. The police were hot on his ____________.
3. Her mother, in whom she confided, said she would support her ____________.
4. He took an oath that he had seen the ____________ leaving the scene of the crime.
5. Mary didn't want to ____________ her values on her family.
6. The ____________ may present evidence as well as witnesses.
7. The Internet makes it very easy for us to ____________ others for their mistakes.
8. I tried to ____________ her, "Don't worry about it. We won't let it happen again".
9. For education she can tap earnings with no ceiling and avoid that 10% ____________.
10. The victory lifted us up ____________.

Background Information

Emergency Response Guide

应急指南

伊利诺伊大学创建于1867年，是美国最具影响力的公立大学之一，拥有"公立常春藤"的美誉，在全世界享有盛名。

伊利诺伊大学警察局发布了一份应急指南，主要对恶劣天气、医疗事故、炸弹威胁、危险物品、枪击事件等各种紧急情况提出应对方法。当遇到紧急情况时，可快速参阅本指南，但提前制定应急计划至关重要。如想了解更多应对紧急情况的方法，请浏览该警局的"跑－躲－打"相关信息。

遇到潜在枪击或危险时：

潜在危险指蓄意对校园造成直接威胁或构成紧急危险的任何行为。

在确保自身安全的情况下，采取以下应对方法。如稍有犹豫，请跟直觉走——毕竟你才是自己的最佳顾问！

室内枪击或危险应对方法：

- 保持镇定。
- 迅速从安全路线撤离室内，远离危险，寻找远离危险区域的另一建筑物躲避。
- 若无法撤离，就近寻找安全场所，尽可能在门后设置遮挡物，关灯，躲到人看不到或听不到的地方，保持安静。切记将手机调到静音模式。
- 一旦安全，马上拨打 911 报警。
- 时刻注意保命，并提醒周围的人也这样做。
- 切记不要开门，除非执法人员建议或收到可靠信息宣布危险已经解除，例如，伊利诺伊安全警报 1 发布的消息。

室外枪击或危险应对方法：

- 保持镇定。
- 就近寻找安全场所。
- 反锁房门；如无法反锁房门，尽可能在门后设置遮挡物。
- 切记不要开门，除非执法人员建议或收到可靠信息宣布危险已经解除，例如，伊利诺伊安全警报 1 发布的消息。

The University of Illinois Police Department publishes an Emergency Response Guide with steps you can take in the event of various kinds of emergencies – like severe weather, medical emergencies, bomb threats, hazardous materials situations, active shooter emergencies, and more. This guide is meant to serve as a quick reference when you are confronted with an emergency, but it is still important to have a plan ahead of time. Explore our Run-Hide-Fight information for more tips on how to prepare for an emergency.

ACTIVE SHOOTER/ACTIVE THREAT

An active threat is defined as any incident which by its deliberate nature creates an immediate threat or presents an imminent danger to the campus community.

Only follow these actions if safe to do so. When in doubt, follow your instincts – you are your best advocate!

If the Active Shooter/Active Threat is inside your building:

- Remain calm.
- Immediately exit building via safest possible route, away from the threat if possible, and seek refuge away from the immediate area inside another building.

• If you cannot evacuate, find the nearest location that provides safety, barricade/block doors by any means possible, shut off lights, move to an area of the room where you cannot be seen or heard, and keep as quiet as possible. Turn cell phones to silent mode.

• As soon as it is safe to do so, notify authorities by calling 911.

• Stay focused on survival and keep others around you focused.

• Do not open the door until a KNOWN law enforcement officer advises it is safe to do so or some other credible information, such as Illini-Alert1, is received advising the threat is over.

If the Active Shooter/Active Threat is NOT inside your building:

• Remain calm.

• Find the nearest location that provides safety.

• Close and lock doors; if doors cannot be locked, barricade/block the door with anything available.

• Do not open the door until a KNOWN law enforcement officer advises it is safe to do so or some other credible information, such as Illini-Alert1, is received advising the threat is over.

(**Source**: https://police.illinois.edu/em/run-hide-fight/)

Vocabulary and Key Notes

1. **sentence** *n.* 判决、宣判 *v.* 判决、宣判
2. **torment** *n.* 痛苦，苦恼；折磨；使人痛苦的（人或物）
v. 折磨，使痛苦；纠缠，作弄；骚扰，捉弄，戏弄
3. **unanimous verdict** 一致裁定；一致裁断
4. **death penalty** 死刑
5. **impose the life sentence** 判处无期徒刑
6. **controversial** *adj.* 有争议的；有争论的
7. **sign an apartment lease** 签订公寓租约
8. **The trial phase** 审判阶段；审理阶段
9. **The penalty phase** 处罚阶段
10. **conviction** *n.* 定罪；证明有罪；确信，坚定的信仰

Translation

***Directions**: Translate the following sentences from Passage 2 into Chinese.*

1. The jury could not reach a unanimous verdict on the death penalty, so a judge imposed the

life sentence.

2. Her disappearance triggered widespread concern in China, with groups set up on the messaging app WeChat to share information about her case.

Supplementary Reading

Accident, Incident, and Hazard Reporting Form

事故、意外事件和危险报告表

THE UNIVERSITY OF AUCKLAND
NEW ZEALAND

Vault Reference Number

Accident, Incident, and Hazard Reporting Form

Report to be completed as soon as possible. (Line Manager or Academic Leader to complete if an injured person is unable to do so and check the accuracy of information) Report to HoD and HSW Service. File one copy in local files and send copy to the HSW Service.

Any health and safety issues or concerns should be reported using this form

Has there been an incident resulting in, or only narrowly avoiding serious harm?

☐ Yes* ☐ No **If yes, ***preserve the scene*** and notify the Health, Safety and Wellbeing (HSW) Service ***immediately*** to determine whether a formal investigation is required.* **For emergency assistance dial 966** (internal) or **0800 373 7550**

Health, Safety and Wellbeing Service: Phone: 09 923 4109 E-mail: HSW@auckland.ac.nz Mobile: 027 209 2763

Section 1. Reporting

1. What Faculty or Service Division does this involve?

Faculty / Service Div.

Department

2. Who is reporting the accident/incident/hazard?

Name		Staff/Student ID (if applicable)	
Contact Details	Phone:	Email:	

3. Details of anyone injured (if applicable and different from above)

Name		Staff/Student ID (if applicable)	
Contact Details	Phone:	Email:	

4. Where and when did it happen/arise?

Building (or location)		Date	
Level (Floor) and room		Time	

5. How was or could have injury, ill-health or damage been caused?

☐ Being hit by objects or things
☐ Biological factors
☐ Body stressing
☐ Chemicals/substances
☐ Heat, radiation or energy
☐ Hitting objects with part of the body
☐ Psychosocial (inc. mental health)
☐ Sound or pressure
☐ Slip, trip or fall
☐ Vehicle accidents
☐ OOS or RSI
☐ Something else: ________

6. Description of accident/incident/hazard

(If not enough room, please attach separate sheet or sheets. Attach Witness statements, diagrams and photos.)

E.G.: I was putting away some files when door slammed shut and caught my finger in filing cabinet door.

7. What action have you or others taken to make the area safe and/or preserve the scene?

(If not enough room, please attach separate sheet or sheets.)

E.G.: I locked the cabinet and labelled it "do not use."

8. Who witnessed the accident/incident?

Name		Name	
Contact		Contact	

9. Signature of reporting person:

Date:

Ensure the Head of Department/Line Manager has been informed

10. Was anybody injured or made ill (harmed)?

☐ **Yes.** Proceed to section 2. (If it is serious, inform the HSW Service without delay)
☐ **No.** Proceed to section 3 to see if there are any 'opportunities to learn'.

This is an approved template in the Health, Safety and Wellbeing Management system.
Once data entered or document printed this document is uncontrolled.

Version: 3
Issue data: 18 March 2019

Section 2. Harm (if applicable)

11.Injured person

Name		Date of Birth	
Contact Details	Phone:	Email:	
Residential address			

12.Role or job title of injured person:

Job Title:		Faculty:
☐ Staff ☐ Student ☐ Other		Staff/Student ID No.
Gender:	Signature:	Date:

13.Period of employment of injured person: (if applicable)
☐ 1st week ☐ 1st month ☐ 1-6 months ☐ 6 months - 1 year ☐ 1-5 years ☐ Over 5 years

14.Time at work prior to injury: (if applicable)
Started work at ______ am / pm Incident occurred at ______ am / pm Hours on shift ______ hours

15.Treatment of injury:
☐ Nil ☐ First-aid ☐ Doctor/Emergency Dept. (not hospitalised) ☐ **Hospitalised (admitted)**

16.Where were they treated?
Location ______ Doctor (if known)) ______

17.What caused the injury? (Agency of harm)
☐ Human factors (unsafe acts or behaviours)
☐ Chemical or chemical products
☐ Machinery or (mainly) fixed plant
☐ Powered equipment, tools or appliances
☐ Animal, human or plant/vegetation (biological agency)
☐ Environmental (e.g. heat, cold)
☐ Material or substance
☐ Non-powered hand tool or equipment
☐ Other biological factors (e.g. Bacterial or viral)
☐ Exposure (e.g. dust, gas, noise, etc.)
☐ Mobile plant or transport
☐ Other______

18.Nature of injury or damage (Specify all):
☐ Abrasion/scratches
☐ Amputation
☐ Bruising/crushing
☐ Burn/scald
☐ Concussion
☐ Dislocation
☐ Puncture wound
☐ Reaction
☐ Disease
☐ Mental Health
☐ Other______
☐ Eye injury
☐ Foreign body
☐ Fracture
☐ Internal injury
☐ Laceration/cut
☐ Sprain or strain
☐ Contamination/poisoning/toxic
☐ Occupational Hearing Loss
☐ Gradual process/OOS or RSI
☐ Fatal

Body part:
☐ Head ☐ Neck ☐ Trunk
☐ Arms/hands ☐ Legs/feet ☐ Multiple locations
☐ Systemic (internal organs)

Side of Body:
☐ Left ☐ Right ☐ Not Applicable

☐ Other (specify)

19.Description of Injury
(As much detail as possible)

E.G.: Crushed middle finger on left hand

Office use only – HSW Service Injury Claims Manager to complete
Do you accept this as a work related injury? ☐ Yes ☐ No ☐ Unsure ☐ Not applicable
I, the undersigned, declare that the details above have been completed accurately, truthfully and fully to the best of my knowledge and belief, and I understand that providing a false or misleading statement is an offence.
Signature of Injury Claims Manager: ______ Date: ______

This is an approved template in the Health, Safety and Wellbeing Management system.
Once data entered or document printed this document is uncontrolled.
Version: 3
Issue data: 18 March 2019

Further Discussion

1. How to stay safe when studying abroad?
2. What can students do to avoid becoming a sexual victim?
3. How to create a safe college campus?

小语说语：misdemeanor

n. a crime less serious than a felony 轻罪；品行不端

● **原文**

It is a misdemeanor to ride a bicycle under the influence of alcohol, drugs or both (CA Vehicle Code Section 21200.5) . 使用酒精、毒品或两者后骑自行车是轻罪（美国加州车辆法规第 21200.5 条）。

● **词根引申**

词根：misdemean

misdemeanour *n.* 行为不端；轻罪；不轨行为

misdemean *n.* 不端正的行为

misdemean *vi.* 做不规矩事；行为不正

misdemean *vt.* 使行为不端

● **例句**

例 1：However, what may be a misdemeanor in one state could be a felony in another.

然而，在一个州中是轻罪的在另一个州就有可能成为重罪。

例 2：Committing a forgery is a felony, but driving an automobile in excess of the speed limit is a misdemeanor.

伪造是犯重罪，但超速驾驶属于轻罪。

● **国内外法条学习**

例 1：An offense under this section constitutes **a petty misdemeanor** if the offender defies an order to leave personally communicated to him or her by the owner of the premises or other authorized person. Otherwise it is a violation.

违规者不服从房屋所有人或其他获授权的人亲自通知他或她离开的命令，则本条规定的罪行构成轻罪。否则就是违规。（《美国联邦法规》第 11.411 条）

例 2：It is a **misdemeanor** to operate a daycare center or group daycare facility within this state without first obtaining a daycare license from the Department or to operate a daycare center or group daycare facility without posting the license in a place easily seen by a parent or the general public.

在本州范围内经营日托中心或开放集体日托设施，如未事先从相关部门获得日托许可证，或未将日托许可证张贴在显眼处便于家长或公众查看，均属轻罪。（《美国爱达荷州行政法典》第 16.06.02.395 条）

例 3：Any person charged with a **misdemeanor**, other than a petty offense may elect, however, to be tried before a district judge for the district in which the offense was committed.

然而，任何被指控犯有轻罪的人都可以选择由罪行发生地的一名地区法官进行审判。（美国法典第 3401 条）

Supplementary Poster Reading (flyer/brochure)

10/2/2019 Lock It or Lose It | Central Michigan University

Skip navigation

In the United States, a motor vehicle is stolen every 44 seconds. Don't be the next victim!

Nearly half of vehicle theft is the result of driver error, such as leaving a key in the ignition or a door unlocked. An unlocked door or window is an easy target for thieves.

The estimated total value of vehicles stolen nationwide each year exceeds $4.3 billion!

Only half of vehicles reported stolen are recovered.

Some tips for keeping your vehicles and valuables safe:

1. **Always close windows, lock doors, and take the key with you**
2. **Never leave your vehicle unattended while running.**
3. **Park in a garage if available. Lock BOTH the car and the garage.**
4. **Don't leave your keys unattended, especially in easily accessible areas.**
5. **Keep vehicle registration and proof of insurance on you; DON'T leave these documents in your glove compartment.**
6. **Always park in well-lit areas.**
7. **Never leave valuables or packages in your vehicle, especially WHERE THEY CAN BE SEEN. Put them in the trunk!**
8. **Report suspicious activity by calling 911.**

(Content provided by the Michigan Auto Theft Prevention Authority, of the Michigan State Police)

Central Michigan University • 1200 S. Franklin St. • Mount Pleasant, Mich. 48859 • 989-774-4000
CMich.edu

HARVARD
Campus Services
ENVIRONMENTAL HEALTH, SAFETY & EMERGENCY MANAGEMENT

Date: 10/6/08 Toolbox Talk #8

DEFENSIVE DRIVING

Always scan ahead for any potential hazards

Watch for bike and pedestrian traffic when traveling around campus

In all cases, while operating a motor vehicle, drivers should practice defensive driving techniques. Defensive driving is the art of driving so as to prevent and avoid traffic crashes, regardless of the unsafe conditions and actions created by other drivers and adverse road and or weather conditions.

A good defensive driver will practice the following eight techniques:

- Glance well ahead in the direction of travel. Look 2 or 3 vehicles ahead to observe driving conditions in front of you. This allows you to consider a condition before you reach it.
- Get the "big picture"; learn to see the entire roadway. Sweep the scene, sides and back. Avoid "tunnel vision". Keep your eyes moving; Position vehicle slightly offset to traffic to increase your field of vision.
- Always allow an escape route, leave a cushion by slowing or moving ahead of the vehicles beside you.
- Keep your vehicle visible and signal your intentions early.
- When stopped prior to making left turns across incoming traffic leave wheels straight to prevent being pushed into oncoming traffic in the event of a rear-end crash.
- When entering intersections practice looking left/right/left. Be sure to come to a full stop before proceeding.
- Learn to compensate for hazards such as weather, debris, potholes, loose gravel, or sand.
- ALWAYS maintain a cautious driving attitude. Remember, when entering a Rotary that Massachusetts law requires you to yield to vehicles already in the Rotary.

Environmental Health, Safety & Emergency Management

Cambridge Campus
46 Blackstone St.
Cambridge MA, 02139
(617) 495-2060

Longwood Campus
107 Ave. Louis Pasteur
Boston, MA 02115
(617) 432-1720

第三章 食品安全案例

导读

2018 年 12 月联合国将 6 月 7 日定为世界食品安全日。食品安全是联合国 17 项可持续性发展目标的重要内容之一。据估计，每年全球有 6 亿人因食用受污染的食品而患病，并有 42 万人因此死亡。这表明食品安全是一个非常重要而且需要人类共同关注的话题。让我们一起去看看澳大利亚和新加坡两国为食品安全做过什么努力吧！

案例阅读

Passage 1

Salmonella Enteritidis (SE) Linked to Eggs

带有肠炎沙门氏菌的鸡蛋

State and territory food regulators, health authorities and agriculture departments in Australia are investigating a rare strain of Salmonella **(Salmonella Enteritidis)** associated with human illness and egg consumption.

Public health officials investigate Salmonella **outbreaks** using a nationally standardized **questionnaire**, and coordinate **epidemiological** investigation through OzFoodNet. DNA Genetic fingerprinting is performed on Salmonella bacteria isolated from ill people by using **whole genome sequencing (WGS)**, which gives a more detailed DNA fingerprint picture than any other typing method. ① WGS performed on bacteria isolated from ill people showed that they were closely related genetically.

This means that ill people in this outbreak were more likely to share a common source of infection. Confirmed human cases linked to this strain have been found in NSW, Victoria, Queensland and Tasmania. As at 17 June 2019 there are a total 235 human cases linked to this outbreak, of which 224 have been confirmed by WGS.

Onset of illness ranges from 18 May 2018 to 23 May 2019. The majority of human cases reside in NSW, but cases have also been detected in Victoria, Queensland, Tasmania and South Australia. Some of the cases from outside NSW are believed to have been infected when travelling in NSW.

Detections of this strain have also occurred on chicken layer farms in NSW, and one farm in Victoria. **Food Standards Australia New Zealand (FSANZ)** is coordinating the response by food regulators under the National Food Incident Response Protocol.

The investigation has already resulted in a small number of food recalls coordinated by FSANZ, in the first half of this year and in September last year. Biosecurity measures and other regulatory action are being applied to affected farms by the relevant authorities. ②

It is important to know that not all eggs are impacted, but if you have purchased recalled eggs, we recommend that you return the products to the place of purchase for **a full refund**, or **discard** the eggs into your garbage, and not into your garden. ③ You should not feed these eggs to your pets, or **livestock**.

Australian authorities will continue to monitor and respond to this issue.

- **What if I have eaten affected eggs?**

It is unlikely you will get sick if you have eaten eggs that have been handled safely and cooked thoroughly. If you are concerned about your own health or your family's health, see your doctor.

- **How can I prevent getting sick from Salmonella?**

To prevent illness:

1) Keep hands and equipment clean when preparing and eating food.

2) Avoid cross **contamination** — for example use separate cutting boards and knives for raw and ready-to-eat food, and store cooked food separately from raw foods.

3) Cook eggs thoroughly.

4) Avoid using dirty or cracked eggs and wash hands after handling eggs.

(**Source**: https://www.foodstandards.gov.au/consumer/safety/Pages/Salmonella-Enteritidis-linked-to-eggs.aspx)

Comprehension Check

Directions: *Tell whether each of the following statements is true or false according to the information from Passage 1.*

1. Confirmed human cases linked to SE have been found in some places of Australia.

2. Some of the human cases from outside NSW are believed to have been infected when paying a visit to NSW.

3. Pets can eat these affected eggs because they are only harmful to human beings.

4. If someone eat the affected eggs, he will certainly get sick and should see his doctor quickly.

5. We should use separate knives for raw and ready-to-eat food in order to avoid cross pollution.

Background Information

Food Standards Australia New Zealand (FSANZ)

澳新食品标准局

澳新食品标准局（FSANZ）前身为澳大利亚新西兰食品管理局 Australia New Zealand Food Authority（ANZFA），它是根据 1991 年澳大利亚新西兰食品标准法（FSANZ Act）成立的，负责制定澳大利亚和新西兰食品标准的政府机构。

FSANZ 制定的食品安全标准包括：食品中的成分、加工助剂、色素、添加剂、维生素、矿物质的限量使用；某些食品如乳制品、肉类、饮料以及转基因食品等通过新技术开发的食品；包装和散装食品的标签要求，例如强制性的明确警告说明或指导性说明；以及澳大利亚境内的农产品生产和加工标准。

FSANZ 不仅为食品企业制定了相关的食品安全标准、召回和监管政策，还为消费者提供了食品标准规范指南，保障公众身体健康。

食品安全标准规定澳大利亚食品生产者有义务生产安全且适宜食用的食品，食品生产经营者对所经营食品有健康和卫生义务，旨在降低食源性疾病的发病率。作为澳大利亚和新西兰食品监管体系的一部分，FSANZ 在食品安全方面发挥着重要作用。

Food Standards Australia New Zealand (FSANZ) is an independent statutory agency established by the Food Standards Australia New Zealand Act 1991 (FSANZ Act). FSANZ is part of the Australian Government's Health portfolio.

FSANZ develops standards that regulate the use of ingredients, processing aids, colorings, additives, vitamins and minerals. The Food Standards Code also covers the composition of some foods, such as dairy, meat and beverages as well as foods developed by new technologies such as genetically modified foods. We are also responsible for some labelling requirements for packaged and unpackaged food, for example specific mandatory warnings or advisory labels. FSANZ also develops Australia-only primary production and processing standards.

The food safety standards aim to lower the incidence of foodborne illness. They place obligations on Australian food businesses to produce food that is safe and suitable to eat, and also place health and hygiene obligations on food handlers.

There are five food safety standards:

1. Interpretation and application

This standard defines the terms used in the food safety standards, specifies these standards apply to Australia only and that food businesses and food handlers must comply with their respective requirements.

2. Food safety programs

This standard enables states and territories to require food businesses to implement a food safety program and sets out the general requirements for these programs. A food safety program identifies the food safety hazards associated with a business's food handling activities and indicates how the business will monitor and control these hazards.

3. Food safety practices and general requirements

This standard specifies food handling controls related to the receipt, storage, processing, display, packaging, transportation, disposal and recall of food. Other requirements relate to the skills and knowledge of food handlers and their supervisors, the health and hygiene of food handlers, and the cleaning, sanitizing and maintenance of food premises and equipment.

4. Food premises and equipment

This standard sets out Australian requirements for the design and construction of food premises, fixtures, fittings, equipment and food transport vehicles. It aims to ensure that, where possible, the layout of the premises minimizes opportunities for food contamination. These requirements should help food businesses meet the food safety requirements of Standard.

5. Food safety programs for food service to vulnerable persons

This standard requires Australian food businesses that prepare food for service to vulnerable people to implement a food safety program. This includes businesses providing food to hospital patients, aged care residents and children in childcare centers, who are generally at greater risk of foodborne illness. It usually also includes delivered meal organizations.

(**Source**: https://www.foodstandards.gov.au/about/Pages/default.aspx)

Vocabulary and Key Notes

1. **Salmonella Enteritidis** 肠炎沙门氏菌

2. **outbreak** *n.* the sudden start of sth. unpleasant, especially violence or a disease（暴力、疾病等坏事的）爆发，突然发生

3. **questionnaire** *n.* a written list of questions that are answered by a number of people so that information can be collected from the answers 调查表；问卷

4. **epidemiology** *n.* the study of the way diseases spread, and how to control them 流行病学 epidemiological *adj.* 流行病学的

5. **Whole Genome Sequencing (WGS)** 全基因组测序

6. **Food Standards Australia New Zealand (FSANZ)** 澳大利亚新西兰食品标准局

7. **a full refund** 全额退款

8. **discard** *v.* to get rid of sth. that you no longer want or need 丢弃；抛弃

9. **livestock** *n.* the animals kept on a farm, for example cows or sheep 牲畜；家畜

10. **contamination** *n.* a process of contaminating; a state of being contaminated 污染

Translation

Directions: *Translate the following sentences from Passage 1 into Chinese.*

1. DNA Genetic fingerprinting is performed on Salmonella bacteria isolated from ill people by using whole genome sequencing (WGS), which gives a more detailed DNA fingerprint picture than any other typing method.

2. Biosecurity measures and other regulatory action are being applied to affected farms by the relevant authorities.

3. It is important to know that not all eggs are impacted, but if you have purchased recalled eggs, we recommend that you return the products to the place of purchase for a full refund, or discard the eggs into your garbage, and not into your garden.

Passage 2

The Singapore Food Agency (SFA)

新加坡食品管理局

The Singapore Food Agency (SFA) publishes food safety statistics biannually (in January and June) to improve the public's understanding of SFA's risk-based, farm-to-fork approach to protecting public health.

Singapore imports over 90% of our food. The volume of food arriving on our shores every day is large. The food can be contaminated anywhere along the supply chain. Therefore, not every single food item in the market can be inspected and tested. Food safety authorities around the world face this challenge.

SFA, as the national authority for food safety, adopts a risk-based approach to food safety. It is guided by a science-based risk assessment and management approach that is consistent with international standards. This means food of higher risks are subjected to more **stringent** checks.

SFA has in place an **integrated** food safety system from farm-to-fork to ensure that food is safe for consumption. This comprises control measures along the food supply such as **accreditation** of overseas sources of food of higher risks (e.g., meat, eggs), licensing of local food establishments, inspections, and testing. ①

- **At the Point of Import**

Imported fruits and vegetables, livestock (poultry and pigs), eggs, meat, and seafood, and processed foods are inspected and sampled at the point of import. Samples are collected during these inspections to ensure the food meet our regulatory standards, which include **microbiological**, pesticides, drug residues, preservatives, contaminants, and additives. ② For food products that fail our tests, SFA follows up with the importers, including rejecting the affected **consignments** and requiring importers to rectify the issue with their suppliers from overseas.

Food that are illegally imported pose a food safety risk. Offenders who illegally import food are liable on conviction to a maximum fine of $50,000 and/or imprisonment for a term not exceeding two years.

- **Local Regulation of Food Establishments**

For food produced, manufactured, and sold locally, SFA licenses and inspects the premises

6. **A person** who is required by a direction to recall food or a food contact article must give written notice to the Director-General of the completion of the recall as soon as practicable after that completion.

7. If a person to whom the direction is given under this section fails or refuses to comply with it, the Director-General may —

1) **take any reasonable steps** necessary to ensure control of the food or food contact article (including entry by authorized officers to a place under a warrant); and

2) **recover the costs and expenses** reasonably incurred in assuming control of the food or food contact article as a debt due from the person to whom the direction was given.

- **Consumers have a role to play**

Food can potentially be contaminated through improper practices from the time it is produced to the time it is consumed. Food safety requires the joint effort of the Government, food industry, and consumers.

Consumers have an important role to play in ensuring food safety as they have direct control over the food they buy, handle, prepare, and consume. To make a more informed choice when deciding which food establishment to patronize or engage, look for track records (grading, number of demerit points and suspension history) of the food establishment on go.gov.sg/sfa-food-retail-license.

In addition, consumers should equip themselves with knowledge of food safety risks and good food safety practices.

Lastly, consumers who come across any errant food operator should report to SFA via the online feedback form.

(**Source:** https://csp.sfa.gov.sg/feedback)

II. The flow chart below can help you better understand food recall in Singapore.

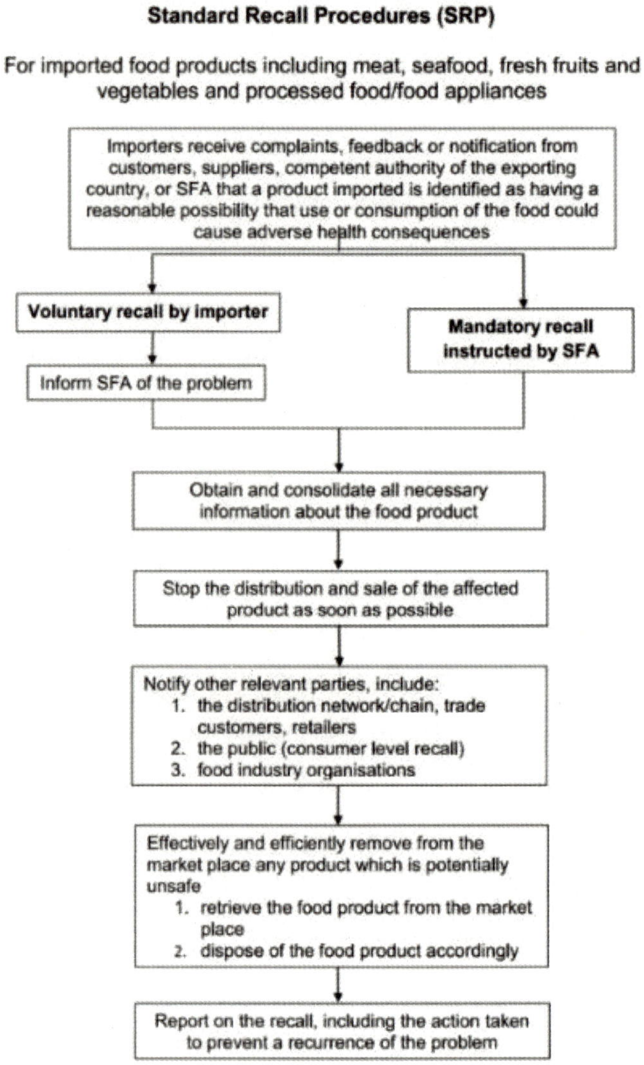

Vocabulary and Key Notes

1. **The Singapore Food Agency (SFA)** 新加坡食品管理局

2. **stringent** *adj*. very strict and that must be obeyed 严格的；严厉的

3. **integrated** *adj*. in which many different parts are closely connected and work successfully together 各部分密切协调的；综合的；完整统一的

4. **accreditation** *n.* official approval given by an organization stating that sb./sth. has achieved a required standard 达到标准；证明合格

5. **microbiological** *n.* studies or tests relating to very small living things such as bacteria and their effects on people 微生物学的；微生物的

6. **consignment** *n.* a quantity of goods that are sent or delivered somewhere 装运的货物；运送物

7. **lapse** *n.* a small mistake, especially one that is caused by forgetting sth. or by being careless 小错；（尤指）记错，过失，疏忽

8. **gastroenteritis** *n.* an illness in which the lining of your stomach and intestines becomes swollen and painful. 肠胃炎

9. **inflammation** *n.* a painful redness or swelling of a part of your body that results from an infection, injury, or illness. 炎症

10. **diarrhea** *n.* an illness in which waste matter is emptied from the bowels much more frequently than normal, and in liquid form 腹泻

11. **vomit** *v.* If you vomit, food and drink comes back up from your stomach and out through your mouth. 呕吐

12. **hygiene** *n.* the practice of keeping yourself and your living and working areas clean in order to prevent illness and disease 卫生

Translation

Directions: *Translate the following sentences from Passage 1 into Chinese.*

1. This comprises control measures along the food supply such as accreditation of overseas sources of food of higher risks (e.g. meat, eggs), licensing of local food establishments, inspections, and testing.

2. Samples are collected during these inspections to ensure the food meet our regulatory standards, which include microbiological, pesticides, drug residues, preservatives, contaminants, and additives.

3. While pathogens can be transmitted through food, viruses such as Norovirus can also be transmitted from person to person, or via environmental surfaces, especially as a result of improper personal hygiene.

Supplementary Reading

Suspension of ** Food (S) Pte Ltd's Food Business Operations

暂停 ** 食品有限公司的一切食品业务运营

The Singapore Food Agency (SFA) has suspended the food business operations of ** Food (S) Pte Ltd, with effect from 20 January 2022 until further notice.

On 19 January 2022, during an inspection of the said premises, widespread cockroach infestations were observed in the food preparation areas. The premises was also found to be dirty and poorly maintained.

In the interest of public health, SFA directed the licensee to rectify the lapses and take necessary measures to improve the food safety practices and the cleanliness of its premises. As a precautionary measure, SFA has also directed the company to dispose the bean curd "tau kwa" that was manufactured on the day of inspection. None of the implicated foods were distributed (i.e. not available for sale).

Food safety is a joint responsibility as food can be contaminated anywhere along the food chain. While SFA continues to be vigilant and works to ensure that regulatory measures are in place and properly enforced, the industry and consumers must also play their part.

All food operators should ensure that their premises are clean and well maintained, and staff are adequately trained on proper food safety management. SFA will take enforcement action against food operators who do not adhere to regulations or comply with food safety requirements. Offenders are liable on conviction to a fine not exceeding $10,000 or to imprisonment for a term not exceeding 12 months or to both.

Members of the public who come across poor food safety practices in food establishments are advised not to patronize them and provide feedback via our online feedback form (www.sfa.gov.sg/feedback) with details for our follow-up investigations.

(**Source:** https://www.sfa.gov.sg/docs/default-source/default-document-library/sfa-media-release---suspension-of-hensin-food-(s)-pte-ltd-s-food-business-operations.pdf)

Further Discussion

Answer the following questions:

1. Have you ever eaten affected food? What did you do? How did you feel? And how did

you deal with the food?

2. Do you have any suggestions for expired food?

3. What is food safety and why is food safety important?

小语说语：mitigate

v. lessen or to try to lessen the seriousness or extent of sth. (punishment) 缩减，安慰，缓和，减轻

- **原文**

… if the Director-General has reasonable grounds to believe that the direction is necessary to mitigate the adverse consequences of a serious danger to public health.

……如果总干事有合理理由相信该召回指令对减轻严重危害公共健康的不利后果是必要的。

- **短语引申**

mitigated injury 轻度伤害

mitigated offense 减轻犯

mitigate the risks 化解风险

- **例句**

例 1：Parties should be mindful of drafting and negotiating carefully the relevant provisions to eradicate or at least mitigate the risks.

缔约方应谨慎对待有关规定的起草和交涉，以消除或至少减轻风险。

例 2：An amount that is more than 30% of the actual losses suffered by the innocent party may be considered as “excessively high” and may be mitigated by the court.

赔偿金超过无过错方所受实际损失的 30% 以上，可能会被视为“过高”，并可能被法院裁定减轻。

- **国内外法条学习**

例 1：Where an infringed person is also at fault for the occurrence or aggravation of the same damage to himself, the liability of the tortfeasor may be **mitigated**.

被侵权人对同一损害的发生或者扩大有过错的，可以减轻侵权人的责任。（《中华人民共和国民法典》第一千一百七十三条）

例 2：When the penalty is for a violation which may have had an effect on a known Indian tribal religious or cultural site on public lands, the Federal land manager should consult with and consider the interests of the affected tribe(s) prior to proposing to **mitigate** or remit the penalty.

针对可能影响公共土地上已知的印第安部落宗教或文化遗址的违法行为，联邦土地管理者应在提出减轻或免除处罚前与受影响部落协商并考虑其利益。（《美国联邦法规》第229.16条）

例3：If a person who has attained to the age of 14 but not to the age of 18 commits an act against the administration of public security, he shall be given a relatively light or **mitigated** penalty.

已满十四周岁不满十八周岁的人违反治安管理的，从轻或者减轻处罚。（《中华人民共和国治安处理处罚法》第十二条）

Supplementary Poster Reading (flyer/brochure)

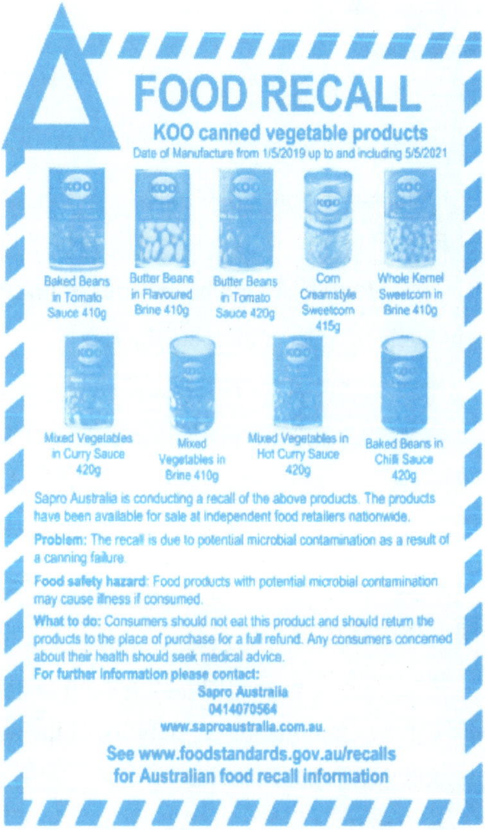

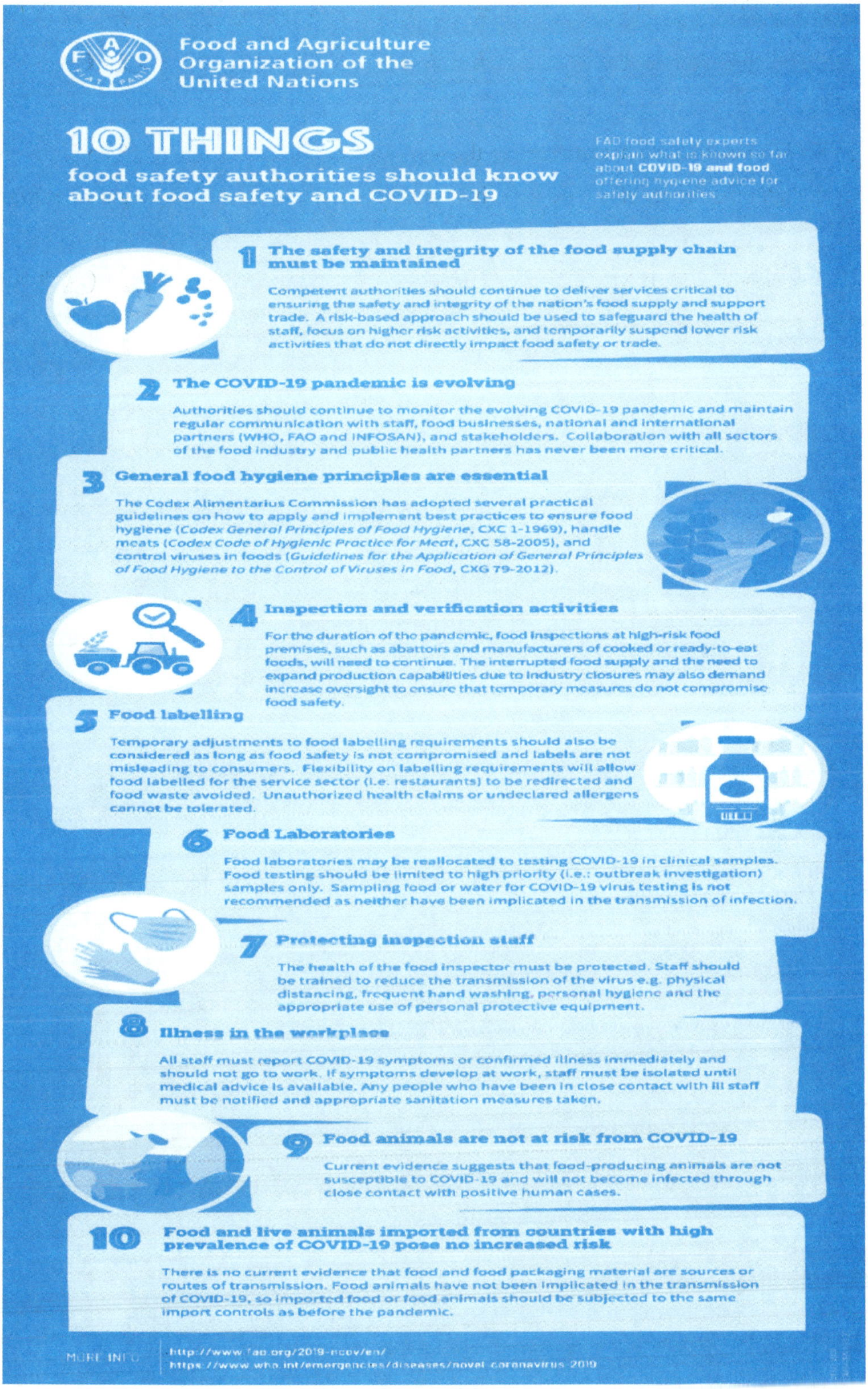
Food and Agriculture Organization of the United Nations
10 THINGS
food safety authorities should know about food safety and COVID-19
FAO food safety experts explain what is known so far about COVID-19 and food offering hygiene advice for safety authorities
1 The safety and integrity of the food supply chain must be maintained
Competent authorities should continue to deliver services critical to ensuring the safety and integrity of the nation's food supply and support trade. A risk-based approach should be used to safeguard the health of staff, focus on higher risk activities, and temporarily suspend lower risk activities that do not directly impact food safety or trade.
2 The COVID-19 pandemic is evolving
Authorities should continue to monitor the evolving COVID-19 pandemic and maintain regular communication with staff, food businesses, national and international partners (WHO, FAO and INFOSAN), and stakeholders. Collaboration with all sectors of the food industry and public health partners has never been more critical.
3 General food hygiene principles are essential
The Codex Alimentarius Commission has adopted several practical guidelines on how to apply and implement best practices to ensure food hygiene (Codex General Principles of Food Hygiene, CXC 1-1969), handle meats (Codex Code of Hygienic Practice for Meat, CXC 58-2005), and control viruses in foods (Guidelines for the Application of General Principles of Food Hygiene to the Control of Viruses in Food, CXG 79-2012).
4 Inspection and verification activities
For the duration of the pandemic, food inspections at high-risk food premises, such as abattoirs and manufacturers of cooked or ready-to-eat foods, will need to continue. The interrupted food supply and the need to expand production capabilities due to industry closures may also demand increase oversight to ensure that temporary measures do not compromise food safety.
5 Food labelling
Temporary adjustments to food labelling requirements should also be considered as long as food safety is not compromised and labels are not misleading to consumers. Flexibility on labelling requirements will allow food labelled for the service sector (i.e. restaurants) to be redirected and food waste avoided. Unauthorized health claims or undeclared allergens cannot be tolerated.
6 Food Laboratories
Food laboratories may be reallocated to testing COVID-19 in clinical samples. Food testing should be limited to high priority (i.e.: outbreak investigation) samples only. Sampling food or water for COVID-19 virus testing is not recommended as neither have been implicated in the transmission of infection.
7 Protecting inspection staff
The health of the food inspector must be protected. Staff should be trained to reduce the transmission of the virus e.g. physical distancing, frequent hand washing, personal hygiene and the appropriate use of personal protective equipment.
8 Illness in the workplace
All staff must report COVID-19 symptoms or confirmed illness immediately and should not go to work. If symptoms develop at work, staff must be isolated until medical advice is available. Any people who have been in close contact with ill staff must be notified and appropriate sanitation measures taken.
9 Food animals are not at risk from COVID-19
Current evidence suggests that food-producing animals are not susceptible to COVID-19 and will not become infected through close contact with positive human cases.
10 Food and live animals imported from countries with high prevalence of COVID-19 pose no increased risk
There is no current evidence that food and food packaging material are sources or routes of transmission. Food animals have not been implicated in the transmission of COVID-19, so imported food or food animals should be subjected to the same import controls as before the pandemic.
MORE INFO
http://www.fao.org/2019-ncov/en/
https://www.who.int/emergencies/diseases/novel-coronavirus-2019

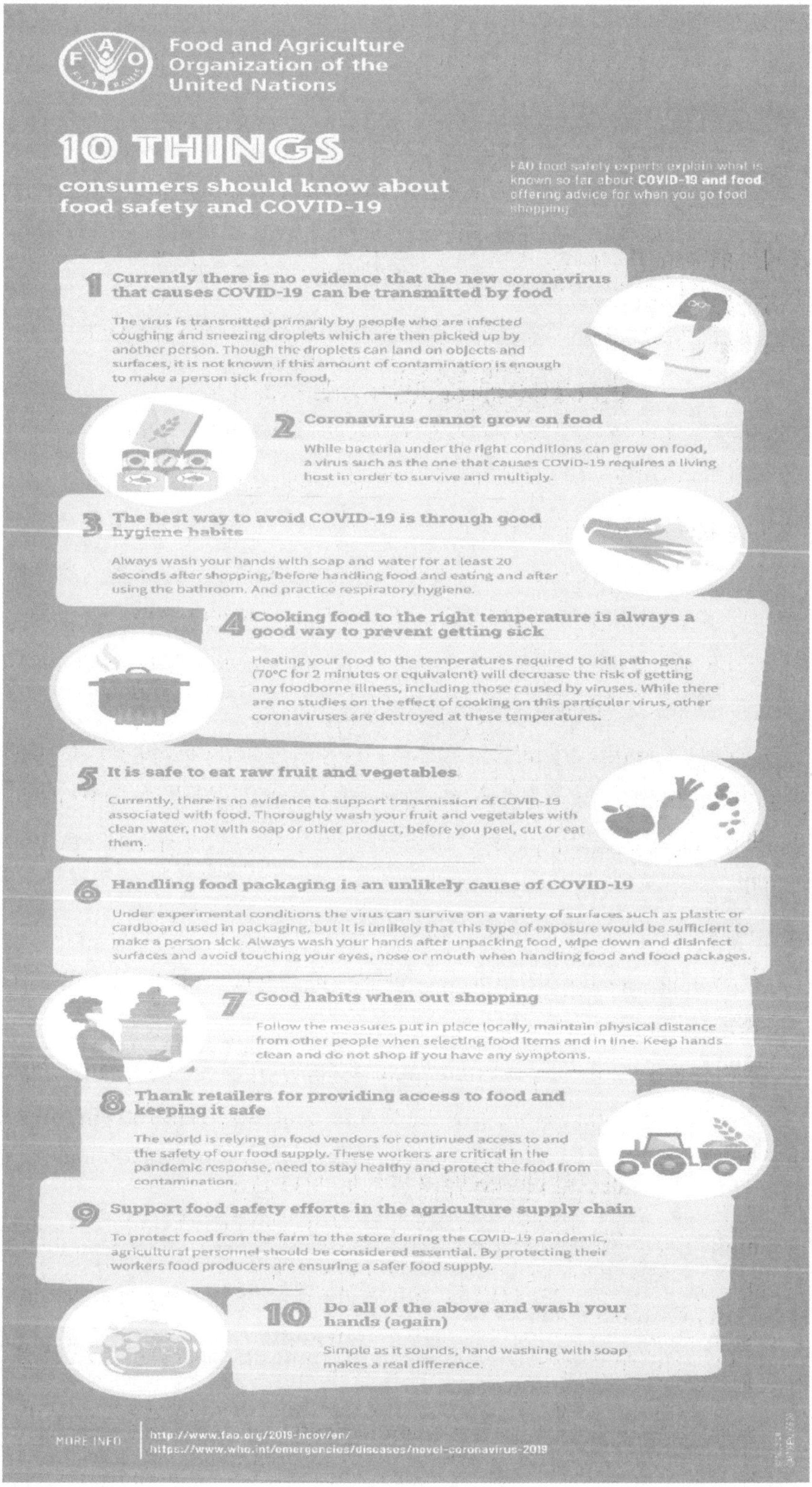
Food and Agriculture
Organization of the
United Nations
10 THINGS
consumers should know about
food safety and COVID-19
FAO food safety experts explain what is known so far about COVID-19 and food, offering advice for when you go food shopping
1 Currently there is no evidence that the new coronavirus that causes COVID-19 can be transmitted by food
The virus is transmitted primarily by people who are infected coughing and sneezing droplets which are then picked up by another person. Though the droplets can land on objects and surfaces, it is not known if this amount of contamination is enough to make a person sick from food.
2 Coronavirus cannot grow on food
While bacteria under the right conditions can grow on food, a virus such as the one that causes COVID-19 requires a living host in order to survive and multiply.
3 The best way to avoid COVID-19 is through good hygiene habits
Always wash your hands with soap and water for at least 20 seconds after shopping, before handling food and eating and after using the bathroom. And practice respiratory hygiene.
4 Cooking food to the right temperature is always a good way to prevent getting sick
Heating your food to the temperatures required to kill pathogens (70°C for 2 minutes or equivalent) will decrease the risk of getting any foodborne illness, including those caused by viruses. While there are no studies on the effect of cooking on this particular virus, other coronaviruses are destroyed at these temperatures.
5 It is safe to eat raw fruit and vegetables
Currently, there is no evidence to support transmission of COVID-19 associated with food. Thoroughly wash your fruit and vegetables with clean water, not with soap or other product, before you peel, cut or eat them.
6 Handling food packaging is an unlikely cause of COVID-19
Under experimental conditions the virus can survive on a variety of surfaces such as plastic or cardboard used in packaging, but it is unlikely that this type of exposure would be sufficient to make a person sick. Always wash your hands after unpacking food, wipe down and disinfect surfaces and avoid touching your eyes, nose or mouth when handling food and food packages.
7 Good habits when out shopping
Follow the measures put in place locally, maintain physical distance from other people when selecting food items and in line. Keep hands clean and do not shop if you have any symptoms.
8 Thank retailers for providing access to food and keeping it safe
The world is relying on food vendors for continued access to and the safety of our food supply. These workers are critical in the pandemic response, need to stay healthy and protect the food from contamination.
9 Support food safety efforts in the agriculture supply chain
To protect food from the farm to the store during the COVID-19 pandemic, agricultural personnel should be considered essential. By protecting their workers food producers are ensuring a safer food supply.
10 Do all of the above and wash your hands (again)
Simple as it sounds, hand washing with soap makes a real difference.
MORE INFO
http://www.fao.org/2019-ncov/en/
https://www.who.int/emergencies/diseases/novel-coronavirus-2019

第四章 旅行安全案例

导读

互联网上的旅游出行信息真假难辨，给不法分子以可乘之机。旅游诈骗案例究竟有多少？都是如何诈骗的？

本文将带您揭开那些布满鲜花的陷阱，这份防诈骗宝典请收好哦！

案例阅读

Passage 1

Beware of Holiday Fraud as Travel Restrictions Ease

旅行限制放宽　谨防假日欺诈

Action Fraud, the national reporting center for fraud and **cyber-crime**, received 1,907 reports of holiday and travel related fraud in 2020/21 financial year — a decrease of over 70 per cent when compared to the previous financial year. ①

However, although a decline in reporting was predicted due to the fact travel was banned for large periods of the year, losses by victims still totaled £2,205,251 during this time — an average loss of £1,242 per victim.

Action Fraud has launched a national awareness campaign (Monday 17 May 2021) to remind the public to think twice before handing over their money and personal information when booking holidays, following the government's recent announcement on international travel resuming. ②

Pauline Smith, Head of Action Fraud, said: "We are all more eager than ever to go on a holiday and relax with family and friends, following the **coronavirus** pandemic. However, criminals will stop at nothing when it comes to **defrauding** innocent people out of a well-deserved break and their **hard-earned** cash. ③

"Criminals are increasingly using more **sophisticated** ways to trick their victims, which is why it's important that we all do our research when booking a holiday and making travel arrangements. ④ Regardless of whether you're planning on travelling abroad, or going on a domestic holiday this year, remember, if a deal sounds too good to be true, it probably is."

Last year, criminals targeted **unsuspecting** holidaymakers booking airline tickets (56 per cent) and holiday accommodation (29 per cent). Almost three quarters of victims were aged between 19 to 50 years old (73 per cent).

Almost a third (32 per cent) of reports stated the victim had contact with the suspect after they responded to an approach, or advertisement, on a social media platform.

Out of these reports, Facebook was the most common platform (62 per cent) where victims were defrauded.

Online booking platforms, such as Airbnb and Booking.com, were mentioned in almost 10 per cent of reports made. Online booking platforms act as a platform for third parties to advertise accommodation.

Whilst many accommodation providers who make use of online booking platforms are legitimate, some criminals will use these platforms to defraud victims by advertising **bogus** accommodation.

Some victims (7 per cent) reported falling victim to suspects **impersonating legitimate** travel companies, including clone comparison websites, airline websites and holiday accommodation websites. ⑤

In some cases, victims have searched for flight tickets online and have found a website they believe to be the company's genuine website. In other cases, victims have used what they believe to be legitimate flight comparison websites to search for flights.

In both instances, victims reported being contacted by someone **purporting to** be from the airline, or flight comparison website, to take them through the booking procedure and take payment.

Sadly, some victims have only become aware that they have been the victim of fraud when they arrive at the airport and are unable to **check-in**.

(**Source**: https://www.actionfraud.police.uk/alert/beware-of-holiday-fraud-as-travel-restrictions-ease)

Comprehension Check

Directions: *Tell whether each of the following statements is true or false according to the information from Passage 1.*

1. Action Fraud had a decline in reporting of holiday and travel related fraud in 2020/21 financial year compared to the previous financial year.

2. Losses by victims are still serious during 2020/21 financial year due to the fact travel was banned for large periods of the year.

3. Criminals will spare no efforts to defraud innocent people out of a well-deserved break and their hard-earned cash.

4. Criminals are increasingly using more naive ways to trick their victims.

5. Some criminals will use legitimate online booking platforms to defraud victims.

Background Information

Action Fraud

反诈骗行动机构

反诈骗行动机构（Action Fraud）是英国国家欺诈和网络犯罪报告中心。如果涉案方身在英国或该诈骗行为发生在英国，或该诈骗行为虽发生在网上但与英国有关，您都可以向“反诈骗行动机构”举报这些诈骗行为。反诈骗行动机构是提供相关反诈骗知识、识别诈骗行为并对诈骗行为受害者提供帮助的组织。

Action Fraud is the UK's national reporting center for fraud and cyber-crime where you should report fraud if you have been scammed, defrauded or experienced cyber-crime.

Vocabulary and Key Notes

1. **cyber-crime** *n.* crime committed using a computer and the internet to steal a person's identity or sell contraband or stalk victims or disrupt operations with malevolent programs 网络犯罪；计算机犯罪

2. **coronavirus** *n.* species in the genera of virus belonging to the subfamily coronaviridae; enveloped viruses with a positive-sense RNA genome and with a nucleocapisd of helical symmetry 冠状病毒；日冕形病毒

3. **defraud** *v.* to get money illegally from a person or an organization by tricking them 骗取；诈取（……的钱财）

4. **hard-earned** *adj.* 来之不易的

5. **sophisticated** *adj*. having or appealing to those having worldly knowledge and refinement and savoir-faire 复杂的；精致的；久经世故的；富有经验的

6. **unsuspecting** *adj*. feeling no suspicion; not aware of danger or of sth. bad 毫不怀疑的；无危险意识的；无戒备心的

7. **bogus** *adj*. pretending to be real or genuine 假的；伪造的

8. **impersonate** *v*. to pretend to be sb. in order to trick people or to entertain them 冒充；假扮；扮演

9. **legitimate** *adj*. for which there is a fair and acceptable reason 正当合理的; 合情合理的; allowed and acceptable according to the law 合法的；法律认可的；法定的；（of a child 小孩）born when its parents are legally married to each other 合法婚姻所生的

10. **purporting**（动词 + 带 to 的不定式） to claim to be sth. or to have done sth., when this may not be true 自称；标榜

11. **check-in** *n*. the place where you go first when you arrive at an airport, to show your ticket, etc. （机场的）登机手续办理处

Translation

Directions: *Translate the following sentences from Passage 1 into Chinese.*

1. Action Fraud, the national reporting center for fraud and **cyber-crime**, received 1,907 reports of holiday and travel related fraud in 2020/21 financial year — a decrease of over 70 per cent when compared to the previous financial year.

2. Action Fraud has launched a national awareness campaign (Monday 17 May 2021) to remind the public to think twice before handing over their money and personal information when booking holidays, following the government's recent announcement on international travel resuming.

3. Criminals will stop at nothing when it comes to defrauding out of a well-deserved break and their hard-earned cash.

4. Criminals are increasingly using more sophisticated ways to trick their victims, which is why it's important that we all do our research when booking a holiday and making travel arrangements.

5. Some victims (7 per cent) reported falling victim to suspects impersonating legitimate travel companies, including clone comparison websites, airline websites and holiday accommodation websites.

Passage 2

What to Look out for When Buying Travel Insurance

买旅游保险要注意什么

If there is a last-minute **cancellation**, you may lose the money paid for that tour. Buying travel insurance can cover this and other unwelcome possibilities and help you recover some or all the cost **incurred.** ①

1. What to look out for

Get quotations from various travel insurers. Make sure your insurance plan provides coverage for major **contingencies** that can affect your trip.

- Trip cancellation, postponement and delay
- Flight delays and missed flights
- Emergency **evacuation** due to health problem or injury
- **Repatriation** of remains or body on death
- Hospitalization and medical care for listed illnesses and injuries
- Lost money, luggage and travel documents

In addition, you should check the following with your insurer.

(a) Health status

You must inform your insurers about any **pre-existing** health conditions. Otherwise, you may have difficulty getting your insurer to honor some of your claims later. ②

(b) Coverage

Is the insurance plan suitable for your needs? For example, if you are carrying very expensive electronic equipment, you may want to increase the amount insured for lost baggage or buy specific coverage for your equipment. On the other hand, if you are going to ski or climb mountains, make sure your plan covers **hazardous** sports and has sufficient coverage for medical evacuation, including the cost of airlifting if necessary. ③

(c) Excess clauses

An excess or **deductible** component reduces the amount you can claim. As such, it may be better to get a plan offering full insurance pay out.

(d) **Exclusions**

Some plans may not include coverage for places and activities deemed dangerous by the insurer. So if you plan to visit **war-torn** Iraq or climb Mount Everest, make sure your preferred insurance plan covers such areas and activities. If in doubt, seek confirmation that your destination or planned activities are under coverage.

2. Other considerations

(a) Starting date

Some plans kick start before your scheduled departure. Such plans insure you against pre-trip changes. ④

(b) Single versus annual plan

If you travel often, it may be more convenient and economical to buy an annual plan. Usually, such plans offer coverage for up to 90 days per trip, with no restrictions on how often you travel during the period of coverage. ⑤

(**Source:** www.case.org.sg)

Comprehension Check

Directions: *Tell whether each of the following statements is true or false according to the information form Passage 2.*

1. For health status, you must inform your insurers about any pre-existing health conditions.

2. You can increase the amount of the insurance to protect your expensive electronic equipments.

3. An excess or deductible component reduces the amount you can claim.

4. Some plans may not include coverage for places and activities deemed dangerous by the insurer.

5. Buying travel insurance can help you recover all the cost incurred.

Background Information

The Consumers Association of Singapore (CASE)

新加坡消费者协会

新加坡消费者协会（CASE）是一个非营利性的非政府组织，致力于通过信息和教育保护消费者利益，倡导公平环境和合乎道德标准的商业行为。自成立起始，协助有关部门制定了《消费者保障（公平贸易）法》（CPFTA）（第 52A 章）和《消费者自由贸易协定》，并于 2004 年 3 月 1 日实施。

The Consumers Association of Singapore (CASE) is a non-profit, non-governmental organization that is committed towards protecting consumers' interest through information and education, and promoting an environment of fair and ethical trade practices. One of the key achievements is in advocating for the Consumer Protection (Fair Trading) Act (CPFTA) which came into effect on March 1, 2004.

- **Lemon Law 柠檬法 / 产品缺陷法**

新加坡《消费者保障（公平贸易）法》第三部分规定了“柠檬法”条款。“柠檬法”也称为新加坡《产品缺陷法》，于 2012 年 9 月 1 日生效。该法律规定消费者可以在购买商品 6 个月内对缺陷产品提出索赔。卖家有义务维修、更换、退还或降价处理有缺陷的产品。柠檬法的规定是消费者保障法的第 12A 至 12F 条。

The Lemon Law took effect on 1 September 2012. It is a law that protects consumers against goods that do not conform to contract or are not of satisfactory quality or performance standards at the time of delivery. Under the Lemon Law, businesses are obligated to repair, replace, reduce the price or provide a refund for a defective good.

Vocabulary and Key Notes

1. **cancellation** *n.* a decision to stop sth. that has already been arranged from happening; a statement that will not happen 取消；撤销；something that has been cancelled 被取消了的事物；the fact of making sth. no longer valid 作废；废除；取消；中止

2. **incur** *v.* to suffer or bring on oneself (a liability or expensc) 招致；遭受；引起

3. **contingency** *n.* an event that may or may not happen 可能发生的事；偶发（或不测、意外）事件

4. **evacuation** *v.* to move people from a place of danger to a safer place （把人从危险的地方）疏散、转移、撤离

5. **repatriation** *n.* to send or bring sb. back to their own country 遣送回国；遣返

6. **pre-existing** *adj.* 先已存在的，早已存在的

7. **hazardous** *adj.* involving risk or danger, especially to sb.'s health or safety 危险的；危害的

8. **deductible** *adj.* that can be taken away from an amount of money you earn, from tax, etc. 可扣除的；可减免的

9. **exclusion** *n.* ~ (of sb./sth.) (from sth.) the act of preventing sb./sth. from entering a place or taking in sth. 排斥；排除在外；an insurance-policy provision that excepts certain events or conditions from coverage 除外条款

10. **war-torn** *adj.* a war-torn country or area is severely affected by the fighting that is taking place there 受战争严重破坏的；饱受战争蹂躏的

Translation

Directions: *Translate the following sentences from Passage 2 into Chinese.*

1. If there is a last-minute cancellation, you may lose the money paid for that tour. Buying travel insurance can cover this and other unwelcome possibilities and help you recover some or all the cost incurred.

2. You must inform your insurers about any pre-existing health conditions. Otherwise, you may have difficulty getting your insurer to honor some of your claims later.

3. On the other hand, if you are going to ski or climb mountains, make sure your plan covers hazardous sports and has sufficient coverage for medical evacuation, including the cost of airlifting if necessary.

4. Some plans kick start before your scheduled departure. Such plans insure you against pre-trip changes.

5. Usually, such plans offer coverage for up to 90 days per trip, with no restrictions on how often you travel during the period of coverage.

Supplementary Reading

Beware of Holiday and Travel Booking Scams

谨防度假及旅游预订诈骗

When using the Internet to research or book your holiday or other travel arrangements, the world is literally at your fingertips. However, there are risks associated with doing so — some specific to holiday and travel booking and some which are in common with other types of online purchases.

Fraud resulting from making payments over unsecured web pages.

Flight scams:

Where you book a flight and receive a fake ticket, or pay for a ticket that never arrives.

Holiday scams:

Fake websites and email offers for holidays or villas that do not exist. They require you to pay a deposit, which you never see again.

Fake competition scams defrauding you out of a fee to secure a holiday.

Inadvertently advertising the fact that your house will be empty when you are away, by posting on social networking or travel tracking sites. Some insurance companies are now rejecting claims if homes are targeted by burglars while the owners are away on holiday and made reference to it on social networking sites.

Safe booking

Ensure that any holiday or travel company unfamiliar to you is reputable by researching them online. Ensure that they are a member of a recognized travel authority which offers financial protection and a complaints service.

When possible, pay for holidays and travel using your credit card as this offers additional financial protection over other methods. Please note that your holiday or travel company may levy a surcharge for credit card payments.

Double check all details such as travel dates, itineraries, destinations and travelers before confirming payment, as you may be charged for amendments.

Take out travel insurance adequate for your destination, activities and everyone in your party.

Do not reply to unsolicited emails from companies you don't recognize.

If renting a private apartment or villa, call the owner/agent directly to ensure that it is legitimate. If the number is not provided, email and request it. Check reviews on TripAdvisor or similar sites. Get the full address of the property and find it on Google maps to check its location and legitimacy.

Prior to payment, obtain a contract setting out terms and conditions of the rental, deposits, payment terms etc.

Before entering payment card details on a website, ensure that the link is secure, in two ways:

There should be a padlock symbol in the browser window frame, which appears when you attempt to log in or register. Be sure that the padlock is not on the page itself… this will probably indicate a fraudulent site.

The web address should begin with "https://". The "s" stands for "secure",

The above indicate only that the link between you and the website owner is secure, and not that the site itself is authentic. You need to do this by carefully checking the address for subtle misspellings, additional words and characters and other irregularities.

Some websites will redirect you to a third-party payment service (such as WorldPay). Ensure that these sites are secure before you make your payment.

Safeguard and remember the password you have chosen for the extra verification services used on some websites, such as Verified by Visa.

On sites such as Facebook Marketplace, other social media buying and selling platforms and forums, you may encounter requests for payment that are not guaranteed to safe, meaning that you could lose your money:

When making a payment to a company or individual, never transfer the money directly into their bank account but use a secure payment site such as PayPal, where money is transferred between two electronic accounts.

Remember that if a seller asks for payment by PayPal Friends & Family, this will be so that they can avoid PayPal charges, but will deny you any payment protection which PayPal may otherwise provide.

And always remember…

Always log out of sites into which you have logged in or registered details. Simply closing your browser is not enough to ensure privacy.

Keep receipts for all online holiday or travel bookings and payments.

Check credit card and bank statements carefully after booking to ensure that the correct amount has been debited, and also that no fraud has taken place as a result of the booking.

Before you post details of your travel dates on social networking or travel tracking sites, ensure that the correct privacy settings are in place.

Ensure you have effective and updated antivirus/antispyware software and firewall running before you go online.

If you think you have been a victim of fraud:

Report it to Action Fraud, the UK's national fraud reporting center by calling 0300 123 20 40 or by visiting www.actionfraud.police.uk. If you are in Scotland, contact Police Scotland on 101.

(**Source**: https://www.getsafeonline.org/personal/articles/holiday-and-travel-booking/)

Further Discussion

1. Many women travel safely each year without incident. However, when it comes to health and security, women travelers are more likely to be affected by religious and cultural beliefs of the foreign countries they visit. Do you have some tips for women when travelling alone?

2. When we suffer holiday fraud, what can we do to protect our interests?

小语说语：impersonate

v. to pretend to be sb. in order to trick people or to entertain them 冒充；假扮；扮演

- **原文**

Some victims (7 per cent) reported falling victim to suspects ***impersonating*** legitimate travel companies, including clone comparison websites, airline websites and holiday accommodation websites.

7% 的受害者报告他们成为嫌疑人的受害者。这些嫌疑人冒充合法旅游公司，其行为包括克隆比较网站、航空公司网站和度假住宿网站。

- **短语**

impersonate somebody 模仿某人

role impersonate 角色扮演

impersonation *n.* 扮演；模仿；装扮

- **国内外法条学习**

例 1：Whoever ***impersonates*** a functionary of a State organ to go about and deceive people shall be sentenced to fixed-term imprisonment of not more than three years, criminal detention, public surveillance or deprivation of political rights.

冒充国家机关工作人员招摇撞骗的，处三年以下有期徒刑、拘役、管制或者剥夺政治权利。（《中华人民共和国刑法》第二百七十九条第一款）

例 2：Whoever ***impersonates*** a people's policeman to go about and deceive people shall be imposed a heavier penalty in accordance with the provisions of the preceding paragraph.

冒充人民警察招摇撞骗的，依照前款的规定从重处罚。（《中华人民共和国刑法》第二百七十九条第二款）

例 3：Whoever ***impersonates*** a serviceman to go about and deceive people shall be sentenced to fixed-term imprisonment of not more than three years, criminal detention, public surveillance or deprivation of political rights.

冒充军人招摇撞骗的，处三年以下有期徒刑、拘役、管制或者剥夺政治权利。（《中华人民共和国刑法》第三百七十二条）

Supplementary Poster Reading (flyer/brochure)

£2.2m was lost to holiday fraudsters in the 2020 / 21 financial year
If you think you've fallen victim to holiday fraud, tell your bank immediately and report to Action Fraud at www.actionfraud.police.uk or by calling 0300 123 2040.
ActionFraud
ABTA
Travel with confidence
#HolidayFraud

COLUMBIA UNIVERSITY DEPARTMENT OF
PUBLIC SAFETY
PRIDE • PROFESSIONALISM • SERVICE

Crime Prevention News

March 2015

Spring Break 2015: Have Fun & Be SAFE

Personal safety is the theme, once again, of our March newsletter. As we noted last year in this space, it is imperative that students exercise caution, especially when travelling abroad for Spring Break. Concerns over violence in Ukraine and the continuous possibility of political and social unrest in the Middle East have prompted the State Department to issue travel alerts for those areas. Note that travel alerts are issued when short-term conditions pose a significant risk to the safety and security of U.S. citizens. Travel warnings are issued to advise Americans to avoid travel to countries where long-term, protracted conditions make a country dangerous or unstable. Several countries meet that criteria, including Mexico, a popular spring break destination. And while resorts and tourist destinations generally do not see the level of violent crime that plagues border region cities and states such as Tijuana, Ciudad de Juarez, and Nuevo Leon, you should be aware that instances of crime and violence can occur anywhere. Columbia University's Department of Public Safety urges students to conduct diligent research before venturing out of the country. Following a few simple safety precautions can help make your Spring Break adventure a more enjoyable experience. (Check out the U.S. Department of State's website listed below. You can find valuable information, such as what to do if you are the victim of a crime or lose your passport. You can also sign up to receive travel alerts via Facebook and Twitter).

Before leaving

- Secure your dorm room or apartment.
- Unplug all appliances.
- Make sure all windows are closed and locked.
- Leave a copy of your travel itinerary with someone back home.

Use the buddy system

There is safety in numbers and it is best to do things as a group. Try to have at least three members of your group with you at all times when leaving your hotel. Don't leave a friend behind. If you go out together, come home together!

Drinking

If you are of legal drinking age and you do decide to drink, do so responsibly. Reports indicate that 98% of spring breakers who suffered injuries were intoxicated at the time. Note also that drinking to intoxication leaves a person more susceptible to becoming the victim of a sexual assault or other serious crime. Keep your drink in sight at all times. If you must leave an unfinished drink to go to the bathroom or dance floor, discard it and purchase a new one when you return. Leaving a drink unattended gives anyone (including bar personnel) the opportunity to tamper with it.

Traveling

- If travelling abroad, check the U.S. State Department's Travel Alerts and Warnings at www.travel.state.gov
- Conduct an internet search of the local Newspapers / Crime Stats / Trends of the area you will be visiting.
- Respect your host country and its people by following their laws and customs.
- Practice the country's language ahead of time. Bring a language dictionary to help.
- Avoid carrying large amounts of cash.
- Leave credit cards and ATM cards locked in a secure place.
- Keep track of your baggage and personal belongings at all times.

DO NOT DRINK AND DRIVE Use a designated driver or choose public transportation.

The most important spring break safety tip we can give you is to ask you to use common sense. Trust your instincts! If someone, or someplace, doesn't feel right to you, chances are it isn't. With these safety tips in mind, stay safe, and enjoy your sun-filled spring break! Please watch this short video of a special report from CNN on Spring Break-
http://www.youtube.com/watch?v=0UhzYX9ubZQ

COLUMBIA UNIVERSITY DEPARTMENT OF PUBLIC SAFETY
WWW.COLUMBIA.EDU/CU/PUBLICSAFETY
LOW LIBRARY ROOM 111 - 212-854-2797
BLACK BUILDING ROOM 109 - 212-305-8100

COLUMBIA UNIVERSITY DEPARTMENT OF
PUBLIC SAFETY
PRIDE • PROFESSIONALISM • SERVICE

Crime Prevention News

December 2016

Holiday Safety Reminders

As we embrace the holiday spirit, it is important to remember that not everyone shares our merriment. There are Grinches lurking about, ready to swoop in and steal your joy. Don't let that happen to you. Follow these simple crime prevention tips to make it harder for an opportunistic thief to ruin your holiday.

Don't shop 'til you drop:

- Stay alert and be aware of what is going on around you.
- Park your car in a well-lighted area; close the windows and lock the door.
- Don't leave packages and boxes visible through car windows. Lock them in the trunk or take them directly home.
- Don't carry large amounts of cash. Pay with checks, debit, or credit cards whenever possible.
- Don't get overburdened with packages; always keep one hand free. Don't leave your packages unattended; thieves are always looking for unattended packages and shopping bags.
- Keep your purse close to your body, not dangling loosely. Put your wallet in your front pants pocket or in an inside coat pocket.

When shopping online, use common sense to protect against fraud or ID theft:

- Familiarize yourself with the rules and policies of online stores and auction sites.
- Only shop with companies you know and make sure that the sites comply with industry security standards.
- Keep your personal information private and keep your passwords secure. Do not respond to requests for a password or credit card information unless you initiate the transaction.

Don't make your office a target for crooks looking for extra holiday cash:

- Do not leave gifts lying around an empty office. Secure them in a safe place or lock your office door if possible.
- Always keep your keys and wallet with you. Secure purses and other valuables in a locked drawer or cabinet.
- Don't be embarrassed to challenge an unfamiliar face in the office.
- Remember If you see something say something, call Public Safety immediately **212-854-5555 (MS Campus); 212-305-7979 (Medical Center)** to report suspicious activity or persons.
- Secure your office when stepping out, even for a minute.
- Don't announce that you are leaving town during the holidays. Don't offer information about co-workers' plans to callers.
- Keep petty cash in a secured area.

Students going home for the Holidays : Please make sure to secure your room doors and windows.

Watch this short video on the "Twelve Scams of Christmas": Click Here- Holiday Scams

Columbia University Public Safety Wishes You & Your Family a Happy & Safe Holiday Season!

Like us on Facebook

Columbia University Public Safety's Facebook Page

Are you on Facebook? Columbia University has some great pages on Facebook. We invite you to check out and like CU Public Safety's Facebook page :https://www.facebook.com/cupublicsafety . It's great way to get informed.

COLUMBIA UNIVERSITY DEPARTMENT OF PUBLIC SAFETY
WWW.COLUMBIA.EDU/CU/PUBLICSAFETY
Low Library Room 111 [illegible]
Black Building Room 109 212-305-8100

第五章 网络安全案例

导读

网络是把双刃剑，既能拉近人与人之间的距离，也存在着许许多多的隐患。本文便是这些隐患的真实案例，希望对您有所帮助！让我们共筑网络安全，守护绿色家园。

案例阅读

Passage 1

Online Coloring Book App Recolor Settles FTC Allegations It Illegally Collected Kids' Personal Information

FTC 指控涂色书网络软件非法收集儿童个人信息案达成和解

The operators of an online coloring book app will be required to notify parents and offer **refunds** to current underage subscribers to settle **Federal Trade Commission allegations** that they violated a children's privacy law by **collecting and disclosing personal information** about children who used the app without notifying their parents and obtaining their consent. ①

In a complaint filed by the Department of Justice on behalf of the FTC, the Commission alleged that the Toronto-based Kuuhuub Inc., along with its Finnish subsidiaries Kuu Hubb Oy and Recolor Oy, violated **the Children's Online Privacy Protection Act Rule (COPPA Rule).** The Rule requires websites and apps to provide notice to parents and obtain verifiable parental consent before collecting personal information from children if the website or app — or even a portion of the website or app — is directed at children under 13.

"The law is clear: the personal information of children is **off limits**, and the FTC will continue to investigate companies like Recolor that break or bend the law," said Samuel Levine, Acting Director of the FTC's Bureau of Consumer Protection. "Even if only a portion of an app or website is directed to kids, companies cannot collect their personal information without parental consent, especially if their app or website offers social media features."

The companies operate the Recolor coloring book app, which provides images that users can digitally color on their mobile devices. While billed as a "coloring book for adults," a portion of the coloring book app was directed to children. The images are organized in a library with categories such as Movies and Animals. One popular category, called Kids, included images that would appeal to children, such as animated characters and cartoonish animals.

In addition to the coloring feature, the app, which generates **revenues** from ads and paid subscriptions, offers social media features such as the ability to upload images for others to view, comment on, and like. To access these social media features, users must register for an account by providing an email address, screen name, and an optional profile description and picture, which are made public to other users.

The FTC alleged that some children including those under 13 were able to register for accounts and use some of the social media features. The companies received dozens of complaints from parents and users who said that children were using the app's social media features such as posting **selfies** and interacting with other users including adults.

In its complaint, the FTC alleged that the Recolor app collected personal information from children under the age of 13 who used the app's social media features and allowed third-party advertising networks to collect personal information from users in the form of persistent identifiers, also known as cookies, for targeted ads. The companies failed to instruct the ad networks to refrain from using children's persistent identifiers for behavioral advertising, according to the complaint. The FTC also alleged that the companies failed to provide notice to parents or obtain verifiable parental consent before collecting personal information from underage users of the Recolor app in violation of the COPPA Rule.

Under the **settlement**, the companies must delete all the personal information they collected from children under 13 unless they obtain parental consent, and must offer current paid subscribers of the Recolor app a refund if they were under the age of 18 when they signed up for the app. ② The companies also agreed to a $3 million **monetary penalty**, which will be suspended upon payment of $100,000 due to their inability to pay the full amount. They will be required to pay the full amount if they have misrepresented their finances. In addition, if they sell the app within a year following entry of the order, they must **remit** the **net proceeds** from the sale to the FTC, after the payment of debts and other related expenses.

The companies must notify users of the app about the alleged COPPA Rule violations and the steps that users can take in response to the settlement.

The Commission voted 4-0 to authorize the Department of Justice to file the complaint and **stipulated final order**. The complaint and proposed **consent decree** were filed in the U.S. District Court for the District of Columbia.

(**Source:** https://www.ftc.gov/news-events/press-releases/2021/07/online-coloring-book-app-recolor-settles-ftc-allegations-it)

Comprehension Check

Directions: *Tell whether each of the following statements is true or false according to the information from Passage 1.*

1. FTC is short for Federal Teenagers Commission.

2. In a complaint filed by the Department of Justice on behalf of the FTC, the Commission alleged that the Toronto-based Kuuhuub Inc., along with its American subsidiaries Kuu Hubb Oy and Recolor Oy, violated the Children's Online Privacy Protection Act Rule (COPPA Rule).

3. In its complaint, the FTC alleged that the Recolor app collected personal information from children under the age of 18.

4. In addition, if they sell the app within a year following entry of the order, they must remit the net revenue from the sale to the FTC, after the payment of debts and other related expenses.

5. Recolor app allowed cookies to collect the children's personal information without any notice.

Background Information

Kids' Privacy (COPPA)

美国儿童在线隐私保护法案

美国国会在 1998 年通过了《儿童在线隐私保护法案》，该法案要求网络从业者要确实告知（actual notice）其网站的隐私权政策，并且在收集 13 岁以下儿童个人信息前，必须首先获得其家长的同意。《儿童在线隐私保护法》已于 2000 年 4 月 21 日开始施行，根据这项法律，美国在线等著名网络服务提供商已将所有未满 13 岁的登录者的个人信息全部删除。以后，13 岁以下的用户将使用一种处于美国在线家长监控系统监测之下的个人信息登记表，而且未成年用户在网上的活动也会受到一定的限制。

Vocabulary and Key Notes

1. **refunds** *n.* an amount of money that is given back to you, especially because you are not happy with a product or service that you have bought （尤指因为对购买的产品或服务不满意而追回的）退款，返还款，偿还金额

2. **Federal Trade Commission allegation** 联邦贸易委员会

联邦贸易委员会（FTC）是美国政府的一个独立机构，其主要任务是执行美国民事（非刑事）反垄断法（反托拉斯法）和促进消费者保护。联邦贸易委员会与美国司法部反垄断司共同管辖美国的联邦民事反垄断执法。它的总部设在华盛顿特区的联邦贸易委员会大楼内。

3. **collect and disclose personal information** 收集和泄露个人信息

4. **Children's Online Privacy Protection Act Rule (COPPA Rule)** 美国儿童在线隐私权保护法

2000 年 4 月 21 日生效的一项美国法律，要求网站在某些情况下必须得到家长的同意下才能收集 13 岁以下儿童的个人身份信息。

5. **allegation** *n.* a statement, made without giving proof, that someone has done something wrong or illegal（未经证实的）指责，指控……

6. **off-limits** if an area of land is off-limits, you are not allowed to enter it 禁止入内的

7. **selfie** *n.* 自拍照

8. **revenue** *n.* the income that a government or company receives regularly（政府的）税收;（公司的）收益

9. **settlement** *n.* an official agreement that finishes an argument. 协议，和解协议

10. **monetary** *adj.* relating to the money in a country 货币的，金融的

11. **penalty** *n.* a punishment, or the usual punishment, for doing something that is against a law 刑罚，惩罚，处罚

monetary penalty 罚款处分，罚款

12. **remit** *v.* to send (money) to a person or place especially in payment of a demand, account, or draft 汇款

13. **net proceed** 净得，净收益

14. **stipulated** *v.* to say exactly how something must be or must be done 规定，约定

15. **consent decree [law]** 双方同意的判决

Translation

Directions: *Translate the following sentences from Passage 1 into Chinese.*

1. The operators of an online coloring book app will be required to notify parents and offer refunds to current underage subscribers to settle Federal Trade Commission allegations that they violated a children's privacy law by collecting and disclosing personal information about children who used the app without notifying their parents and obtaining their consent.

2. Under the settlement, the companies must delete all the personal information they collected from children under 13 unless they obtain parental consent, and must offer current paid subscribers of the Recolor app a refund if they were under the age of 18 when they signed up for the app.

Passage 2

Cyberbullying

网络霸凌

Instructions: The following hypothetical scenarios are meant to provide further guidance, and act as an example, when using the TxSSC's Bullying Checklist for Schools. Each of the examples below provide a hypothetical scenario and then apply each component of the checklist to the situation, ultimately determining if the action or actions meets the legal definition of bullying according to the Texas Education Code.

Scenario 1

Taylor and Devin communicate through text and social media every day. Taylor and Devin are both interested in **dating** a student named Ryan. At some point, Devin starts spreading false rumors to Ryan about Taylor, in order to get Ryan to dislike Taylor. After leaving school, Devin starts texting unflattering photos of Taylor to Ryan and making social media posts "**bashing**" Taylor. ① These texts and photos, as well as social media posts, are NOT done while at school, only while at home or at other friends' houses. Devin is from a wealthy family and their parents hold high positions in the community, while Taylor is from a moderate income, single-parent family.

Other students are beginning to **shun** Taylor at school, resulting in Taylor **socially withdrawing** at school and no longer wanting to attend that school. When Taylor and Devin are in class together, they have had to be separated, as they obviously do not get along together in school.

Scenario 2

Jordan and Dakota are longtime friends and their families are friends as well. They are the same age and live a few blocks from each in the same neighborhood. They are both on the baseball team and both are well connected socially at school. Lately, they have been more competitive in their sports activities and have **grown** further **apart**. At times, they have been observed at school trading verbal **taunts** about each other and making fun of each other's family members. No physical **altercations** have occurred, but they are both **aligning** with other friends to go "against" each other. ②

Scenario 3

Logan and Cameron attend the same school and live in the same neighborhood. They ride the bus to school together every morning and afternoon. Logan is well-known around the school and has lots of friends, while Cameron is shy and does not have many. Recently, Logan has started to "pick on" Cameron on the bus. He throws paper planes at him and **rounds up** other students on the bus to make fun of him. This has occurred for the last several weeks. Logan does not talk to Cameron while at school. Cameron has started to miss several days of school, because he is afraid that Logan's taunts will start happening while at school.

Scenario 4

Parker and Morgan go to the same school and walk home every day. One day, after leaving the school campus, Parker decides to tease Morgan on their walk home. Parker pushes Morgan to the ground and **dumps out** her backpack. Parker is much bigger than Morgan, so it was easy for her to push her down. Morgan runs home crying. Morgan's mom has called up to the school to report that Morgan is the victim of bullying.

Scenario 5

Jayden and Avery go to high school together. Jayden is a **junior** and Avery is a **freshman**. They play basketball together every Saturday. One Saturday at the basketball court, Jayden stole Avery's basketball. When Avery **confronts** Jayden, Jayden denies doing it. That evening, Avery gets on Twitter and notices that Jayden posted a short video of Avery missing a basketball shot with the caption "This is what sucking at **bball** looks like". ③ Avery notices that the video has been shared over 50 times by classmates and others. On Monday morning, students in school were laughing at Avery while walking through the halls. Avery has been unable to focus in class because of the laughing.

(**Source**: txssc.txstate.edu)

Comprehension Check

After reading the 5 scenarios above, please determine which of them are cases of bullying and explain why by using the background information.

1. Is Scenario 1 bullying?
2. Is Scenario 2 bullying?
3. Is Scenario 3 bullying?
4. Is Scenario 4 bullying?
5. Is Scenario 5 bullying?

Background Information

David's Law

大卫法

DEFINING CYBERBULLYING

"Cyberbullying" as defined in David's Law means bullying arising from a pattern of acts or one significant act that is done through the use of any electronic communication device, including a cellular or other type of telephone, a computer, a camera, electronic mail, instant messaging, text messaging, a social media application, an Internet website, or any other Internet-based communication tool.

网络霸凌的定义

《大卫法》把网络霸凌定义为：通过使用任何电子通信设备，包括手机或其他类型的电话、电脑、相机、电子邮件、即时通信、短信、社交媒体应用程序、互联网网站或任何其他基于互联网的通信工具，而产生的一系列霸凌行为或某一严重霸凌行为。

ENGAGING IN CERTAIN BULLYING

This law authorizes a school to remove a student who is engaging in bullying activity from class and place them in a disciplinary alternative education program or expel them if they encourage a student to commit or attempt to commit suicide; incite violence against a student through group bullying; or release or threaten to release intimate visual material of a minor or of a student who is 18 years of age or older without the student's consent.

学校的处置方式

根据《大卫法》，学校有权将在课堂上有霸凌行为的学生赶出课堂，并让其接受与之替代的惩戒性的教育计划；学校有权开除有下列行为的学生：教唆同学自杀或教唆同学试图自杀；用集体欺凌来鼓动对同学的暴力；在未经同学同意的情况下，发布或威胁发布未成年人或 18 岁或以上同学的不雅照片。

COUNSELOR'S ROLE

David's Law provides that in addition to a school counselor's responsibilities, the counselor will serve as an impartial, non-reporting resource for interpersonal conflicts and discord involving two or more students, including accusations of bullying. This role will not exempt a school counselor from any mandatory reporting requirements imposed by other provisions of law.

辅导员的作用

《大卫法》规定，除了学校辅导员的职责外，辅导员将作为一个中立的、非报告的角色，处理涉及两名或两名以上学生之间的冲突与纷争，包括对于霸凌行为的指控。这一角色不会免除学校辅导员履行其他法律条款规定的强制性的报告性义务。

PREVENTION

The new law adds the following to the areas that are to be covered by the list prepared and maintained by the Department of State Health Services of recommended best practice-based programs for implementation in public schools (from which school districts may select for implementation in the district):

- Early mental health intervention;
- Mental health promotion;
- Substance abuse prevention;
- Substance abuse intervention;
- Suicide prevention;
- Grief-informed and trauma-informed practices;
- Skills related to managing emotions, establishing and maintaining positive relationships, and responsible decision-making;
- Positive behavior interventions and supports and positive youth development;
- Safe and supportive school climate

如何预防校园欺凌

针对推荐在公立学校实行的基于最佳实践的项目，州卫生服务部准备了一个列表并对其进行维护，新法在此列表包含的领域中增加了如下内容，供各学区从中选择实行）：

- 早期心理健康干预。
- 促进心理健康。
- 药物滥用预防及干预。
- 自杀预防。
- 悲痛知情及创伤知情的实践。
- 关于如何管理情绪、建立和维持积极的人际关系以及如何负责任地决策的技能。
- 积极的行为干预和积极的支持，以及乐观向上的青少年成长路程。
- 安全且有所支持的学校氛围。

Vocabulary and Key Notes

1. **date** *n.* & *v.* a social meeting planned before it happens, especially one between two people who have or might have a romantic relationship （异性间的）约会，幽会

2. **bash** *v.* criticize someone severely 严厉批评，猛烈抨击

3. **socially withdraw** 不合群

4. **shun** *v.* to avoid something 避开，避免

5. **grow apart** （关系）变得有隔阂，逐渐疏远

6. **taunts** *v.* to intentionally annoy and upset someone by making unkind remarks to them, laughing unkindly, etc. 嘲笑；讥讽；嘲弄

7. **altercation** *n.* a loud argument or disagreement 争辩；争吵；口角

8. **align** *v.* to put two or more things into a straight line 使成一条直线；对准；校直

9. **round up** a bringing together of people, animals, things, etc. 聚拢，聚集

10. **dump out** 倾卸，倾倒，倾销

11. **junior** *n.* someone who has a job at a low level within an organization; a student in the next-to-the-last year before graduating from an educational institution 地位（或等级）较低者；年资较浅者，晚辈；（美国四年制中学或大学的）三年级学生

12. **freshman** （中学或大学的）一年级新生

13. **confront** *v.* to face, meet, or deal with a difficult situation or person 面对，面临；遭遇；直面，正视

14. **bball** basketball 的缩写

Translation

Directions: *Translate the following sentences from Passage 2 into Chinese.*

1. After leaving school, Devin starts texting unflattering photos of Taylor to Ryan and making social media posts "bashing" Taylor.

2. No physical altercations have occurred, but they are both aligning with other friends to go "against" each other.

3. That evening, Avery gets on Twitter and notices that Jayden posted a short video of Avery missing a basketball shot with the caption "This is what sucking at bball looks like".

Supplementary Reading

Shop Safely Online

网上购物安全指南

Online shopping offers many advantages, from lower prices to exclusive items not available in Singapore. But there are risks, like non-delivery of goods or non-refund of damaged goods. A few simple practices can prevent you from becoming another sad statistic.

Where you can buy from

- Big, well-known online retailers like Amazon.
- Online auction sites like eBay.
- Smaller, less well-known operations.
- Other online users, like from Web forums.
- "Sprees" or mass orders, where a person coordinates a bulk purchase to try and get discounts.

The risks

- Buying goods that do not get delivered.
- Goods received don't match the description.
- Delays and hassles with online purchases.
- Poor after-sales service.
- Misuse of your credit card details.

Do your research and only deal with reputable sellers

- Check forums, seller feedback channels and consumer organizations to find out what others say about the seller, especially when buying from individuals.

- Do a search for the seller's physical address, telephone number and other contact details.
- Don't judge a person or company solely by their Web online "personality".
- Read the fine print, and in some instances, click the links describing the purchase agreement.
- Be especially cautious, when buying from a foreign retailer or someone overseas.

Know the retailer or seller's return policy. Issues to look out for include

- What happens if purchased items are not received?
- What is the timeframe in which a buyer must contact a merchant and return the items?
- Will the merchant offer a full refund or a merchandise credit?
- If an item has been opened, can it be returned?
- How will refunds be handled for returned items?
- What buyer protection programs does the site offer?

...

If things go wrong

- Contact the seller to see what has happened.
- If there is a third party involved, for example you bought the items from an auction Web site or a Web forum, contact this third party for assistance.
- If you paid with a credit card, call the bank to see if the payment can be halted or reversed.
- If you paid another third party payment provider, such as PayPal, contact them directly or visit their Web site to learn how to file a claim or see if you are covered under a buyer protection program.
- Make a police report, and remember to bring all your correspondence with you.
- Consumer watch organizations like the Consumer Association of Singapore (CASE) can help mediate a solution.
- You may wish to engage a lawyer to pursue the case for you if you believe you have a case and a clearly identified seller, but be warned that this is an expensive process and there is no guarantee it will work, especially if the seller is overseas.

(**Source:** Singapore Online Safety Guide 2006)

Further Discussion

Answer the following questions:

1. Have you ever witnessed cyberbullying? What did you do? How did you feel? What would you do if you were a target?

2. What do you need to do to protect yourself against cybercrimes?

小语说语：settlement

n.

(1) the conveyance or disposition of property for the interest of a person（财产的）处置；转让

(2) an agreement achieved between the litigants to solve the dispute before judgment in a trial, or before the trial begins （纠纷或诉讼的）和解；解决

(3) the transfer of funds between a payer bank and collecting bank in order to complete transactions for customers （银行）清算

(4) the meeting in which the ownership of real property actually transfers from seller to buyer （地产买卖）最后交易程序

• 原文

Under the **settlement**, the companies must delete all the personal information they collected from children under 13 unless they obtain parental consent, and must offer current paid subscribers of the Recolor app a refund if they were under the age of 18 when they signed up for the app.

根据**和解协议**，若非得到父母的同意，上述公司须删除其收集的 13 岁以下的儿童用户的个人信息，且须给注册 Recolor 应用程序时年龄在 18 岁以下的现有付费用户退款。

• 短语

advice of settlement 结算通知书

assets settlement 资产决算

clearing and settlement 清算与结算

a settlement sheet 地产成交清单

judicial settlement 司法解决

• 例句

例 1：Any capital **settlement** for interbank borrowing that can be implemented inside a same bank shall be conducted by way of capital transfer.

同业拆借的资金清算可以在同一银行完成的，应以资金转移方式进行。

例 2：Article 58 When a privately-run school is to be terminated, it shall make financial **settlement** according to law.

第五十八条 民办学校终止时，应当依法进行财务清算。

• 国内外法条学习

例 1：Voluntary **settlement** procedures shall be for a period not to exceed 75 days, unless extended with the concurrence of the Chief Administrative Law Judge.

未经首席行政法法官同意延长的情况下，自愿和解程序的期限不应超过 75 天。（《美国联邦法规》第 2200.120 条）

例 2：Termination of the relationship of rights and obligations under a contract does not affect the validity of the contract clauses regarding **settlement** and liquidation.

合同的权利义务关系终止，不影响合同中结算和清理条款的效力。（《中华人民共和国民法典》第五百六十七条）

例 3：Arbitration shall be made based on true facts and relative laws to give out a fair and reasonable settlement for parties concerned.

仲裁应当根据事实，符合法律规定，公平合理地解决纠纷。（《中华人民共和国仲裁法》第七条）

Supplementary Poster Reading (flyer/brochure)

Scammers know millions of people use online dating sites. They are there, too, hiding behind fake profiles.

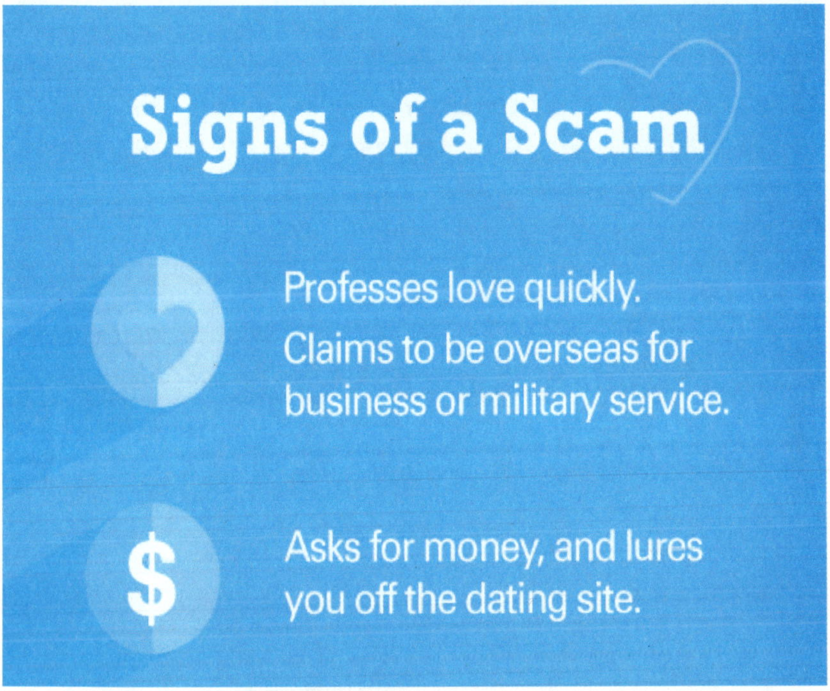
Signs of a Scam
Professes love quickly.
Claims to be overseas for business or military service.
$
Asks for money, and lures you off the dating site.

What to do

1. **Slow down** — and talk to someone you trust. Don't let a scammer rush you.

2. **Never transfer money** from your bank account, buy gift cards, or wire money to an online love interest. You won't get it back.

3. **Contact your bank right away** if you think you've sent money to a scammer.

4. Report your experience to:
   - The online dating site
   - Federal Trade Commission: **ftc.gov/complaint**
   - Federal Bureau of Investigation: **ic3.gov**

Top 10 Tips to Stay Safe Online
1 Don't share your personal information
2 Only talk to people that you know
3 Don't meet up with anyone you have only met online
4 Only accept friend requests from people you know personally
5 Always think carefully about what you post
6 Make use of the privacy settings on all of your social media accounts
7 Remember that not everyone online is who they say they are
8 Report inappropriate content immediately
9 Only share images that you'd be comfortable with your friends and family seeing
10 Never share your passwords
High Speed Training
Images from www.flaticon.com

第六章 交易安全案例

导读

科技的发展使得交易变得便捷高效，与此同时，线上交易的风险也在增加，线上欺诈的手段和途径更是层出不穷，殊不知，近年新冠疫情的来袭使得犯罪分子们找到了坑骗的“新门道”，疫情期间我们该如何保护好自己的“钱袋子”呢？我们一起在下面的文章中找答案。

案例阅读

Passage 1

Shopping Online? Know Your Retailer and Your Rights

网购？须了解你的卖家及自己的权利

COVID opened the door for **scammers** to double down on their worst practices, while **preying on** consumers during an unprecedented global **pandemic**. ① That includes some ***bad actors*** who have been taking advantage of online shoppers in search of hard-to-find items like face masks and other personal protective equipment (PPE).

Today, the Federal Trade Commission **filed a complaint against** one of those bad actors. The Commission alleged that Frank Romero (doing business as Trend Deploy) failed to deliver advertised PPE on time — if at all. What's more, Romero didn't tell customers about shipping delays, offer **order cancellations**, or give **refunds**. ② And even worse, although consumers thought Romero was selling them N95 masks, in reality Romero sent them cloth masks that did not have the protective qualities he promised. ③ This case is part of the **FTC**'s continuing effort to address "online shopping" fraud that seeks to exploit high demand for PPE and other COVID-related products.

When you shop online, sellers are supposed to ship your order within the time stated in their ads, or within 30 days if the ads don't give a time. ④ If a seller can't ship within the promised time, it has to give you a revised shipping date, with the chance to either cancel your order for **a full refund** or accept the new shipping date.

So before you shop online, especially from an unfamiliar retailer, remember these three things:

1. Check out the company or product. Search online for the name plus terms like "review," "complaint," or "scam." See what other people say about it. Read the seller's description of the product carefully. If the seller has name-brand goods at **steeply discounted prices**, they might be fakes.

2. Look at **the terms of the sale**. Make note of the total price, including taxes, shipping, and handling; the expected delivery date; and **policies for refunds**, including who pays for return shipping and if there is a **restocking fee**.

3. Pay by credit card. You'll get protections under federal law, so you don't have to pay for things you ordered but didn't get.

Remember, if you see a scam, or want to report a problem about online shopping, tell the FTC at ReportFraud.ftc.gov.

(**Source**: https://www.consumer.ftc.gov/blog/2021/06/shopping-online-know-your-retailer-and-your-rights-0)

Comprehension Check

Directions: *Tell whether each of the following statements is true or false according to the information from Passage 1.*

1. Consumers have been scammed during the unprecedented global pandemic.

2. Bad actors refer to some public figures with excellent acting skills but bad conduct.

3. Romero didn't tell customers about shipping delays, offer order cancellations, but gave refunds.

4. Romero was complained only because of the poor quality of his products.

5. When the advertisement does not specify the arrival time of the goods, it is the default that the goods will be sent to the buyer within 30 days.

Background Information

Federal Trade Commission (FTC)

美国联邦贸易委员会

联邦贸易委员会（Federal Trade Commission，FTC）是一个美国政府独立机构，成立于1914年。其主要任务是促进消费者利益的保护及消除强迫性垄断等反竞争性商业行为。联邦贸易委员会与美国司法部反托拉斯司共同拥有对美国联邦民事反托拉斯执法的管辖权。它的总部设在华盛顿特区的联邦贸易委员会大楼。

自成立以来，联邦贸易委员会通过执法、宣传和教育等方式，防止反竞争、欺诈以及不公正的商业行为，以保护消费者和正当竞争，同时不过度增加合法商业活动的负担。

多年来，在国会的支持下，相关立法逐步完善，该机构已具备足够的权力与经验以监督经济领域的反竞争行为。

About Federal Trade Commission (FTC)

- History of the FTC

When the FTC was created in 1914, its purpose was to prevent unfair methods of competition in commerce as part of the battle to "bust the trusts". Over the years, Congress passed additional laws giving the agency greater authority to police anticompetitive practices. In 1938, Congress passed a broad prohibition against "unfair and deceptive acts or practices." Since then, the Commission also has been directed to administer a wide variety of other consumer protection laws, including the Telemarketing Sales Rule, the Pay-Per-Call Rule and the Equal Credit Opportunity Act. In 1975, Congress gave the FTC the authority to adopt industry-wide trade regulation rules.

- How FTC Benefits Consumers

As a consumer or business person, you may be more familiar with the work of the Federal Trade Commission than you think. The FTC deals with issues that touch the economic life of every American.

The FTC is the only federal agency with both consumer protection and competition jurisdiction in broad sectors of the economy. The FTC pursues vigorous and effective law enforcement; advances consumers' interests by sharing its expertise with federal and state legislatures and U.S. and international government agencies; develops policy and research tools through hearings, workshops, and conferences; and creates practical and plain-language educational programs for consumers and businesses in a global marketplace with constantly changing technologies. FTC's work is performed by the Bureaus of Consumer Protection, Competition and Economics. That work is aided by the Office of General Counsel and seven regional offices.

(Source: https://www.ftc.gov/about-ftc**)**

Vocabulary and Key Notes

1. **scammer** *n.* a person who perpetrates a scam; swindler 诈骗犯；骗子

2. **pandemic** *n.* a disease that spreads over a whole country or the whole world （全国或全球性）流行病；大流行病

3. **refund** *n.* an amount of money that is given back to you, especially because you are not happy with a product or service that you have bought （尤指因为对购买产品或服务不满意而追回的）退款，返还款，偿还金额

4. **FTC** abbreviation for **the Federal Trade Commission**: a US government organization that is responsible for preventing unfair or dishonest business activities 美国联邦贸易委员会

5. **prey on sb.** to hurt or deceive a group of people, especially people who are weak or can easily be hurt or deceived 伤害，欺骗，坑害（尤指弱势人群）

6. **restocking fee** an amount of money charged by a company or store for accepting returned goods and giving the customer their money back 退订费

7. **file a complaint against sb.** 控告某人；呈交诉状

8. **order cancellations** 撤单；订单取消

9. **policies for refunds** 退款规定

10. **a full refund** 全额退款

11. **steeply discounted prices** 超低折扣价

12. **the terms of the sale** 销售条款；销售条件

Translation

Directions: *Translate the following sentences from Passage 1 into Chinese.*

1. COVID opened the door for scammers to double down on their worst practices, while preying on consumers during an unprecedented global pandemic.

2. What's more, Romero didn't tell customers about shipping delays, offer order cancellations, or give refunds.

3. This case is part of the FTC's continuing effort to address "online shopping" fraud that seeks to exploit high demand for PPE and other COVID-related products.

Passage 2

FTC Charges Two Florida-based Companies with Helping Student Debt Relief Scammers

联邦贸易委员会指控两家佛罗里达州公司协助学生减免债务诈骗

Two Florida companies and their CEO will be permanently **barred from** offering payment-processing services to settle Federal Trade Commission **allegations** that they aided a criminal student debt relief scam that **bilked** $62 million from thousands of students and their families.

According to the FTC's **complaint**, Moneta Management, LLC, Moneta Management, Inc., and their CEO Michael Todd Greene knowingly provided false or deceptive information to credit card and ACH processors to obtain merchant processing for the scam operated by Brandon Frere and his three companies. Frere and his companies **reached a settlement** with the FTC in November 2020 and also **pleaded guilty** to federal criminal charges in 2019. ①

Greene and his companies **submitted payment processing applications** that concealed Frere's scam, denied that Frere and his companies were offering consumers prohibited debt relief services, and ignored repeated warnings and direct evidence that Frere's scam was defrauding consumers and violating **the Telemarketing Sales Rule**, according to the complaint. ② The accounts that Greene and his companies helped create for Frere's scam allowed the processing of credit card and debit payments from consumers.

As part of the settlement with the FTC, Greene and his two companies will be barred from payment processing, acting as a sales agent or independent sales organization, and from assisting and facilitating unfair and deceptive trade practices. The proposed **final order** also imposes a monetary judgment of $ 28.6 million on Greene and his companies, which will be partially suspended after payment of $ 20,493 due to their inability to pay the full amount. ③ They will be required to pay the full amount if they are found to have **misrepresented** their finances.

The Commission voted 4-0-1 to **file the complaint** and proposed final order. Chair Lina Khan did not participate. The FTC filed the complaint and final order in the U.S. District Court for the Southern District of Florida. The Court approved the final order on July 8, 2021.

(**Source:** https://www.ftc.gov/news-events/press-releases/2021/07/ftc-charges-two-florida-based-companies-helping-student-debt)

Comprehension Check

Part I

Directions: *Tell whether each of the following statements is true or false according to the information from Passage 2.*

1. Michael Todd Greene and his companies are accused of debt relief scam against students.
2. Frere and his companies reached a settlement with the FTC in 2020 and also pleaded guilty to federal criminal charges in November 2019.
3. Greene and his companies received many same warnings from FTC.
4. Greene and his companies will pay full $28.6 million immediately if they are found to have misrepresented their finances.
5. Greene and his companies created many fraudulent accounts for Frere.

Part II

Directions: *Fill in the blanks with the following words. Make additions or changes where necessary.*

bilk	conceal	violate	bar
impose	suspend	file	facilitate

1. The new ramp will __________ the entry of wheelchairs.
2. The council has __________ a ban on alcohol in the city parks.
3. The police __________ charges against the two suspects.
4. They were charged with __________ federal law.
5. The players are __________ from drinking alcohol the night before a match.
6. He __________ clients out of tens of millions of dollars.
7. It was said that the police __________ vital evidence.
8. Mr. Young was given a six-month jail sentence, __________ for two years (= if he commits another crime within two years, he will have to go to prison for six months for his original crime).

Background Information

Telemarketing Sales Rule — TSR

电话营销规定

《电话营销规定》（TSR）是实施 The Telemarketing and Consumer Fraud and Abuse Prevention Act（《电话营销和消费者欺诈及滥用预防法》）的一项监管规则，于 1995 年 12 月 31 日生效。

TSR 主要规定以下五个方面：

要求电话营销人员具体披露重要信息；

禁止虚假陈述；

限制电话销售人员给消费者打电话的时间；

禁止向要求不再拨打电话的消费者拨打电话；

对某些商品和服务的销售设定付款限制。

2002 年，联邦贸易委员会（FTC）宣布对 TSR 进行重大修改，其中大部分于 2003 年 3 月 31 日生效，特别是规定了一份全国性的“谢绝来电”（DNC）名单。除了“国家谢绝来电名单”外，修订后的规则还限制了“追加销售”（也称“向上推销”，试图说服顾客购买额外或者更昂贵的产品）、否定期权、免费转付费、预先获得的账户信息和预测拨号器的使用。虽然大部分修订规则于 2003 年 3 月生效，但 DNC 名单于 2003 年 10 月开始运作。

PS：“国家谢绝来电登记处”（The National Do Not Call Registry）

“国家谢绝来电登记处”由美国消费者保护机构联邦贸易委员会（FTC）管理。它的设立是为了帮助企业和消费者阻隔一些不必要的销售电话。

企业或者消费者可以免费在“国家谢绝来电登记处”登记姓名及号码，那么在 31 天的有效期内，登记在列的号码就不会收到电话营销的来电。

联邦条例规章（Code of Federal Regulations）

Title 16: Commercial Practices

PART 310 — TELEMARKETING SALES RULE

§310.3(a) (2) Misrepresenting, directly or by implication, in the sale of goods or services any of the following material information:

…

(x) Any material aspect of any debt relief service, including, but not limited to, the amount of money or the percentage of the debt amount that a customer may save by using such service; the amount of time necessary to achieve the represented results; the amount of money or the percentage of each outstanding debt that the customer must accumulate before the provider of the debt relief service will initiate attempts with the customer's creditors or debt collectors or make a bona fide offer to negotiate, settle, or modify the terms of the customer's debt; the effect of the service on a customer's creditworthiness; the effect of the service on collection efforts of the customer's creditors or debt collectors; the percentage or number of customers who attain the represented results; and whether a debt relief service is offered or provided by a non-profit entity.

§310.3 (b) Assisting and facilitating. It is a deceptive telemarketing act or practice and a violation of this Rule for a person to provide substantial assistance or support to any seller or telemarketer when that person knows or consciously avoids knowing that the seller or telemarketer is engaged in any act or practice that violates §310.3(a), (c) or (d), or§310.4 of this Rule.

(Source: https://www.ecfr.gov/cgi-bin/retrieveECFR?gp=&SID=f72acee1f30754c1a397ed350a0d5f98&mc=true&n=pt16.1.310&r=PART&ty=HTML#se16.1.310_14)

Vocabulary and Key Notes

1. **bar** *v.* to prevent something or someone from doing something or going somewhere, or to not allow something 阻挡，阻挠；防止，禁止

be barred from 被禁止

2. **allegation** *n.* a statement, made without giving proof, that someone has done something wrong or illegal （未经证实的）指责，指控

3. **bilk** *v.* to get money from someone unfairly or dishonestly 诈骗

4. **misrepresent** *v.* to describe falsely an idea, opinion, or situation, often in order to get an advantage 不如实地叙述（或说明）；误传；歪曲；诈称

5. **reach a settlement** 达成和解；达成一致的意见

6. **plead guilty** 服罪；认罪

7. **submitt applications** 提交申请

8. **The Telemarketing Sales Rule** 电话营销规定

9. **final order** 终审裁定

Translation

Directions: *Translate the following sentences from Passage 2 into Chinese.*

1. Frere and his companies reached a settlement with the FTC in November 2020 and also pleaded guilty to federal criminal charges in 2019.

2. Greene and his companies submitted payment processing applications that concealed Frere's scam, denied that Frere and his companies were offering consumers prohibited debt relief services, and ignored repeated warnings and direct evidence that Frere's scam was defrauding consumers and violating the Telemarketing Sales Rule, according to the complaint.

3. The proposed final order also imposes a monetary judgment of $28.6 million on Greene and his companies, which will be partially suspended after payment of $20,493 due to their inability to pay the full amount.

Supplementary Reading

Gift Card Scams

购物卡诈骗

Someone might ask you to pay for something by putting money on a gift card, like a Google Play or iTunes card, and then giving them the numbers on the back of the card. If they ask you to do this, they're trying to scam you. No real business or government agency will ever insist you pay them with a gift card. Anyone who demands to be paid with a gift card is a scammer. Read on to learn more about gift card scams.

- What Gift Card Scams Looks Like

Gift cards are for gifts, not for payments. But they're popular with scammers because they're easy for people to find and buy, and they have fewer protections for buyers compared to some other payment options. They're more like cash: once you use the card, the money on it is gone. Scammers like this.

If someone calls you and demands that you pay them with gift cards, you can bet that a scammer is behind that call. Once they have the gift card number and the PIN, they have your money. Scammers may tell you many stories to get you to pay them with gift cards, but this is what usually happens:

1. The caller says it's urgent. The scammer says you have to pay right away or something terrible will happen. But you don't, and it won't.

2. The caller usually tells you which gift card to buy. They might say to put money on an eBay, Google Play, Target, or iTunes gift card. They might send you to a specific store — often Walmart, Target, CVS, or Walgreens. Sometimes they say to buy cards at several stores, so cashiers won't get suspicious. And, the caller might stay on the phone with you while you go to the store and load money onto the card. These are all signs of a scam.

3. The caller asks you for the gift card number and PIN. The card number and PIN on the back of the card let the scammer get the money you loaded onto the card. And the scammer gets it right away.

- How Scammers Convince You To Pay With Gift Cards

Scammers pretend to be someone they're not to convince you to pay with gift cards. They want to scare or pressure you into acting quickly, so you don't have time to think or talk to someone you trust. Here's a list of common gift card scams and schemes:

1. The caller says they're from the government — maybe the IRS or the Social Security Administration. They say you have to pay taxes or a fine, but it's a scam.

2. Someone calls from tech support, maybe saying they're from Apple or Microsoft, saying there's something wrong with your computer. But it's a lie.

3. You meet someone special on a dating website, but then he needs money and asks you to help him. This romance scammer makes up any story to trick you into sending him gift cards.

4. The scammer pretends to be a friend or family member in an emergency and asks you to send money right away – but not tell anyone. This is a scam. If you're worried, hang up and call your friend or relative to check that everything is all right.

5. Someone says you've won a prize but first, you have to pay fees or other charges with a gift card. Remember: no honest business or agency will ever make you pay with a gift card. But also — did you even enter that sweepstakes?

6. The caller says she's from your power company, or another utility company. She threatens to cut off your service if you don't pay immediately. But utility companies don't work that way. It's a scam.

7. You get a check from someone for way more than you expected. They tell you to deposit the check, then give them the difference on a gift card. But that check will be fake and you'll be out all that money.

- What to Do If You Paid a Scammer With Gift Cards

If you paid a scammer with a gift card, tell the company that issued the card right away.

(**Source**: https://www.consumer.ftc.gov/articles/gift-card-scams)

Further Discussion

Answer the following questions:

1. Have you seen other trading security incidents during the pandemic? What did the parties do? What would you do if you were a target?

2. What can you do to bring about the most transaction security?

小语说语：complaint

n. (1) in a civil action, the initial pleading setting out the facts on which the claim is based（民事）起诉状

(2) in criminal law, a formal charge against a person who has committed an offense, usually a misdemeanor（刑事）指控状（通常针对轻罪）

- **原文**

The Commission voted 4-0-1 to file the **complaint** and proposed final order. 委员会以 4 比 0 比 1 的投票结果提出申诉，并提出了最终裁决。

- **短语**

fresh complaint　及时告发（指性受害者在合理时间内立即向警察、父母、朋友等告发侵害事件）此种告发可作为支持受害者的可信性证据

counter-complaint　反诉诉状

third-party complaint　第三方诉状（由被告提出，指称第三方对原告向被告提出的索赔负有责任）

- **例句**

例 1：People familiar with the matter say Goldman was given no opportunity to settle before the **complaint** was announced last Friday.

知情人士表示，（证交会）上周五宣布起诉前，并没有给高盛（一家投资银行）任何机会来达成和解。

例 2：They argue that none of them is named in the **complaint** and point out that the bank's robust defence means no heads will roll.

他们表示，证交会的起诉书中没有提到他们中任何一人的名字，而高盛的强力抗辩意味着，没有人会因此下台。

● 国内外法条学习

例 1：After the filing of a complaint for forfeiture under this section, the Attorney General may seek dismissal of the **complaint** in favor of forfeiture proceedings under State or local law.

在根据本条规定提出没收申诉后，司法部长可根据州或地方法律要求驳回申诉，以支持没收诉讼程序。（《美国法典》第 981.04 条）

例 2：A youth shall file a **complaint** with the complaint mediator or superintendent within 5 days from the day on which an incident occurred.

青少年应在意外事件发生后 5 天内向申诉调解员或学监提出申诉。（《美国威斯康星行政法典》第 380.04 条）

例 3：Any **complaint** in a reasonable form (letter or email) which is signed by the complainant, or his/her representative, and includes sufficient information to initiate an investigation must be treated as if it were a properly completed Complaint/Referral Form filed in person.

原告或其代理人以任何合理形式（信件或电子邮件）签署的申诉状，如包含足够资料以展开调查，则视为申诉人按照合理程序当面提交的申诉状。（《美国联邦法规》第 658.411 条）

例 4：Where one of the parties, without notifying the other party, requests the rescission of the contract by directly filing a lawsuit or applying for arbitration in accordance with law, and the people's court or arbitration institution confirms such request, the contract shall be rescinded when a duplicated copy of the **complaint** or the application letter for arbitration is is served on the other party.

当事人一方未通知对方，直接以提起诉讼或者申请仲裁的方式依法主张解除合同，人民法院或者仲裁机构确认该主张的，合同自起诉状副本或者仲裁申请书副本送达对方时解除。《中华人民共和国民法典》第五百六十五条）

例 5：The network service provider shall timely terminate the measures taken where, within a reasonable period of time after the forwarded declaration reaches the right holder, it fails to receive notice that the right holder has filed a **complaint** or a lawsuit.

网络服务提供者在转送声明到达权利人后的合理期限内，未收到权利人已经投诉或者提起诉讼通知的，应当及时终止所采取的措施。（《中华人民共和国民法典》第一千一百九十六条）

例 6：When a people's court receives **a bill of complaint**, it shall, upon examination, file a case within seven days or decide to reject the complaint. If the plaintiff refuses to accept the decision, he may appeal to a people's court.

人民法院接到起诉状，经审查，应当在七日内立案或者作出裁定不予受理。原告对裁定不服的，可以提起上诉。（《中华人民共和国行政诉讼法》第四十二条）

Supplementary Poster Reading (flyer/ brochure)

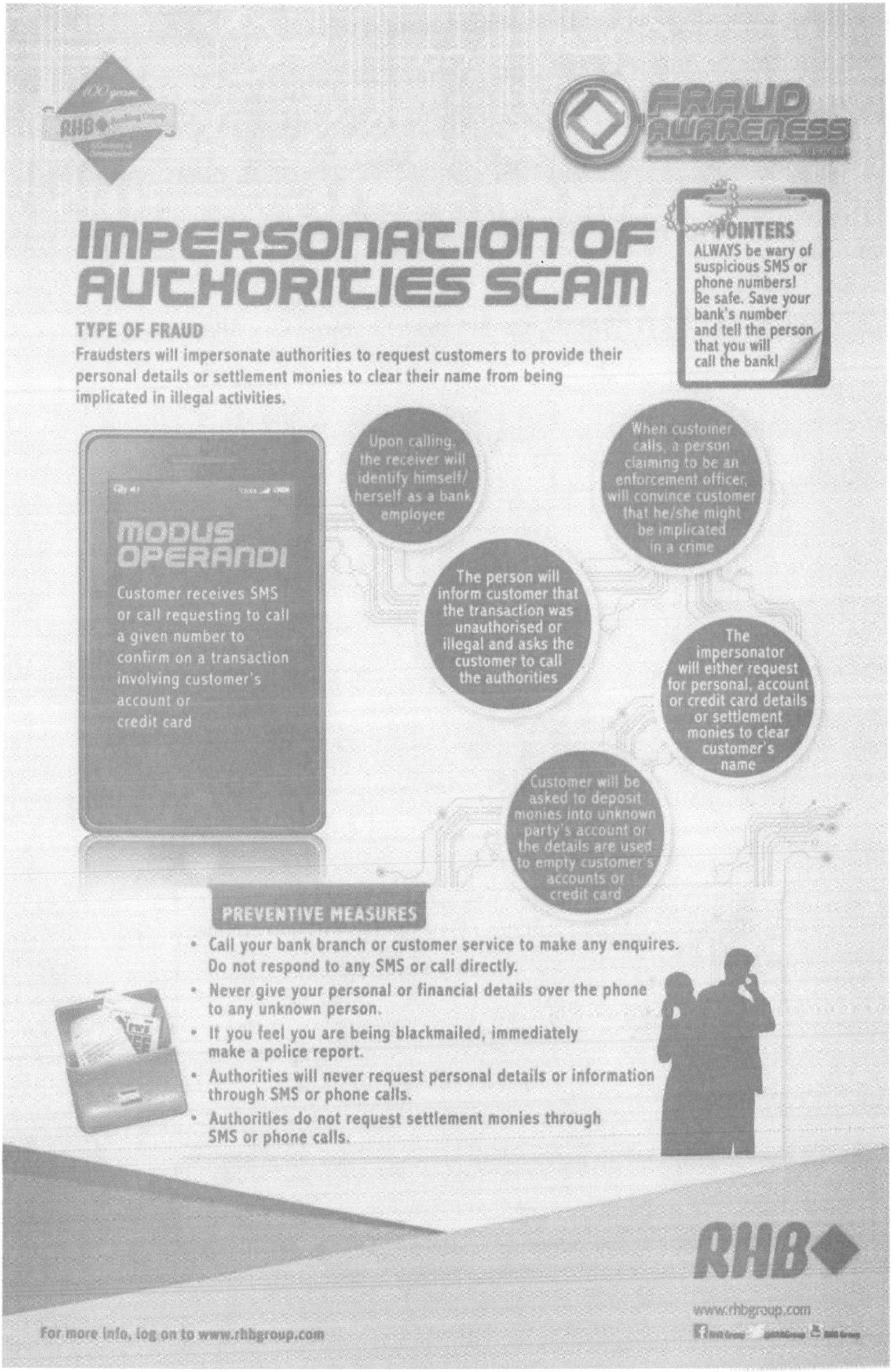
RHB Banking Group
FRAUD AWARENESS
IMPERSONATION OF AUTHORITIES SCAM
POINTERS
ALWAYS be wary of suspicious SMS or phone numbers!
Be safe. Save your bank's number and tell the person that you will call the bank!
TYPE OF FRAUD
Fraudsters will impersonate authorities to request customers to provide their personal details or settlement monies to clear their name from being implicated in illegal activities.
MODUS OPERANDI
Customer receives SMS or call requesting to call a given number to confirm on a transaction involving customer's account or credit card
Upon calling, the receiver will identify himself/herself as a bank employee
When customer calls, a person claiming to be an enforcement officer, will convince customer that he/she might be implicated in a crime
The person will inform customer that the transaction was unauthorised or illegal and asks the customer to call the authorities
The impersonator will either request for personal, account or credit card details or settlement monies to clear customer's name
Customer will be asked to deposit monies into unknown party's account or the details are used to empty customer's accounts or credit card
PREVENTIVE MEASURES
• Call your bank branch or customer service to make any enquires. Do not respond to any SMS or call directly.
• Never give your personal or financial details over the phone to any unknown person.
• If you feel you are being blackmailed, immediately make a police report.
• Authorities will never request personal details or information through SMS or phone calls.
• Authorities do not request settlement monies through SMS or phone calls.
RHB
www.rhbgroup.com
For more info, log on to www.rhbgroup.com

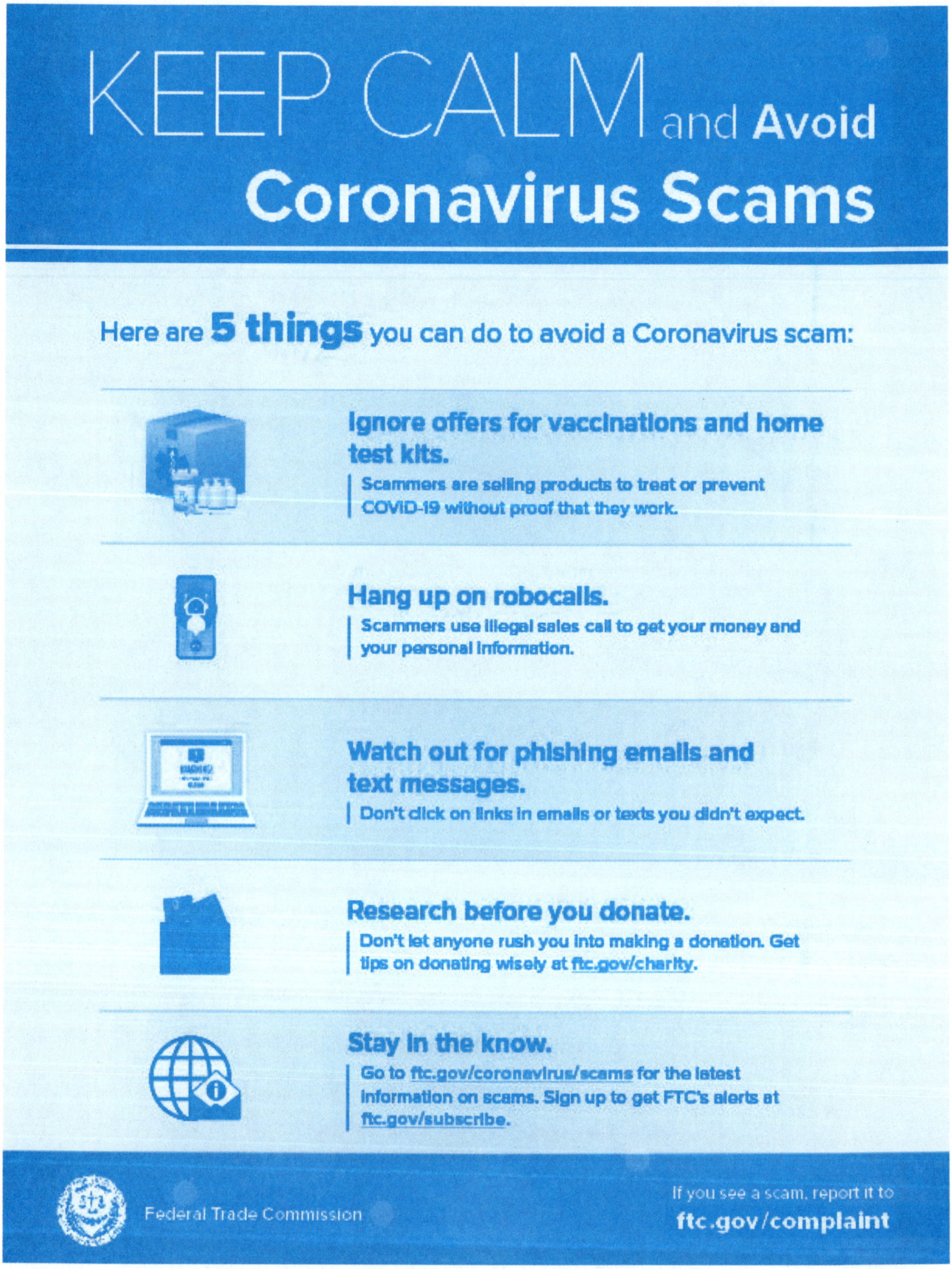
KEEP CALM and Avoid
Coronavirus Scams
Here are 5 things you can do to avoid a Coronavirus scam:
Ignore offers for vaccinations and home test kits.
Scammers are selling products to treat or prevent COVID-19 without proof that they work.
Hang up on robocalls.
Scammers use illegal sales call to get your money and your personal information.
Watch out for phishing emails and text messages.
Don't click on links in emails or texts you didn't expect.
Research before you donate.
Don't let anyone rush you into making a donation. Get tips on donating wisely at ftc.gov/charity.
Stay in the know.
Go to ftc.gov/coronavirus/scams for the latest information on scams. Sign up to get FTC's alerts at ftc.gov/subscribe.
Federal Trade Commission
If you see a scam, report it to
ftc.gov/complaint

4 TIPS TO
PROTECT YOUR BUSINESS
from Credit Card Processing Scams
FOLLOW THESE TIPS TO KEEP YOUR BUSINESS SAFE
1
ALWAYS ASK THE CALLER WHAT COMPANY THEY WORK FOR
Scams:
Claim to "represent" Visa, MasterCard, or "your bank"
Evasive
A reputable company like BASYS:
Forthcoming with company name
Proud to share their website, a phone #, and a BBB rating
2
NEVER GIVE OUT YOUR ACCOUNT INFORMATION
Scams:
"Your account has been locked"
You need to "update your account information"
A reputable company like BASYS:
Places company contact info on every terminal
Protects your account information
3
NEVER SIGN A DOCUMENT TO GET A PRICE QUOTE
Scams:
Want you to sign a document to get a quote on credit card processing
A reputable company like BASYS:
Only needs basic contact info, and statements from your current credit card processor, to give you a quote
4
NEVER SIGN A DOCUMENT WITHOUT READING IT THOROUGHLY
DOCUMENT
Scams:
Want you to sign documents for "quotes", or "updating account information"
Those documents likely commit you to:
Leased equipment you don't need
High-priced, low-quality services
A reputable company like BASYS:
Encourages you to read a document completely
Happy to thoroughly answer any questions before you sign
BASYS® PROCESSING
(800) 386-0711 basyspro.com 15423 W. 100th Terrace · Lenexa, KS 66219

第二篇

民法典案例

第七章 平等原则案例

导读

《民法典》被称为“社会生活的百科全书”，是人民权利的宣告书。《民法典》规定民事主体在从事民事活动时，相互之间在法律地位上都是平等的，任何一方不得将自己的意志强加给对方，他们的合法权益也受到法律的平等保护。本章将从“奥运健儿姓名被恶意抢注商标”和“嘟嘟 App 下架”两个案例学习《民法典》的平等原则如何保障未成年、消费者和妇女等主体的合法权益。

案例阅读

Passage 1

The Names of Olympic Athletes Have Been Registered as Trademarks

奥运健儿姓名被恶意抢注商标

The National Intellectual Property Administration rejected 109 applications for trademark registration using names of Olympic athletes on Thursday **in a bid to** protect the name rights of public figures.

Any signs, including words, graphs, letters, numerals, three-dimensional symbols, color combinations, sound or any combination thereof, that are capable of distinguishing the goods of a **natural person, legal person** or other organizations from those of others may be applied for registration as trademarks. ①

A trademark submitted for registration shall **bear noticeable characteristics** and be readily **distinguishable**, and it may not conflict with **the legitimate rights** obtained by others earlier.

Some enterprises attempted to **maliciously** use the names of Olympic players to apply for trademarks.

The behavior, which is to benefit from others' reputation, has not only harmed Olympic athletes' rights and interests, but also brought negative effects to society, according to the note. ②

It said the administration will intensify efforts to fight malicious trademark registrations and keep a sound business environment, adding applicants or agencies that use improper means to apply for trademarks will be punished **in line with** the law. ③

Without getting permission from the Olympic athletes or **guardians** of players who are minors, no one should maliciously register their names as trademarks or take other action infringing on the right of their names or other rights, the committee said.

"If such acts occur, the application for trademark registration should be **suspended** or withdrawn **in a timely manner,**" it said, adding that the athletes or guardians of young players have the right to sue **infringers**.

In the "Civil Code of the People's Republic of China":

A natural person enjoys the right to name and **is entitled to** determine, use, change, or allow others to use his name **in accordance with** law, provided that public order and good morals are not offended. ④

No organization or individual may infringe upon other's **rights to name or rights to entity name** by means such as interference, **misappropriation, impersonation**, or the like. ⑤

(**Source**: https://mp.weixin.qq.com/s/c7TKGr0s5l-eevLqUi7i_Q)

Comprehension Check

Short Answer Questions

Directions: *There are three short answer questions based on the passage 1. Please consider and answer the following questions.*

1. What kinds of elements can be applied for trademark registration in China?
2. What are the requirements for applying for trademark registration?
3. After reading the passage, what are the articles of law about the right to name in the "Civil Code of the People's Republic of China"?

Background Information

（一）案例速览

8月18日，中国奥林匹克委员会通过官方微博发布提示，针对近期发生的杨倩、陈梦、全红婵等奥运健儿姓名被申请注册商标事宜，社会各界开展相关商业活动，应当保持理性，切实尊重运动员合法权益，遵守《中华人民共和国民法典》《中华人民共和国商标法》《中华人民共和国反不正当竞争法》等相关法律法规规定。

提示强调，如未获得运动员本人或未成年运动员监护人授权，不得以奥运健儿姓名恶意抢注商标或其他侵犯运动员姓名权等合法权益的行为；有上述行为的，应及时撤回和停止实施商标注册申请。运动员及未成年运动员监护人有依法追究相关侵权行为人法律责任的权利。

（二）《中华人民共和国民法典》相关法条速览

Article 1012 A natural person enjoys the right to name, and is entitled to determine, use, change, or allow others to use his name in accordance with law, provided that public order and good morals are not offended.

第一千零一十二条　自然人享有姓名权，有权依法决定、使用、变更或者许可他人使用自己的姓名，但是不得违背公序良俗。

Article 1014 No organization or individual may infringe upon other's rights to name or rights to entity name by means such as interference, misappropriation, impersonation, or the like.

第一千零一十四条　任何组织或者个人不得以干涉、盗用、假冒等方式侵害他人的姓名权或者名称权。

Article 1017 With regard to a pseudonym, stage name, screen name, translated name, trade name, abbreviation of a name or entity name of a social popularity, where the use of which by others will suffice to cause public confusion, the relevant provisions on protection of the rights to name and the rights to entity name shall be applied mutatis mutandis.

第一千零一十七条　具有一定社会知名度，被他人使用足以造成公众混淆的笔名、艺名、网名、译名、字号、姓名和名称的简称等，参照适用姓名权和名称权保护的有关规定。

（三）《中华人民共和国商标法》相关法条速览

Article 7 Any user of a trademark shall be responsible for the quality of the goods in respect of which the trademark is used. The administrative authorities for industry and commerce at different levels shall, through the administration of trademarks, stop any practice that deceives consumers.

第七条　申请注册和使用商标，应当遵循诚实信用原则。商标使用人应当对其使用商标的商品质量负责。各级工商行政管理部门应当通过商标管理，制止欺骗消费者的行为。

Article 8 In respect of any visual sign capable of distinguishing the goods or service of one natural person, legal entity or any other organization from that of others, including any word, design, letters of an alphabet, numerals, three-dimensional symbol, combinations of colors, and their combination, an application may be filed for registration.

第八条　任何能够将自然人、法人或者其他组织的商品与他人的商品区别开的标志，包括文字、图形、字母、数字、三维标志、颜色组合和声音等，以及上述要素的组合，均可以作为商标申请注册。

Article 9　Any trademark in respect of which an application for registration is filed shall be so distinctive as to be distinguishable, and shall not conflict with any prior right acquired by another person.

第九条　申请注册的商标，应当有显著特征，便于识别，并不得与他人在先取得的合法权利相冲突。

Article 10　The following signs shall not be used as trademarks:

(1) those identical with or similar to the State name, national flag, national emblem, military flag, or decorations, of the People's Republic of China, with names of the places where the Central and State organs are located, or with the names and designs of landmark buildings;

(2) those identical with or similar to the State names, national flags, national emblems or military flags of foreign countries, except that the foreign state government agrees otherwise on the use;

(3) those identical with or similar to the names, flags or emblems or names, of international intergovernmental organizations, except that the organizations agree otherwise on the use or that it is not easy for the use to mislead the public;

(4) those identical with or similar to official signs and hallmarks, showing official control or warranty by them, except that the use thereof is otherwise authorized;

(5) those identical with or similar to the symbols, or names, of the Red Cross or the Red Crescent;

(6) those having the nature of discrimination against any nationality;

(7) those having the nature of exaggeration and fraud in advertising goods; and

(8) those detrimental to socialist morals or customs, or having other unhealthy influences.

第十条　下列标志不得作为商标使用：

（一）同中华人民共和国的国家名称、国旗、国徽、国歌、军旗、军徽、军歌、勋章等相同或者近似的，以及同中央国家机关的名称、标志、所在地特定地点的名称或者标志性建筑物的名称、图形相同的；

（二）同外国的国家名称、国旗、国徽、军旗等相同或者近似的，但经该国政府同意的除外；

（三）同政府间国际组织的名称、旗帜、徽记等相同或者近似的，但经该组织同意或者不易误导公众的除外；

（四）与表明实施控制、予以保证的官方标志、检验印记相同或者近似的，但经授权的除外；

（五）同“红十字”、“红新月”的名称、标志相同或者近似的；

（六）带有民族歧视性的；

（七）带有欺骗性，容易使公众对商品的质量等特点或者产地产生误认的；

（八）有害于社会主义道德风尚或者有其他不良影响的。

(**Source:** https://flk.npc.gov.cn/detail2.html?ZmY4MDgwODE2ZjEzNWY0NjAxNmYyMTc2NDU0NTFiMzU%3D; http://english.www.gov.cn/archive/laws_regulations/2014/08/23/content_281474983043626.htm)

Vocabulary and Key Notes

1. **in a bid to** 为了
2. **natural person** 自然人
3. **legal person** 法人
4. **bear** *n*. to show sth.; to carry sth. so that it can be seen 显示；带有
5. **noticeable** *adj*. easy to see or notice; clear or definite 显著的；显而易见的
6. **characteristic** *n*. a typical feature or quality that sth./sb. has 特征；特点；品质
7. **distinguishable** *adj*. able to be discerned 可识别的
8. **the legitimate rights** 合法权利
9. **malicious** *adj*. having or showing hatred and a desire to harm sb. or hurt their feelings 怀有恶意的；恶毒的
10. **in line with** 符合；与……一致
11. **guardian** *n*. a person who is legally responsible for the care of another person 监护人
12. **suspend** *n*. to officially stop sth. for a time; to prevent sth. from being active, used, etc. for a time 暂停；中止；使暂停发挥作用（或使用等）
13. **in a timely manner** 及时
14. **infringer** *n*. 侵权行为人
15. **rights to name** 姓名权
16. **rights to entity name** 名称权

17. **misappropriation** *n.* wrongful use, especially the dishonest or inappropriate use of others' money, data, etc. 侵占；挪用

18. **impersonation** *n.* the act of pretending to be someone else, with intent to mislead or deceive 假冒

Translation

Directions: *Translate the following sentences from Passage 1 into Chinese.*

1. Any signs, including words, graphs, letters, numerals, three-dimensional symbols, color combinations, sound or any combination thereof, that are capable of distinguishing the goods of a natural person, legal person or other organizations from those of others may be applied for registration as trademarks.

2. The behavior, which is to benefit from others' reputation, has not only harmed Olympic athletes' rights and interests, but also brought negative effects to society, according to the note.

3. It said the administration will intensify efforts to fight malicious trademark registrations and keep a sound business environment, adding applicants or agencies that use improper means to apply for trademarks will be punished in line with the law.

4. A natural person enjoys the right to name and is entitled to determine, use, change, or allow others to use his name in accordance with law, provided that public order and good morals are not offended.

5. No organization or individual may infringe upon other's rights to name or rights to entity name by means such as interference, misappropriation, impersonation, or the like.

Passage 2

Dudu Ride-hailing Service Was Pulled from App Stores in China

嘟嘟打车服务从中国应用商店下架

China's **cyberspace regulator** said on Sunday that it had ordered smartphone app stores to stop offering Dudu Global's app after finding that the **ride-hailing giant** had illegally collected users' personal data. ① **The Cyberspace Administration of China (CAC)** said it had told Dudu to make changes to **comply with** Chinese data protection rules, four days after Dudu began trading on the **New York Stock Exchange**, having raised $4.4 billion in an initial public offering.

The CAC did not specify the nature of Dudu's **violation** in a statement on its social media feed.

Dudu responded by saying it had stopped registering new users and would remove its app from app stores. It said it would make changes to comply with rules and protect users' rights. ② Dudu said it would **rectify** the problems and continuously raise its awareness of risk prevention. It added that it would improve its technical ability to protect its users' personal information and data, protect users from internet safety risks and continuously provide safe and convenient service. ③

Dudu made its trading **debut** on Wednesday in an **IPO** that valued the company at $67.5 billion, well down from the $100 billion it had hoped for, which potential investors had resisted. Dudu's app was still working in China for people who had already downloaded it. It offers over 20 million rides in China every day, on average.

CAC on Friday announced an investigation into Dudu to protect "national security and the public interest," prompting a 5.3% fall in its share price to $15.53.

The stock was sold at $14 per share in the IPO – the top of the indicated range.

Dudu, which offers services in China and more than 15 other markets, gathers vast amounts of real-time mobility data every day. It uses some of the data for autonomous driving technologies and traffic analysis.

Dudu had **flagged** Chinese regulations in its IPO **prospectus** and said: "We follow strict procedures in collecting, transmitting, storing and using user data **pursuant** to our data security and privacy policies." ④

A notice on Dudu's China app showed it had updated its user information and data privacy policy on June 29, the day before its trading debut. In a statement to Reuters, Dudu described the move as a "regular update" after adding two new services on the app under its **chauffeur** business. ⑤

Founded by Hill in 2012, the company had previously been subject to regulatory probes in China over safety and its operating license.

(**Source**: https://mp.weixin.qq.com/s/Um_AqyCDp903IPiiZvK2IA)

Comprehension Check

Directions: *Tell whether each of the following statements is true or false according to the information form Passage 2.*

1. Dudu, a popular ride-hailing app, was removed from application stores after the Cyberspace Administration of China verified a report about its illegal collection and usage of personal information

2. Faced with this situation, Dudu made no response.

3. The government has also been ramping up its efforts to safeguard the nation's data security and cybersecurity.

4. Dudu's app was no longer working in China for people who had already downloaded it.

5. Throughout the review period, new user registration for Dudu app will be suspended to stop the spread of risks.

Background Information

（一）案件速览

据国家网信办消息，根据举报，经检测核实，“嘟嘟出行”App存在严重违法违规收集使用个人信息问题。国家互联网信息办公室依据《中华人民共和国网络安全法》相关规定，通知应用商店下架“嘟嘟出行”App，要求嘟嘟出行科技有限公司严格按照法律要求，参照国家有关标准，认真整改存在的问题，切实保障广大用户个人信息安全。

（二）《中华人民共和国民法典》相关法条速览

Article 111 A natural person's personal information is protected by law. Any organization or individual that needs to access other's personal information must do so in accordance with law and guarantee the safety of such information, and may not illegally collect, use, process, or transmit other's personal information, or illegally trade, provide, or publicize such information.

第一百一十一条　自然人的个人信息受法律保护。任何组织或者个人需要获取他人个人信息的，应当依法取得并确保信息安全，不得非法收集、使用、加工、传输他人个人信息，不得非法买卖、提供或者公开他人个人信息。

Article 1032 A natural person enjoys the right to privacy. No organization or individual may infringe upon the other's right to privacy by prying into, intruding upon, disclosing, or publicizing other's private matters.

Privacy is the undisturbed private life of a natural person and his private space, private activities, and private information that he does not want to be known to others.

第一千零三十二条　自然人享有隐私权。任何组织或者个人不得以刺探、侵扰、泄露、公开等方式侵害他人的隐私权。

隐私是自然人的私人生活安宁和不愿为他人知晓的私密空间、私密活动、私密信息。

Article 1034　A natural person's personal information is protected by law.

Personal information is the information recorded electronically or in other ways that can be used, by itself or in combination with other information, to identify a natural person, including the name, date of birth, identification number, biometric information, residential address, telephone number, email address, health information, whereabouts, and the like, of the person.

The provisions on the right to privacy, or, in the absence of which, the provisions on the protection of personal information, shall be applied to the private personal information.

第一千零三十四条　自然人的个人信息受法律保护。

个人信息是以电子或者其他方式记录的能够单独或者与其他信息结合识别特定自然人的各种信息，包括自然人的姓名、出生日期、身份证件号码、生物识别信息、住址、电话号码、电子邮箱、健康信息、行踪信息等。

个人信息中的私密信息，适用有关隐私权的规定；没有规定的，适用有关个人信息保护的规定。

Article 1035　The processing of personal information shall be in compliance with the principles of lawfulness, justification, and within a necessary limit, and shall not be excessively processed; meanwhile, the following conditions shall be satisfied;

(1) consent has been obtained from the natural person or his guardian, unless otherwise provided by laws or administrative regulations;

(2) the rules for processing information are publicized;

(3) the purpose, method, and scope of the information processing are clearly indicated; and

(4) it is not in violation of laws or administrative regulations or against the agreement of both parties.

The processing of personal information includes the collection, storage, use, refinement, transmission, provision, disclosure, and the like, of the personal information.

第一千零三十五条　处理个人信息的，应当遵循合法、正当、必要原则，不得过度处理，并符合下列条件：

（一）征得该自然人或者其监护人同意，但是法律、行政法规另有规定的除外；

（二）公开处理信息的规则；

（三）明示处理信息的目的、方式和范围；

（四）不违反法律、行政法规的规定和双方的约定。

个人信息的处理包括个人信息的收集、存储、使用、加工、传输、提供、公开等。

Vocabulary and Key Notes

1. **cyberspace regulator** 网络监管机构

2. **ride-hailing** 叫车；网约车

3. **giant** *n.* a very large and powerful organization 大公司；强大的组织；巨头

4. **The Cyberspace Administration of China (CAC)** 中国国家互联网办公室

5. **comply with** 遵守；依从

6. **New York Stock Exchange** 纽约证券交易所

7. **violation** *n.* the action of violating someone or something 违反；违背

8. **rectify** *v.* to put right sth. that is wrong 矫正；纠正；改正

9. **debut** *n.* the first public appearance of a performer or sports player （演员、运动员）首次亮相；初次登台（或上场）

10. **IPO (initial public offering)** （公司股票的）首次公开发行，上市

11. **flag** *v.* to put a special mark next to information that you think is important 标示（重要处）

12. **prospectus** *n.* a document that gives information about a company's shares before they are offered for sale （企业的）招股章程，募股章程

13. **pursuant** *adj.* according to or following sth., especially a rule or law 依照，根据，按照（尤指规则或法律）

14. **chauffeur** *n.* a person whose job is to drive a car, especially for sb. rich or important（尤指富人或要人的）司机

Translation

***Directions**: Translate the following sentences from Passage 2 into Chinese.*

1. China's cyberspace regulator said on Sunday that it had ordered smartphone app stores to stop offering Dudu Global's app after finding that the ride-hailing giant had illegally collected users' personal data.

2. Dudu responded by saying it had stopped registering new users and would remove its app from app stores. It said it would make changes to comply with rules and protect users' rights.

3. It added that it would improve its technical ability to protect its users' personal information and data, protect users from internet safety risks and continuously provide safe and convenient service.

4. Dudu had flagged Chinese regulations in its IPO prospectus and said: "We follow strict procedures in collecting, transmitting, storing and using user data pursuant to our data security and privacy policies."

5. A notice on Dudu's China app showed it had updated its user information and data privacy policy on June 29, the day before its trading debut. In a statement to Reuters, Dudu described the move as a "regular update" after adding two new services on the app under its chauffeur business.

Supplementary Reading

Say "No" to Domestic Violence

向家暴坚决说"不"

A man in Xi'an, Shaanxi Province, has been suspended by his company after a video of him beating his wife in front of their child drew widespread criticism online.

In the video, the man was seen repeatedly hitting his wife on the head while she held their child on her lap. After the child moved aside, he threw her onto the sofa, sat on her, and continued to hit her on the head. An older woman later took the child away but did not do much to intervene.

NSR Trading, a subsidiary of Airport Group in Shaanxi, said the company deeply condemned the domestic violence inflicted by Wang, a deputy director of one department of the company.

The company has decided to suspend him and hand him over to its disciplinary inspection division, it said in a statement Thursday, adding that it has sent people to visit Wang's wife.

Police in Xi'an had received a report from Wang's wife and were looking into the case, the Baqiao division of Xi'an's public security bureau said in a statement on Thursday.

An initial investigation found Wang had beaten his wife after they quarreled over a trivial matter.

The incident triggered strong condemnation of Wang from netizens on social media platforms. On the Sina Weibo micro-blog platform, different hashtags about the incident had garnered hundreds of millions of views by Thursday night.

The video was horrifying to watch, said one netizen. Another said that once there are acts of violence in a marriage, there is no point in the couple staying married.

The Shaanxi Women's Federation said it has paid close attention to the incident and strongly condemned Wang's behavior.

China bans any form of domestic violence. The federation will offer necessary legal aid and psychological help to Wang's wife, it said in a statement on Thursday.

Women's legal rights and interests should not be violated and the whole of society is encouraged to pay close attention to them and put an end to any form of domestic violence, the federation said.

According to China's Anti-Domestic Violence Law, any perpetrator of such behavior will receive administrative or criminal punishment based on the severity of the acts.

Women threatened with domestic violence are encouraged to call the police and women's federations and use legal means to protect their rights and interests.

(**Source:** https://mp.weixin.qq.com/s/6Gth8bGaVbbazZXz5l4cYg)

Further Discussion

Answer the following questions:

1. Did you learn about "Minors Protection Law"? Can you list some articles of this law that concern you?

2. In today's big data era, personal information is crucial to our life. Please offer some tips about protection of personal information.

小语说语：Equal/Equally/Equality

平等原则 The Principle of Equality

Article 2 The civil law regulates personal and proprietary relationships among the persons of the civil law, namely, natural persons, legal persons, and unincorporated organizations that are **equal** in status.

第二条 民法调整平等主体的自然人、法人和非法人组织之间的人身关系和财产关系。

Article 4 All persons of the civil law are **equal** in legal status when conducting civil activities.

第四条　民事主体在民事活动中的法律地位一律平等。

Article 14　All natural persons are **equal** in their capacity for enjoying civil-law rights.

第十四条　自然人的民事权利能力一律平等。

Article 113　The proprietary rights of the persons of the civil law are **equally** protected by law.

第一百一十三条　民事主体的财产权利受法律平等保护。

Article 206　The State implements a socialist market economy and protects the **equal** legal status and development rights of all market participants.

第二百零六条　国家实行社会主义市场经济，保障一切市场主体的平等法律地位和发展权利。

Article 207　The real rights of the State, collectives, private individuals, and the other right holders are **equally** protected by law and free from infringement by any organization or individual.

第二百零七条　国家、集体、私人的物权和其他权利人的物权受法律平等保护，任何组织或者个人不得侵犯。

Article 1041　Marriage and family are protected by the State.

A marriage system based on freedom of marriage, monogamy, and **equality** between men and women is implemented.

第一千零四十一条　婚姻家庭受国家保护。实行婚姻自由、一夫一妻、男女平等的婚姻制度。

Article 1043　Husband and wife shall be loyal to each other, respect each other, and care for each other. Family members shall respect the elderly, take care of the young, help each other, and maintain a marital and familial relationship of **equality**, harmony, and civility.

第一千零四十三条　夫妻应当互相忠实，互相尊重，互相关爱；家庭成员应当敬老爱幼，互相帮助，维护平等、和睦、文明的婚姻家庭关系。

Article 1055　Husband and wife are **equal** in marriage and family.

第一千零五十五条　夫妻在婚姻家庭中地位平等。

Article 1058 Both spouses have **equal** rights and joint duties to raise, educate, and protect their minor children.

第一千零五十八条　夫妻双方平等享有对未成年子女抚养、教育和保护的权利，共同承担对未成年子女抚养、教育和保护的义务。

Article 1062 Husband and wife have **equal** rights when disposing of the community property.

第一千零六十二条　夫妻对共同财产，有平等的处理权。

Article 1126 Men and women are **equal** in their right to inheritance.

第一千一百二十六条　继承权男女平等。

第八章 自愿原则案例

导读

本章从自愿实施紧急救助行为造成受助人损害，救助人不承担民事责任的案例出发，对民法典的自愿原则进行学习。自愿原则作为民法基本原则中的核心原则，其实质内涵是意思自治。但是，自愿原则并不意味着为所欲为！如何在私权保护中弘扬传统美德和社会公德？民法典的“自甘风险规则”“紧急救助行为责任豁免规则”等的立法价值取向值得深思。

案例阅读

Passage 1

Promotion of “Good Samaritan Law” Good for Healthy Social Environment

推广实施“好人法”有利于构建健康的社会环境

The Shenyang Intermediate People’s Court recently ruled that a well-meaning drugstore owner was not liable for accidentally breaking a senior citizen’s ribs while giving her **cardiopulmonary resuscitation** (CPR). ①

The case is important as it demonstrates how a “good Samaritan law” can protect first aid givers. Not surprisingly, netizens have **hailed** the verdict.

On Sept 7, 2017, a 70-year-old woman surnamed Qi fainted at a drugstore in Shenyang, capital of Liaoning province. Since he couldn’t feel the woman’s pulse, drugstore owner Sun, who holds a medical license, gave her CPR before an ambulance arrived.

The timely action saved Qi’s life but left her with 12 broken ribs for which she sued Sun, seeking damages for her medical expenses. ②

It is not uncommon to see rib fractures during CPR, as **vigorous cardiac compression** is required to help a patient regain his/her heartbeat.

Technically, the drugstore owner did nothing wrong; according to the first aid principle, the focus should be on saving the life of a patient.

The lawsuit against Sun made many assume that the old **adage**, no good **deeds** go unpunished, holds true. No wonder many people hesitate to help those in trouble for fear of **landing in trouble in** the process. ③

Fortunately, the court ruling has helped **allay** such fears. After consulting medical experts, the court ruled that the drugstore owner's efforts were not in violation of medical rules and he bears no liability. ④ The ruling promotes the healthy social atmosphere of helping people in need.

The case also shows the positive social effects of the Chinese version of a "good Samaritan law".

Article 184 of the general principles of the Civil Law, approved by the **National People's Congress**, China's top legislature, on March 15, 2017, stipulates that rescuers **bear no civil liability** if they cause damage to those being rescued because of their voluntary emergency rescue actions. ⑤

This **exemption** encourages people to extend a helping hand to others during an emergency, and **is conducive to** promoting social justice and creating a healthy social environment.

(**Source**: Promotion of "Good Samaritan Law" Good for Healthy Social Environment — Chinadaily.com.cn)

Comprehension Check

Directions: *Use an appropriate word or phrase from the box with their proper forms to complete each sentence. Each word or phrase can be used once only.*

stipulate	faint	pulse	violation	allay
adage	hail	rule	deed	netizen

1. Ammonia is used as a restorative when a person has ________.

2. In an email to Americans on Saturday, the Trump administration tried to ________ concerns caused by the court decision in the Texas case.

3. The attack on civilians is a flagrant __________ of the peace agreement.

4. That was the moment that I realized how true the old __________ is that looks can be deceiving.

5. The World Health Organization __________ a life-saving breakthrough.

6. A __________ is a particular kind of document. It must be a writing and a writing on paper or its like.

7. The court __________ that the claim was null and void.

8. Because you got your finger on the __________.

9. This feature of ________ contributed to the generation and propagation of false news.

10. Allocation of risk on the pawnage right shall be __________ by statute in accordance with the real situations.

Background Information

（一）案例速览

2017年9月7日，齐老太到药店买药，途中突然昏倒，店主孙老板立即给她做心肺复苏，压断其12根肋骨。同年10月，齐老太将孙老板告上法庭。本案明确指出原告齐老太服用硝酸甘油药品与心脏骤停无必然因果联系，被告孙老板在给原告齐老太实施心肺复苏的过程中不违反诊疗规范，不应承担抢救过错，法院故而驳回齐老太的诉讼请求，二审维持原判。该判决有利于鼓励和倡导普通市民参与紧急现场救护活动，形成“做好事有保护”的社会氛围，促进互帮互助的良性循环的形成。

（二）Good Samaritan laws

Samaritans 原指撒玛利亚人，Good Samaritan（善良的撒玛利亚人）是基督教文化中一个著名成语和口头语，意为好心人、见义勇为者。这个词来源于《圣经》中的一个寓言：一个犹太人被强盗打劫，受了重伤，躺在路边。有祭司和利未人路过但不闻不问。唯有一个撒玛利亚人路过，不顾隔阂，动了慈心照应他，在需要离开时自己出钱把犹太人送进了旅店。

《善良的撒玛利亚人法》（Good Samaritan laws）也是真实存在的一部法律。在美国和加拿大，这部法律给伤者、病人的自愿救助者免除责任，目的在于使人做好事时没有后顾之忧，不用担心因过失造成伤亡而遭到追究，从而鼓励旁观者对伤、病人士施以帮助。有的翻译为《好撒玛利亚人法》，也有的称《无偿施救者保护法》。

向受难者伸出援助之手是中华民族的优良传统之一，但在这个过程中也潜藏着风险，救助人可能会因救助方式不当等因素，而损害受助人的权益，从而引发纠纷。为鼓励见义勇为，避免“好人流血又流泪”，我国《民法典》第一百八十四条规定了紧急救助行为责任豁免规则，被称作我国的“好人法”。

（三）《中华人民共和国民法典》相关法条速览

Article 5 When conducting a civil activity, a person of the civil law shall, in compliance with the principle of voluntariness, create, alter, or terminate a civil juristic relationship according to his own will.

第五条 民事主体从事民事活动，应当遵循自愿原则，按照自己的意思设立、变更、终止民事法律关系。

Article 184 A person who voluntarily engages in rescuing another person in an emergency situation and thus causes harm to the latter person bears no civil liability.

第一百八十四条 因自愿实施紧急救助行为造成受助人损害的，救助人不承担民事责任。

Vocabulary and Key Notes

1. **cardiopulmonary resuscitation** 简称 CPR，心肺复苏术，是针对骤停的心脏和呼吸采取的救命技术

2. **hail** *v.* to call someone in order to attract their attention 招呼，呼喊

3. **vigorous** *adj.* very forceful or energetic 充满活力的；有力量的；精力旺盛的

4. **cardiac** *adj.* of the heart or heart disease 心脏的；心脏病的

5. **adage** *n.* a wise saying 谚语；格言

6. **deed** *n.* ① a thing that sb. does that is usually very good or very bad 行为；行动

② (often plural in British English) a legal document that you sign, especially one that proves that you own a house or a building （尤指房产）契约，证书

deed of confirmation 产权转让确认契据

deed of partition 财产分割契约

title deed 产权证书

7. **land oneself in deep trouble** 陷入困境

8. **allay** *vt.* if you allay a strong emotion felt by someone, such as fear or worry, you cause them to feel it less or to feel calm again. 减轻，缓解（担忧、恐惧等）

9. **National People's Congress** 全国人民代表大会（中国最高国家权力机关）

10. **bear no civil liability** 不承担民事责任

11. **exemption** *n.* freedom from some requirement that other persons must meet 豁免

12. **extend a helping hand** 伸出援助之手

Translation

Directions: *Translate the following sentences from Passage 1 into Chinese.*

1. The Shenyang Intermediate People's Court recently ruled that a well-meaning drugstore owner was not liable for accidentally breaking a senior citizen's ribs while giving her cardiopulmonary resuscitation (CPR).

2. The timely action saved Qi's life but left her with 12 broken ribs for which she sued Sun, seeking damages for her medical expenses.

3. The lawsuit against Sun made many assume that the old adage, no good deeds go unpunished, holds true. No wonder many people hesitate to help those in trouble for fear of landing in trouble in the process.

4. After consulting medical experts, the court ruled that the drugstore owner's efforts were not in violation of medical rules and he bears no liability.

5. Article 184 of the general principles of the Civil Law, approved by the National People's Congress, China's top legislature, on March 15, 2017, stipulates that rescuers bear no civil liability if they cause damage to those being rescued because of their voluntary emergency rescue actions.

Passage 2

Chinese Woman Was Saddled with Ex-husband's US$3 Million in Debts

中国女子背负前夫三百万美元债务

A divorced woman from eastern China has spent six years fighting against court rulings stating that she is liable to pay debts of over 20 million yuan (US $3.1 million) borrowed by her ex-husband during their marriage, according to a newspaper report. ①

The couple was divorced in 2012, but she received **summons** from courts in Hangzhou in Zhejiang province after she and her ex-partner were sued by five different groups of people **claiming** they were owed money borrowed by her former husband, the Qiangjiang Evening News reported. ②

Her ex-partner was a former official working in Hangzhou and he has never appeared in court for any of the **hearings**. The woman, who was not named in the report, said she could not trace him.

"Did I agree to borrow this money? Have I ever used one cent of the loans?" The woman was quoted as saying by the newspaper.

She lives with her son, who is about 12, and has sold one flat for 2.5 million yuan to **pay off** some of the debts.

Most of the woman's salary is also taken away each month to pay some of the money owed, the report said. It leaves her with only 3,000 yuan to support her son.

This woman is among about 100 divorced wives in Hangzhou who have formed chat-groups on the social media app WeChat to **vent** their frustration as they pay off debts run up by their ex-husbands. ③

The Supreme People's Court **issued** regulations in January stipulating that one partner in a marriage does not need to pay debts borrowed by their husband or wife during their marriage unless **creditors** can prove the loans were agreed by both parties, or used for their families' everyday expenses or for their joint business operations. ④

Another divorced woman in Hangzhou has successfully appealed against debt payments, with a court ruling her husband is solely responsible for 1 million yuan borrowed during their marriage, the newspaper reported. ⑤

(**Source**: https://amp.scmp.com/news/china/society/article/2150203/chinese-woman-saddled-ex-husbands-us3-million-debts)

Comprehension Check

Directions: *Tell whether each of the following statements is true or false according to the information from Passage 2.*

1. The divorced woman agreed to borrow the money but her husband did not spend it on her, so she took legal action.

2. According to the newspaper, the woman spent six years fighting legal battles, arguing that she was unaware of her former partner's huge debts during their marriage.

3. According to Article 41 of the Marriage Law, the woman is still required to repay her ex-husband's debt, even though the loan was not used for household expenses and she was not aware of the debt.

4. The divorced woman of the article was not the only one who was stuck with husbands' debt. However, not every one of them had successfully appealed against debt payments.

5. Since her husband is nowhere to be found, the woman has never used 3,000 yuan to

support her son.

Background Information

（一）案例速览

杭州的徐女士在离婚后接到了五个借贷诉讼，其前夫在婚姻存续期间欠下高达三百万美元的债务，而这份债务被要求由双方共同承担。2016 年 8 月，徐女士向杭州市人民检察院申请法律监督，请求检察机关依法抗诉。2017 年 2 月 6 日，杭州市检察院对周董（化名）与海峰（化名）民间借贷合同纠纷案等五个案件提请浙江省检察院抗诉。2017 年 4 月 12 日，浙江省检察院对周董与海峰民间借贷合同纠纷一案向浙江省高级人民法院提出抗诉。2018 年 1 月 3 日，浙江省高级人民法院撤销原判对本案依法改判，判决由周董个人承担案涉债务。

（二）《中华人民共和国民法典》相关法条速览

Article 1064 Debts incurred according to the common expression of intent of both spouses, such as a debt jointly signed by both spouses and a debt signed by one spouse and subsequently ratified by the other spouse, and debts incurred by one of the spouses in his own name during the marriage to meet the daily needs of the family, constitute community debts.

A debt incurred by one of the spouses in his own name during the marriage in excess of the daily needs of the family is not a community debt, unless the creditor may prove that such debt is used for both spouses' daily life or for joint production and operation of the spouses, or such debt incurs according to the common expression of intent of both spouses.

第一千零六十四条　夫妻双方共同签名或者夫妻一方事后追认等共同意思表示所负的债务，以及夫妻一方在婚姻关系存续期间以个人名义为家庭日常生活需要所负的债务，属于夫妻共同债务。

夫妻一方在婚姻关系存续期间以个人名义超出家庭日常生活需要所负的债务，不属于夫妻共同债务；但是，债权人能够证明该债务用于夫妻共同生活、共同生产经营或者基于夫妻双方共同意思表示的除外。

【注解】本条是关于超出家庭日常生活需要所负的债务证明责任分配问题。

相对于家庭日常生活需要所负的债务，实践中还存在大量夫妻一方以个人名义超出家庭日常生活需要所负的债务。这类债务是否属于夫妻共同债务，司法实践中的争议和认定难度都比较大。《最高人民法院关于审理涉及夫妻债务纠纷案件适用法律有关问题的解释》第三条规定：“夫妻一方在婚姻关系存续期间以个人名义超出家庭日常生活需要所负的债务，债权人以属于夫妻共同债务为由主张权利的，人民法院不予支持，但债权人能够证明该债务用于夫妻共同生活、共同生产经营或者基于夫妻双方共同意思表示的除外。”也就是说，**当夫妻一方以个人名义对外所负的债务，尤其是数额较大的债务，超出了家庭日常生活所需的范畴时，认定该债务是否属于夫妻共同债务的标准，是债权人能否证明债务用于夫妻共同生活或者共同生产经营，或者债务的负担系基于夫妻双方共同的意思表示，如果债权人不能证明的，则不能认定为夫妻共同债务。**这一举证证明责任的分配，符合民事诉讼法第六十四条第一款“当事人对自己提出的主张，有责任提供证据”的规定，也与民事诉讼法司法解释第九十条“当事人对自己提出的诉讼请求所依据的事实或者反驳对方诉讼请求所依据的事实，应当提供证据加以证明”的规定相一致。通过合理分配举证证明责任，可以有效平衡债权人和债务人配偶一方的利益保护。这条规定与《解释》第一条相呼应，从合同相对性原则出发，强调在夫妻一方具名举债的情况下，当债务超出家庭日常生活需要范围时，尤其是大额债务，债权人主张该债务属于夫妻共同债务的，应当承担举证证明责任，以此引导债权人在债务形成时尽到充分的谨慎注意义务。

（《最高人民法院关于审理涉及夫妻债务纠纷案件适用法律有关问题的解释》2018年1月18日起施行）

（三）《最高人民法院关于审理涉及夫妻债务纠纷案件适用法律有关问题的解释》相关法条速览

Article 3 Where one spouse incurs a debt in his or her own name during marriage beyond the needs of everyday life of his or her family, if the creditor files any claim on the ground that it is a community debt of husband and wife, the court shall not support the claim, unless the creditor is able to prove that the debt is used to meet the joint needs of life or production or operation of husband and wife or based on their common declaration of will.

第三条 夫妻一方在婚姻关系存续期间以个人名义超出家庭日常生活需要所负的债务，债权人以属于夫妻共同债务为由主张权利的，人民法院不予支持，但债权人能够证明该债务用于夫妻共同生活、共同生产经营或者基于夫妻双方共同意思表示的除外。

（四）《中华人民共和国婚姻法》相关法条速览

Article 41 At the time of divorce, the debts jointly incurred by both husband and wife for the common life shall be paid out of the jointly owned property. If the jointly owned property is not enough to pay the debts or if the property is individually owned, both parties shall agree upon the payment of the debts. If both parties fail to reach any agreement, the people's court shall decide on the payment of the debts.

第四十一条　【共同债务】离婚时，原为夫妻共同生活所负的债务，应当共同偿还。共同财产不足清偿的，或财产归各自所有的，由双方协议清偿；协议不成时，由人民法院判决。

（五）《最高人民法院关于适用〈中华人民共和国婚姻法〉若干问题的解释（二）》速览

Article 24 During the existence of the marriage, if either the husband or wife files a claim for a personal debt in the name of one party, the debt shall be treated as a joint debt of the husband and wife, unless either the husband or wife is able to prove that the creditor and the debtor have clearly stipulated it as a personal debt or to show that the debt is under any of the circumstance as prescribed in the third paragraph of Article 19 of the Marriage Law.

Where a third party claims rights over any debt fabricated by one spouse in collusion with the third party, the people's court shall not support the third party's claim.

Where a third party claims rights over any debt owed by one spouse when he or she commits any violation or crime, such as gambling and drug use, the people's court shall not support the third-party's claim.

第二十四条　债权人就婚姻关系存续期间夫妻一方以个人名义所负债务主张权利的，应当按夫妻共同债务处理。但夫妻一方能够证明债权人与债务人明确约定为个人债务，或者能够证明属于婚姻法第十九条第三款规定情形的除外。夫妻一方与第三人串通，虚构债务，第三人主张权利的，人民法院不予支持。

夫妻一方在从事赌博、吸毒等违法犯罪活动中所负债务，第三人主张权利的，人民法院不予支持。

【注：本条已被《最高人民法院关于适用〈中华人民共和国婚姻法〉若干问题的解释（二）的补充规定》（发布日期：2017 年 2 月 28 日 实施日期：2017 年 3 月 1 日）增加两款，分别作为该条第二款和第三款：“夫妻一方与第三人串通，虚构债务，第三人主张权利的，人民法院不予支持。夫妻一方在从事赌博、吸毒等违法犯罪活动中所负债务，第三人主张权利的，人民法院不予支持。”】

(**Source**: http://en-pkulaw-cn.beijinghangkong.tsg211.com/Display.aspx?lib=law&Cgid=50970; http://en-pkulaw-cn.beijinghangkong.tsg211.com/display.aspx?id=f844c4836826b24abdfb&lib=law&SearchKeyword=&SearchCKeyword=%bb%e9%d2%f6%b7%a8; https://www.lawtime.cn/article/lll94114139416507oo607581)

Vocabulary and Key Notes

1. **take legal action** 提起法律诉讼

2. **running up huge liabilities** 积累巨额负债

3. **liability** *n.* the fact that someone is legally responsible for something （法律上对某事物的）责任，义务

joint and several liability 连带责任

joint liability 共同责任

liability without fault 无过失责任

product liability 产品责任

4. **summons** *n.* a written notice to appear in court as a defendant, witness, juror, etc. （通知到庭应诉、作证、充当陪审员等的）传票

5. **claim** *v.* to demand or ask for sth. because you believe it is your legal right to own or to have it 要求（拥有）；索取

6. **hearing** *n.* a judicial session in which evidence and arguments are presented before a judge （司法程序中的）听审，听证

7. **issue** *v.* officially put forth or announce (a legal or administrative order or regulation) 发布，签发（法律、行政命令等）

8. **creditor** *n.* a person or entity to whom a debt is owed 债权人

lien creditor 有留置权保障的债权人

general creditor 一般债权人

secured creditor 具担保债权人

9. **appeal** *n.* asking a higher court to review a lower court's decision in order to correct mistakes or injustice 上诉

Translation

Directions: *Translate the following sentences from Passage 2 into Chinese.*

1. A divorced woman from eastern China has spent six years fighting against court rulings stating that she is liable to pay debts of over 20 million yuan (US$3.1 million) borrowed by her ex-husband during their marriage, according to a newspaper report.

2. The couple was divorced in 2012, but she received summons from courts in Hangzhou in Zhejiang province after she and her ex-partner were sued by five different groups of people claiming they were owed money borrowed by her former husband, the Qiangjiang Evening News

reported.

3. This woman is among about 100 divorced wives in Hangzhou who have formed chat-groups on the social media app WeChat to vent their frustration as they pay off debts run up by their ex-husbands.

4. The Supreme People's Court issued regulations in January stipulating that one partner in a marriage does not need to pay debts borrowed by their husband or wife during their marriage unless creditors can prove the loans were agreed by both parties, or used for their families' everyday expenses or for their joint business operations.

5. Another divorced woman in Hangzhou has successfully appealed against debt payments, with a court ruling her husband is solely responsible for 1 million yuan borrowed during their marriage, the newspaper reported.

Supplementary Reading

Digital Inheritance Triggers Fierce Debate

数字继承引发激烈争论

In November, Apple released a new feature in its latest operating system update. The program, Digital Legacy, allows users to pass on personal information to family members and friends in the event of the user's death.

A maximum of five "Legacy Users" can be added to a person's iCloud account, so that when that individual dies, these contacts can obtain his or her details through an access key.

Also in November, a picture created by an online painter circulated widely on social media platforms.

The picture introduces a new product concept, "the smart coffin", with users collating their personal details on a flash drive and then following pop-up instructions. After a user dies, the "smart coffin" publishes an obituary, notifies close contacts, transfers passwords to personal accounts, or deletes data, according to the deceased's wishes.

All the user's data is stored in the "smart coffin", which requires password access. In the event of death, the "coffin" can be switched to "dead" status by entering the deceased's death certificate number. Artificial intelligence then takes care of the other procedures required.

Digital Legacy and the "smart coffin" have triggered heated online discussion about arrangements for online inheritance.

Some netizens welcomed the "smart coffin", saying such a product is necessary, while others said they had a considerable amount of data they did not wish family members to see.

As digitalization penetrates further into daily lives, netizens have become increasingly concerned about personal details left on the internet — and how to deal with them properly after death. Young people comprise the group most concerned about digital inheritance, with many of them drawing up wills.

A white paper released by the China Will Registration Center in March, shows that in 2020, nearly 11 percent of the post-'80s generation and just over 21 percent of the post-'90s generation mentioned virtual assets in their wills. They have accounts with Alipay, WeChat, QQ and with video game providers.

Among the post-'90s generation who have made wills, virtual assets ranked third in importance, after bank deposits and real estate.

Ms. Wu, a member of the younger generation who recently planned for her digital afterlife through the China Will Registration Center in Shanghai, said that if she died unexpectedly and didn't make plans in advance, there was a good chance that her digital history would be seen by her parents.

However, the planning process wasn't easy — requiring far more time and research than she expected. From initially consulting the center's professionals, including lawyers, to final approval of her will, the entire procedure took the 26-year-old media worker nearly two months.

The first problem Wu encountered emerged as she was sorting through her digital assets. Currently, there is no law clearly defining virtual property, so Wu didn't know what she could put in her will.

After consulting a lawyer, she divided her accounts into two categories, based on whether they had any real economic value.

For example, her accounts with Alipay and WeChat Pay, as well as for video games, were categorized as economic assets. Social media accounts, on the other hand, were considered non-material assets.

But without a specific judicial interpretation of digital inheritance, the handling of these assets is mainly based on user agreements signed with network providers, which have different rules depending on the service.

Alipay's service agreement states that "property interests" with the online payment platform can be inherited by law. Close family members of the deceased can inherit the balance deposited with Alipay by providing a death certificate, identification card and proof of kinship. WeChat Pay also allows such balances to be passed on.

Dispute has arisen over inheritance of social media accounts. The majority of such providers state in user agreements that an account is for personal use only and cannot be transferred, loaned or inherited.

(**Source**: Digital Inheritance Triggers Fierce Debate — Chinadaily.com.cn)

Further Discussion

Answer the following questions:

1. When you see a passerby fainting, will you go up to help? After studying case 1, please give your answer and reason.

2. What happens to your online stuff when you're no longer around?

小语说语：Voluntary

The principle of voluntariness

自愿原则

Article 5 When conducting a civil activity, a person of the civil law shall, in compliance with the principle of **voluntariness**, create, alter, or terminate a civil juristic relationship according to his own will.

第五条　民事主体从事民事活动，应当遵循**自愿**原则，按照自己的意思设立、变更、终止民事法律关系。

Article 184 A person who **voluntarily** engages in rescuing another person in an emergency situation and thus causes harm to the latter person bears no civil liability.

第一百八十四条　因自愿实施紧急救助行为造成受助人损害的，救助人不承担民事责任。

Article 192 An obligor who agrees to perform a prior obligation after the limitation period expires may not later on use the expiration of the limitation period as a defense, and an obligor who has **voluntarily** performed such a prior obligation may not later on demand for restitution.

第一百九十二条　诉讼时效期间届满后，义务人同意履行的，不得以诉讼时效期间届满为由抗辩；义务人已经**自愿**履行的，不得请求返还。

Article 1006 A person with full capacity for performing civil juristic acts has the right to make a **voluntary** decision in accordance with law to donate his cells, tissues, organs, and remains. No organization or individual may force, deceive, or induce the person to donate such.

第一千零六条　完全民事行为能力人有权依法**自主**决定无偿捐献其人体细胞、人体组织、人体器官、遗体。任何组织或者个人不得强迫、欺骗、利诱其捐献。

Article 1076 The divorce agreement shall include expression of intent of both parties to **voluntarily** divorce and their mutual agreement on such matters as child support, property division, and allocation of debts.

第一千零七十六条　离婚协议应当载明双方**自愿**离婚的意思表示和对子女抚养、财产以及债务处理等事项协商一致的意见。

Article 1078 Upon ascertaining that the divorce is **voluntarily** intended and that the two parties have reached agreement on such matters as child support, property division, and allocation of debts, the marriage registration authority shall register the divorce and issue a divorce certificate.

第一千零七十八条　婚姻登记机关查明双方确实是**自愿**离婚，并已经对子女抚养、财产以及债务处理等事项协商一致的，予以登记，发给离婚证。

Article 1105 The parties to an adoptive relationship may enter into an adoption agreement on a **voluntary** basis.

第一千一百零五条　收养关系当事人**愿意**签订收养协议的，可以签订收养协议。

Article 1161 A successor shall pay the taxes and debts legally payable or owed by the decedent to the extent of the actual value of the portion of the estate he inherits, unless the successor pays **voluntarily** in excess of such limit.

第一千一百六十一条　继承人以所得遗产实际价值为限清偿被继承人依法应当缴纳的税款和债务。超过遗产实际价值部分，继承人**自愿**偿还的不在此限。

Article 1176 Where a person **voluntarily** participates in a recreational or sports activity with certain inherent risks and thus suffers damage due to another participant's act, he may not request the other participant to bear tort liability unless the damage is caused by the latter's intentional act or by his gross negligence.

第一千一百七十六条　**自愿**参加具有一定风险的文体活动，因其他参加者的行为受到损害的，受害人不得请求其他参加者承担侵权责任；但是，其他参加者对损害的发生有故意或者重大过失的除外。

第九章 公平原则案例

导读

公平原则是民法的一项基本原则，它要求当事人在民事活动中应以社会正义、公平的观念指导自己的行为、平衡各方的利益，要求以社会正义、公平的观念来处理当事人之间的纠纷。本章的案例告诉我们，作为民事主体和消费者的我们要敢于用知识、用法律捍卫我们的合法权益。

案例阅读

Passage 1

Snack Food Policy

“禁带饮食”规定

A law school student in Shanghai has taken **Shanghai Dey Resort** to court for not allowing her to bring her own snacks into the park, Chinese news portal Paper.cn reported on Sunday.

The student, who is surnamed Wang and is a junior at East China University of Political Science and Law, said she was told to either throw away or finish the snacks in her backpack, which were worth 46.30 yuan ($6.56), after security personnel caught her **smuggling** food into the park. ① She eventually **discarded** her snacks.

Shanghai Dey Resort has banned outside food, alcohol and non-alcohol beverages over 600 milliliters inside its park since November 2017, according to Paper.cn. ②

Since that visit to the park in late January, Wang has been **filing a series of complaints to** the municipal's public hotlines and regulators. ③ In March, she brought the case to the People's Court of Pudong New Area, where the theme park is located.

She called for the park's ban to be **overturned** and for the park to compensate her loss of 46.30 yuan. The case was heard on April 23 and is still **pending verdict**. ④

The student said that Dey only bans food at its Asia branches and although the rule was published on its websites, she did not receive relevant tips while purchasing the ticket and before entering the park.

Although Shanghai Dey claims the food ban is due to hygiene reasons, that did not stop Chinese net users from **speculating** that Dey is applying double standards in Asia and forcing tourists to buy their food. ⑤

Some users also complained about the high food prices inside Shanghai Dey. For example, a 500 milliliter Pepsi costs 20 yuan, seven times the normal price.

"Guests are allowed to bring food items – such as snacks or foods that do not require heating – into Dey theme parks," Walt Dey World said on its official website.

"Dey has **infringed on tourists' right of choice**. As a US company, it is improper to apply a double standard on Asian countries," Professor Liu, a business law professor at Renmin University of China in Beijing told the Global Times on Sunday.

(**Source**: https://mp.weixin.qq.com/s/J3r_tYvfRNFtn-3T4YGxOQ)

Comprehension Check

Directions: *Use an appropriate word or phrase from the box with their proper forms to complete each sentence. Each word or phrase can be used once only.*

smuggle	discard	pend	complaint	municipal
overturn	verdict	hygiene	speculate	infringe

1. Instead of __________ their old worn-out jeans, customers bring them in to be renewed.

2. The government has introduced some tough new laws on food __________.

3. A spokesman with the Beijing __________ Education Commission said the rule is still in force.

4. Having to wait hours came high on the list of __________.

5. People fear that security cameras could __________ personal liberties.

6. The testimony based on __________ is not admissible.

7. Customs officials foiled an attempt to __________ the paintings out of the country.

8. The company's new president decided to __________ a decision by his predecessor that was unpopular with employees.

9. This petition shall be made to the first Administrative Panel appointed to hear a __________ dispute between the parties.

10. The judge will delay his __________ until he receives medical reports on the offender.

Background Information

（一）案例速览

小王认为 Dey 乐园制定的规则侵犯了自身合法权益，提起诉讼，向法院提出了两点诉讼请求：一、确认上海 Dey 乐园禁止游客携带食品入园的格式条款无效（overturn the no-outside-food-and-drink policy）；二、要求上海 Dey 乐园赔偿原告损失（compensate her loss），包括原告在 Dey 乐园外购买却因被告不合理规则而被迫丢弃的食品费用，共计 46.3 元。

（二）《中华人民共和国民法典》相关法条

《中华人民共和国民法典》从维护公平、保护弱者出发，对格式条款予以限制：

Article 496　A standard clause refers to a clause formulated in advance by a party for the purpose of repeated use which has not been negotiated with the other party when concluding the contract.

Upon concluding a contract, where a standard clause is used, the party providing the standard clause shall determine the parties' rights and obligations in accordance with the principle of fairness, and shall, in a reasonable manner, call the other party's attention to the clause concerning the other party's major interests and concerns, such as a clause that exempts or alleviates the liability of the party providing the standard clause, and give explanations of such clause upon request of the other party. Where the party providing the standard clause fails to perform the aforementioned obligation of calling attention or giving explanations, thus resulting in the other party's failure to pay attention to or understand the clause concerning his major interests and concerns, the other party may claim that such clause does not become part of the contract.

第四百九十六条　格式条款是当事人为了重复使用而预先拟定，并在订立合同时未与对方协商的条款。

采用格式条款订立合同的，提供格式条款的一方应当遵循公平原则确定当事人之间的权利和义务，并采取合理的方式提示对方注意免除或者减轻其责任等与对方有重大利害关系的条款，按照对方的要求，对该条款予以说明。提供格式条款的一方未履行提示或者说明义务，致使对方没有注意或者理解与其有重大利害关系的条款的，对方可以主张该条款不成为合同的内容。

Article 497　A standard clause is void under any of the following circumstances:

(1) existence of a circumstance under which the clause is void as provided in Section 3 of Chapter VI of Book One and Article 506 of this Code;

(2) the party providing the standard clause unreasonably exempts or alleviates himself from the liability, imposes heavier liability on the other party, or restricts the main rights of the other party; or

(3) the party providing the standard clause deprives the other party of his main rights.

第四百九十七条　有下列情形之一的，该格式条款无效：

（一）具有本法第一编第六章第三节和本法第五百零六条规定的无效情形；

（二）提供格式条款一方不合理地免除或者减轻其责任、加重对方责任、限制对方主要权利；

（三）提供格式条款一方排除对方主要权利。

Article 498　Where a dispute arises over the understanding of a standard clause, the clause shall be interpreted in accordance with its common understanding. Where there are two or more interpretations of a standard clause, the clause shall be interpreted in a manner unfavorable to the party providing the standard clause. Where a standard clause is inconsistent with a non-standard clause, the non-standard clause shall prevail.

第四百九十八条　对格式条款的理解发生争议的，应当按照通常理解予以解释。对格式条款有两种以上解释的，应当作出不利于提供格式条款一方的解释。格式条款和非格式条款不一致的，应当采用非格式条款。

Vocabulary and Key Notes

1. **Shanghai Dey Resort** 上海 Dey 度假区

2. **smuggle** *v.* to take, send or bring goods or people secretly and illegally into or out of a country, etc. 走私；私运；偷运

3. **discard** *v.* to get rid of sth. that you no longer want or need 丢弃；抛弃

4. **file a series of complaints to** 提出一系列投诉

5. **overturn** *v.* to officially decide that a legal decision etc. is not correct, and to make it no longer valid 推翻，撤销（判决等）

6. **pending** *adj.* remaining undecided; awaiting decision （诉案、争议等）未决的；待决的
pending verdict 未决判决

7. **speculate** *v.* reach conclusions not based on knowledge or evidence 猜想

8. **infringe on tourists' right of choice** 侵犯游客选择权

Translation

Directions: *Translate the following sentences from Passage 1 into Chinese.*

1. The student, who is surnamed Wang and is a junior at East China University of Political Science and Law, said she was told to either throw away or finish the snacks in her backpack, which were worth 46.30 yuan ($6.56), after security personnel caught her smuggling food into the park.

2. Shanghai Dey Resort has banned outside food, alcohol and non-alcohol beverages over 600 milliliters inside its park since November 2017, according to Paper.cn.

3. Since that visit to the park in late January, Wang has been filling a series of complaints to the municipal's public hotlines and regulators.

4. She called for the park's ban to be overturned and for the park to compensate her loss of 46.30 yuan. The case was heard on April 23 and is still pending verdict.

5. Although Shanghai Dey claims the food ban is due to hygiene reasons, that did not stop Chinese net users from speculating that Dey is applying double standards in Asia and forcing tourists to buy their food.

Passage 2

Chinese Students Sued Company A over not Providing Chargers

中国大学生诉 A 公司不配充电器案

A group of Chinese university students have filed a lawsuit against Compay A, demanding the company provide a **charger** for an Phone they bought.

Following Company A's 2020 decision to no longer include chargers in the box with its Phones, the company has repeatedly faced fines from Brazil. Now it's **subject to** a new lawsuit, this time from a group of students from Dua University and the Bei University of Chemical Technology.

The students took Company A to the Beijing Internet Court, according to a report by *Shanghai Law Journal*, where they **allege** they weren't able to charge their Phone 12 and 12 Pro Max units as advertised on the company's website, and that the included cable isn't **compatible with** most third-party chargers on the market, which still come with a USB-A port. ①

Company A has argued that its box for the Phone 12 Pro Max is clear that it does not include a charger. The company has previously said that the reason for the removal is to reduce carbon waste.

One of the students surnamed Fang began the campaign after buying an Phone 12 Pro Max. It was one of the first without a charger, and her aims include getting Company A to provide a charger.

She also wants the company to pay 100 yuan (approximately $15.50), **presumabl**y per buyer, and pay **litigation costs**.

"Company A has a serious infringement of consumers' **legitimate rights and interests,**" she said during the hearing. "Most consumers and even the Company's employees are equally puzzled and angry about this, but most of them have become a silent majority."

The two parties were in the process of supplying the court with additional evidence, the report said. The case was presented at a competition for **public interest lawsuits** this month. ②

"As a TV remote control box, a charger is a necessary mobile phone accessory," Chang, a lawyer from Beijing Kang Law Firm, told the Global Times on Wednesday, noting that, the Company's charger is its **exclusive accessory**; that is, the mobile phone can't work normally without it, which violates the service contract.

Consumers can negotiate with Company A directly, or conduct investigation and mediation through **consumer associations**, or sue to apply for sales return, Chang said. ③

The case has seen extensive public support on Chinese social media platforms like Weibo.

Many internet users have expressed support for the students for **standing up for** consumers' interests. Some said they had been forced to purchase new chargers and **adapters** when **upgrading** to an Phone 12, but others worried Company A would pass the costs on to consumers if it was asked to give out free adapters. ④

Company A is also facing pressure in other countries regarding Phone chargers.

Earlier this year, Brazil's consumer protection agency imposed a nearly $2 million fine on Company A for selling its Phone 12 series without chargers.

The European Union is proposing a regulation to have a common USB-C charging port for all smartphones to reduce waste and protect consumer interests. Company A has warned the **move** could **stifle innovation**. ⑤

(**Source**: https://mp.weixin.qq.com/s/7h7TGDOmX4fkaAJYqLzFrQ)

Comprehension Check

Directions: *Tell whether each of the following statements is true or false according to the information from Passage 2.*

1. Company A doesn't include chargers in the box with its Phones all the time.

2. According to Company A's statement, the reason for the removal of Company A's chargers is to reduce carbon waste.

3. Company A is also facing pressure in other countries regarding Phone chargers.

4. A few internet users have expressed support for the students for standing up for consumers' interests.

5. Company A may pass the costs on to consumers if it was asked to give out free adapters.

Background Information

（一）案件速览

Bei 大学的法学生方同学购买了 Phone 12 Pro Max 手机，在发现手机并没有配备相应的充电设备后，选择用法律手段维护权益。“根据从物随主物移转和社会交易习惯，购买手机理应配备充电器。”

来自 Bei 大学、Dua 大学的学生们组队将 A 公司告上法庭，2021 年 5 月，方同学及其小组成员向 A 电子产品商贸（北京）有限公司所在的北京市东城区人民法院提出立案申请。请求判令 A 公司交付手机充电器；承担违约责任，支付违约金 100 元并承担诉讼费用。

（二）知识点补充：从物随主物 The accessory follows the principal

主物与从物的划分规则，是指在两个以上的物发生互相附着或者聚合而且在经济上发生密切的关联之后，当物上的权利发生变动时，为确定物的归属所适用的规则。物的主从关系的划分并非人为拟制，而是经济实践的反映。现实中的物常常是由许多单一物结合在一起组成的物。当物上的权利发生变动时，必须考虑各部分是否也随之发生权利的变动，因此制定主物与从物之间的关系规则。

（三）《中华人民共和国民法典》相关法条

Article 320 Where a principal thing is transferred, the accessary thereof shall be transferred concomitantly, unless otherwise agreed by the parties.

第三百二十条　主物转让的，从物随主物转让，但是当事人另有约定的除外。

Article 631　Where a contract is rescinded due to the inconformity of the principal subject matter with the agreed requirements, the effect of the rescission shall be effective against the accessory subject matter. Where a rescission is due to the inconformity of the accessory subject matter with the agreed requirements, the effect of the rescission is not effective against the principal subject matter.

第六百三十一条　因标的物的主物不符合约定而解除合同的，解除合同的效力及于从物。因标的物的从物不符合约定被解除的，解除的效力不及于主物。

（四）《中华人民共和国消费者权益保护法》相关法条

Article 4　When conducting transactions with consumers, business operators shall abide by the principles of voluntariness, equality, fairness, good faith.

第四条　经营者与消费者进行交易，应当遵循自愿、平等、公平、诚实信用的原则。

（五）修订后的《消费者权益保护法》以下内容成为网购消费者的维权利器

The revised consumer rights law stipulates that:

- 7 天后悔权

经营者采用网络、电视、电话、邮购等方式销售商品，消费者有权自收到商品之日起七日内退货，且无需说明理由，但根据商品性质不宜退货的除外。

Business operators shall unconditionally make refunds within seven days of a transaction via Internet, television, phone and post, excluding products unsuitable for such unconditional return.

- 网交平台担责

网络交易平台提供者不能提供销售者或者服务者的真实名称、地址和有效联系方式的，消费者也可以向网络交易平台提供者要求赔偿。

Consumers can seek compensation from online trading platforms if they are unable to provide true names, addresses and valid contact details for vendors using their networks.

- 霸王条款无效

经营者不得以格式条款、通知、说明、店堂告示等方式，作出排除或限制消费者权利、减轻和减免经营者责任、加重消费者责任等对消费者不公平、不合理的规定。

Business owners should not impose unfair and unreasonable conditions on consumers in forms such as standard terms in contracts, notices and bulletins at outlets which have the aim of creating a significant imbalance in the parties' rights and obligations to the detriment of the consumer, and relieving or exempting the business' obligations.

- **禁止信息骚扰**

经营者未经消费者同意或者请求，或者消费者明确表示拒绝的，不得向其发送商业性信息。

Business operators should not send commercial information to consumers without their approval or after their rejection.

- **耐用品举证倒置**

经营者提供的机动车、计算机、电视机、电冰箱、空调器、洗衣机等耐用商品或者装饰装修等服务，消费者自接受商品或者服务之日起六个月内发现瑕疵，发生争议的，由经营者承担有关瑕疵的举证责任。

Businesses selling durable commodities (such as vehicles, computers, TVs, refrigerators, air conditioners and washing machines) and decoration services are legally liable to provide proof of the integrity of their products in disputes if buyers find flaws in the products within six months after they receive them or the first six months of use.

- **消费者和经营者发生消费者权益争议的，可以通过下列途径解决：**

In case of disputes with business operators over consumer rights and interests, consumers may settle the disputes in the following manner:

（1）与经营者协商和解；

Consult and conciliate with business operators;

（2）请求消费者协会调解；

Request mediation through consumer associations;

（3）向有关行政部门申诉；

Appeal to relevant administrative departments;

（4）根据与经营者达成的仲裁协议提请仲裁机构仲裁；

Apply to arbitral organizations for mediation according to agreements with business operators;

（5）向人民法院提起诉讼。（新《消法》规定，省级以上消费者协会有权代表消费者提起公益诉讼。）

Institute legal proceedings in the people's court. (Consumer associations at provincial levels and above have been designated as those that can file public interest litigation on behalf of consumers under the revised consumer rights law.)

(**Source**: https://mp.weixin.qq.com/s/6aQrH8a89psM_mZnEy6Bfw)

Vocabulary and Key Notes

1. **charger** *n.* a piece of equipment for loading a battery with electricity 充电器

2. **subject to** governed by 受……支配的；likely to be affected in some indicated way 会遭受……的

3. **allege** *v.* to state sth. as a fact but without giving proof（未提出证据）断言，指称，声称

4. **compatible with** 与……和谐相处；与……相配的

5. **presumably** *adv.* used to say that you think that sth. is probably true 很可能；大概；想必是

6. **litigation costs** 诉讼成本；诉讼费用

7. **legitimate rights and interests** 合法权益

8. **public interest lawsuits** 公共利益诉讼

9. **exclusive accessory** 独家配件

10. **consumer associations** 消费者协会

11. **standing up for** 支持

12. **adapter** *n.* device that enables something to be used in a way different from that for which it was intended or makes different pieces of apparatus compatible（电器设备的）转接器，适配器

13. **upgrade** *v.* to make a piece of machinery, computer system, etc. more powerful and efficient 使（机器、计算机系统等）升级；提高；改进

14. **move** *v.* make a motion; submit a formal request to the court 提出动议；向法院提出正式请求

15. **stifle innovation** 扼杀创新

Translation

Directions: *Translate the following sentences from Passage 2 into Chinese.*

1. The students took Company A to the Beijing Internet Court, according to a report by *Shanghai Law Journal,* where they allege they weren't able to charge their Phone 12 and 12 Pro Max units as advertised on the company's website, and that the included cable isn't compatible with most third-party chargers on the market, which still come with a USB-A port.

2. The case was presented at a competition for public interest lawsuits this month.

3. Consumers can negotiate with Company A directly, or conduct investigation and

mediation through consumer associations, or sue to apply for sales return, Chang said.

4. Some said they had been forced to purchase new chargers and adapters when upgrading to an Phone 12, but others worried Company A would pass the costs on to consumers if it was asked to give out free adapters.

5. The European Union is proposing a regulation to have a common USB-C charging port for all smartphones to reduce waste and protect consumer interests. Company A has warned the move could stifle innovation.

Supplementary Reading

Facial Recognition Misuse Shows Need for "Data Fence"

人脸识别遭滥用　急需"数据门槛"

A new energy vehicle company in Shanghai was recently punished for collecting customers' biometric data without their consent. The company had installed facial recognition cameras at seven stores, collecting and uploading 430,000 facial photos in over six months to analyze customer flow, including the number of people entering the stores, gender ratio and age analysis. Earlier, a sanitary product brand was found collecting customer's facial information without their consent, underlining the urgency to strengthen the protection of biometric data and other personal information.

With the wide application of digital technology, almost anyone can produce, use and even become the owner of digital assets. Big data can make use of such data to reap economic and social benefits. However, the ease with which digital assets can be copied and spread makes their protection difficult, ultimately restricting the development of the digital economy.

Therefore, to build a sound protection system for digital assets, prevent the illegal use and dissemination of digital assets, and realize the efficient allocation and orderly circulation of digital assets in the market it is not only necessary to promote the healthy development of the digital industry, but also to promote the construction of digital China.

From the legal perspective, the authorities should build a firm "legal fence" for data information protection. Considering the potential risks to the protection of digital assets and applications, relevant laws and regulations should focus on data security and user privacy, especially in the aspect of merchants collecting personal information.

In the era of big data, data information and digital assets should not be monopolized or dominated by specific subjects, and necessary legal guidance and intervention should be carried out in accordance with the principle of equal rights and obligations.

Advanced technologies such as blockchain and big data should be better applied for digital asset protection in order to promote the rapid flow and effective use of data assets, such as effective identity verification, ownership verification, ownership transfer and contract execution.

Accelerating the establishment of a stronger data information protection system will not only protect the legal rights and interests of the obligee, but will also address the issue of social equity brought about by the "free use" of personal data, effectively defuse the competition risks behind the application of digital assets, and maximize the development of the digital economy.

(**Source**: http://www.chinadaily.com.cn/a/202201/12/WS61de1816a310cdd39bc80732.html)

Further Discussion

Answer the following questions:

1. Things don't always go right. Sometimes you don't get what you ordered; sometimes you get an item of the blue. What tips and strategies can help you resolve the problem?

2. What should be done in order to better protect our digital information?

3. Does facial recognition technology violate personal freedoms?

小语说语：Fairness

The principle of fairness

公平原则

Article 6 When conducting a civil activity, a person of the civil law shall, in compliance with **the principle of fairness,** reasonably clarify the rights and obligations of each party.

第六条　民事主体从事民事活动，应当遵循公平原则，合理确定各方的权利和义务。

Article 288 The persons entitled to adjacent rights in immovable property shall properly deal with adjacent relationships in accordance with **the principles of** facilitation to production, convenience for daily lives, solidarity and mutual assistance, and **fairness** and reasonableness.

第二百八十八条　不动产的相邻权利人应当按照有利生产、方便生活、团结互助、公平合理的原则，正确处理相邻关系。

Article 533 The people's court or an arbitration institution shall rectify or rescind the contract in compliance with **the principle of fairness**, taking into account the actual circumstances of the case.

第五百三十三条　人民法院或者仲裁机构应当结合案件的实际情况，根据公平原则变更或者解除合同。

第十章 诚信原则案例

导读

诚信，作为社会主义核心价值观和民法典的基本原则，在我们生活中有着举足轻重的作用。民无诚信不立，国无诚信不兴。本章的案例为我们敲响了怎样的警钟？

案例阅读

Passage 1

Case of Dispute over Unfair Competition

不正当竞争案

As an important resource in the information age, big data contains enormous economic and social value. With the boom of industries related to the big data industry, it is also urgent to establish industry norms and governance standards. This case clarified that using **web crawler technology** to steal big data resources for a similar business **constitutes an unfair competition**. ① This rule aims to encourage the big data industry players to follow the business ethics and carry out fair and **benign** competition.

From November 2015 to May 2016, Wuhan Y Science & Technology Co., Ltd. to expand the market share and information **query** accuracy of **the intelligent bus app "C"**, Mr. Shao, the company's **legal representative** and president then, authorized Chen, the company's technical director to instruct employees surnamed Liu and others to use web crawler technology to obtain a large number of real-time bus information data of "K", the like app run by **Shenzhen G Technology Co., Ltd.** ("G"), use it for its own app "C" and provide inquiry service to the public. G Technology Co. **sued** to the court for the break of **business ethics and the principle of good faith** by Y Technology Co. and relevant responsible persons which constituted unfair competition. ②

The court **held** that the commercially valued big data resources legally obtained by the right owner of the plaintiff G through collection, analysis, edition and compilation are protected by the relevant law. ③ The plaintiff G provides free data query to the public for reasons of its business model or other needs, but the defendant Y uses web crawler technology to steal the data and use it to run its similar business. Y Technology Co. had **the subjective intention** of seeking its own competitive advantages by destroying others' market competitive advantages, which seriously **disrupted** the market order, and thus constituted unfair competition. ④ On May 23, 2018, Shenzhen Intermediate People's Court **made a civil judgment**, which ordered the defendant Wuhan Y Technology Co., Ltd. to **compensate** the plaintiff Shenzhen G Technology Co., Ltd. for the economic losses and reasonable costs of RMB 500,000 yuan. ⑤ After **the first instance judgment** was pronounced and served, neither the plaintiff nor the defendant **appealed**, and the judgment has become effective.

(**Source**: https://english.court.gov.cn/2019-12/04/c_766705.htm)

Comprehension Check

Directions: *Use an appropriate word or phrase from the box with their proper form to complete each sentence. Each word or phrase can be used once only.*

enormous	constitute	benign	plaintiff	compensate
norm	market order	clarify	disrupt	hold

1. Reporters asked him to __________ his position on economic and political reforms.

2. While printing __________ increased access to books by making cheap, high-volume production possible; it also reduced choice.

3. It's an aggressive approach, exploiting the weaknesses of our __________ case.

4. The draft also clarified the legal responsibilities and punishment for illegal acts to safeguard __________, the meeting said.

5. Court case verdicts do not __________ binding precedents. However, they are used for the purposes of judicial reference and guidance.

6. If any provision of this agreement is __________ to be unenforceable, it shall not affect any other provisions of this Agreement.

7. Now social __________ are rules of behavior that are socially and culturally accepted in a society.

8. They enjoyed an especially __________ climate.

9. The firm will __________ workers for their loss of earnings.

10. New companies displace old ones. New business models __________ established ones.

Background Information

（一）案例速览

本案明确指出武汉 Y 公司未经许可利用网络爬虫技术盗用大数据资源，用于经营同类应用程序，破坏他人市场竞争优势、谋取自身竞争优势，违背了商业道德和诚实信用原则，严重破坏了市场秩序，构成不正当竞争。本案判决被告 Y 公司向原告 G 公司赔偿 50 万元。该判决有利于确立大数据行业行为规范，促进经营者遵循商业道德，开展公平、良性竞争。

（二）《中华人民共和国民法典》相关法条速览

Article 86 A for-profit legal person shall, when engaging in operational activities, observe commercial ethics, maintain the security of transactions, subject itself to the supervision of the government and the public, and assume social responsibilities.

第八十六条　营利法人从事经营活动，应当遵守商业道德，维护交易安全，接受政府和社会的监督，承担社会责任。

（三）《中华人民共和国反不正当竞争法》速览

1. The definition of unfair competition 不正当竞争的定义

Unfair competition refers to any business operator's act of participating in the production and operation activities in violation of the provisions herein to disrupt the competition order in the market and infringe the legitimate rights and interests of other business operators or consumers.

本法所称的不正当竞争，是指经营者违反本法规定，损害其他经营者的合法权益，扰乱社会经济秩序的行为。

2. 相关法条学习

Article 2 While carrying out production or business activities, a business operator shall follow the principles of voluntariness, equality, fairness, and good faith, abide by laws and observe business ethics.

第二条　经营者在生产经营活动中，应当遵循自愿、平等、公平、诚信的原则，遵守法律和商业道德。

Article 9 A business operator shall not engage in any of the following infringements of commercial secrets:

(1) obtaining an obligee's commercial secrets by theft, bribery, intimidation, electronic

intrusion or other improper means;

第九条　经营者不得实施下列侵犯商业秘密的行为：

（一）以盗窃、贿赂、欺诈、胁迫、电子侵入或者其他不正当手段获取权利人的商业秘密；

Article 17　A business operator that violates this Law and thus causes damage to others shall bear civil liability for such damage in accordance with the law. A business operator whose lawful rights and interests are infringed by an unfair competition act may file a lawsuit with a people's court.

The amount of compensation for damage caused by any unfair competition act to a business operator shall be determined depending on the actual losses suffered by such operator as a result of the infringement; where it is truly difficult to work out the actual losses, such amount shall be determined in accordance with the benefits obtained by the infringer from the infringement. Where a business operator is maliciously engaged in the infringement of commercial secrets, if the circumstance is serious, the amount of compensation may be determined between one time to five times the amount determined according to the above method. The amount of compensation shall also include the reasonable expenses paid by the damaged business operator to stop the infringement.

第十七条　经营者违反本法规定，给他人造成损害的，应当依法承担民事责任。经营者的合法权益受到不正当竞争行为损害的，可以向人民法院提起诉讼。

因不正当竞争行为受到损害的经营者的赔偿数额，按照其因被侵权所受到的实际损失确定；实际损失难以计算的，按照侵权人因侵权所获得的利益确定。经营者恶意实施侵犯商业秘密行为，情节严重的，可以在按照上述方法确定数额的一倍以上五倍以下确定赔偿数额。赔偿数额还应当包括经营者为制止侵权行为所支付的合理开支。

(**Source**: Law of the People's Republic of China against Unfair Competition 中华人民共和国反不正当竞争法 http://www.doc88.com/p-50087081198768.html)

Vocabulary and Key Notes

1. **web crawler technology** 网络爬虫技术
2. **constitute an unfair competition** 构成不正当竞争
3. **benign** *adj.* kind and gentle; not hurting anybody 善良的；和善的；良性的
4. **query** *n.* a question, especially one asking for information or expressing a doubt about sth. 疑问；询问

5. **the intelligent bus app** 智能公交应用程序

6. **legal representative** 法人代表；法定代表人

7. **sue** *v.* to make a claim against sb. in court about sth. that they have said or done to harm you 控告；提起诉讼

8. **business ethics** 商业道德；企业道德；职业道德

9. **the principle of good faith** 诚信原则

10. **hold** *v.* to consider that sth. is true 认为；相信

11. **the subjective intention** 主观目的

12. **disrupt** *v.* to make it difficult for sth. to continue in the normal way 扰乱；使中断；打乱

13. **make a civil judgment** 作出民事判决

14. **compensate** *v.* to pay sb. money because they have suffered some damage, loss, injury, etc. 给（某人）赔偿（或赔款）

15. **the first instance judgment** 一审判决

16. **appeal** *v.* to make a formal request to a court or to sb. in authority for a judgement or a decision to be changed 上诉；申诉

Translation

Directions: *Translate the following sentences from Passage 1 into Chinese.*

1. This case clarified that using web crawler technology to steal big data resources for a similar business constitutes an unfair competition.

2. G Technology Co. sued to the court for the break of business ethics and the principle of good faith by Y Technology Co. and relevant responsible persons which constituted unfair competition.

3. The court held that the commercially valued big data resources legally obtained by the right owner of the plaintiff G through collection, analysis, edition and compilation are protected by the relevant law.

4. Y Technology Co. had the subjective intention of seeking its own competitive advantages by destroying others' market competitive advantages, which seriously disrupted the market order, and thus constituted unfair competition.

5. On May 23, 2018, Shenzhen Intermediate People's Court made a civil judgment, which ordered the defendant Wuhan Y Technology Co., Ltd. to compensate the plaintiff Shenzhen G

Technology Co., Ltd. for the economic losses and reasonable costs of RMB 500,000 yuan.

Passage 2

Subtitle Website Founder Was Jailed for Film Piracy

字幕网站创始人因盗版电影入狱

The Shanghai No.3 Intermediate People's Court sentenced surnamed Liang, the founder of a website that hosted pirated films with Chinese subtitles, to three years and six months in prison on Monday for **copyright infringement** and also fined him 1.5 million yuan ($235,000). ①

The court also sought to recover **illegal gains** and **confiscate** the funds and tools used for his criminal acts. ②

It said Liang founded two companies and instructed another person, surnamed Wang, to develop the website of RY Subtitle Group, known as YT, and apps for mobile platforms in 2018.

He also instructed another person, surnamed Xie, to have translators produce Chinese subtitles for films and television series acquired from overseas. These shows were then uploaded to the companies' websites and apps for public viewing and downloading without legal authorization or permission for distribution. ③

The website of YT and related apps had hosted 32,824 videos and **garnered** 6.83 million members before they were shut down.

The court said Liang earned around 12 million yuan from membership fees, advertisements and the sale of hard drives with pirated copies of films.

Liang was arrested on Jan 6 and **confessed**.

The court said Liang's actions constituted copyright infringement to a serious degree, but he was given lighter punishment due to his confession and cooperation. ④

On China's **Sina Weibo microblogging platform**, the official account of YT said on Monday that it had admitted its guilt and the website and apps would not reopen because copyright issues could not be resolved.

Yao, deputy secretary-general of **Chinese Intellectual Property Law Research Association**, said the group had infringed the copyrights of owners, who were often overseas.

"The case reflected the government's emphasis on protecting intellectual property for **foreign entities** in China and creating a level and fair business environment for all," he said. "It has fulfilled its obligation as a responsible member of the World Trade Organization."

The protection of intellectual property will encourage more new creations and society should promote the spread of intellectual creations through lawful and proper means ⑤ , he added. Zheng, a lawyer with Shanghai Y Law Firm who specializes in IP protection, said he agreed with the court's **verdict** as the sharing of unauthorized films online for profit is illegal, and could be compared to the selling of pirated DVDs in the early 2000s. ⑥

"The environment for IP protection in China has improved a lot in the past decade," he said. "The verdict sent yet another warning to people that regardless of the forms of distribution, piracy will always be punished here."

(**Source:** https://www.chinadaily.com.cn/a/202111/23/WS619c45fba310cdd39bc76ea0.html)

Comprehension Check

Directions: *Tell whether each of the following statements is true or false according to the information from Passage 1.*

1. The court sentenced the founder of the website to more than three years in prison and also fined him less than 2 million yuan.

2. In 2018, Liang has already confessed part of his illegal actions.

3. Under the guidance of Liang, Xie created YT and found translators to produce Chinese subtitles for films.

4. Due to his confession, Liang was lucky to get a lighter punishment.

5. At the beginning of 21st century, if someone copies DVDs to sell to others, he would be dropped across for his illegal action.

Background Information

（一）案例速览

1. 2021 年 11 月 22 日，上海市第三中级人民法院公开审理了上海市人民检察院第三分院提起公诉的被告人梁某某涉嫌犯著作权罪一案，并当庭作出一审判决，以侵犯著作权罪判处被告人梁某某有期徒刑三年六个月，并处罚金人民币一百五十万元；违法所得予以追缴，扣押在案的供犯罪所用的本人财物等予以没收。

2. What is copyright? 什么是著作权？

Copyright is a type of intellectual property that protects original works of authorship as soon as an author fixes the work in a tangible form of expression. In copyright law, there are a lot of different types of works, including paintings, photographs, illustrations, musical compositions, sound recordings, computer programs, books, poems, blog posts, movies, architectural works, plays, and so much more!

著作权是知识产权的一种，它指的是只要作者将作品付诸一种有形的表达形式上，该作者的原创作品就会获得保护。在版权法中，有很多不同类型的作品都受法律保护，包括绘画、照片、插图、音乐作品、录音、计算机程序、书籍、诗歌、博客、电影、建筑作品、戏剧等等！

（二）《中华人民共和国民法典》相关法条速览

Article 123 The persons of the civil law enjoy intellectual property rights in accordance with law.

Intellectual property rights are the exclusive rights enjoyed by the right holders in accordance with law over the following subject matters:

(1) works;

(2) inventions, new utility models, or designs;

(3) trademarks;

(4) geographical indications;

(5) trade secrets;

(6) layout designs of integrated circuits;

(7) new plant varieties; and

(8) the other subject matters as provided by law.

第一百二十三条　民事主体依法享有知识产权。

知识产权是权利人依法就下列客体享有的专有的权利：

（一）作品；

（二）发明、实用新型、外观设计；

（三）商标；

（四）地理标志；

（五）商业秘密；

（六）集成电路布图设计；

（七）植物新品种；

（八）法律规定的其他客体。

Article 1185 In case of an intentional infringement of another person's intellectual property rights, where the circumstances are serious, the infringed person has the right to request for corresponding punitive damages.

第一千一百八十五条　故意侵害他人知识产权，情节严重的，被侵权人有权请求相应的惩罚性赔偿。

（三）《中华人民共和国著作权法》相关法条速览

Article 3 "Works" mentioned in this Law shall refer to ingenious intellectual achievements in the fields of literature, art and science that can be presented in a certain form:

(1) written works;

(2) oral works;

(3) musical, dramatic, quyi, choreographic and acrobatic art works;

(4) works of fine art and architecture;

(5) photographic works;

(6) audiovisual works;

(7) drawings of engineering designs and product designs, maps, sketches and other graphic works as well as model works;

(8) computer software;

(9) other intellectual achievements that meet the characteristics of works.

第三条　本法所称的作品，包括以下列形式创作的文学、艺术和自然科学、社会科学、工程技术等作品：

（一）文字作品；

（二）口述作品；

（三）音乐、戏剧、曲艺、舞蹈作品；

（四）美术、摄影作品；

（五）电影、电视、录像作品；

（六）工程设计、产品设计图纸及其说明；

（七）地图、示意图等图形作品；

（八）计算机软件；

（九）法律、行政法规规定的其他作品。

Article 9 "Copyright owners" shall include:

(1) authors;

(2) other natural persons, legal entities and unincorporated organizations enjoying copyright in accordance with this Law.

第九条　著作权人包括：

（一）作者；

（二）其他依照本法享有著作权的自然人、法人或者非法人组织。

Article 10　"Copyright" shall include the following personal rights and property rights:

...

(12) The right of dissemination via information networks, that is, the right to provide works that may be obtained by the public at the time and place selected by the public by wire or wireless means.

...

(15) the right of translation, that is, the right to transform the language of a work into another language.

第十条　著作权包括下列人身权和财产权

……

（十二）信息网络传播权，即以有线或者无线方式向公众提供、使公众可以在选定的时间和地点获得作品的权利。

……

（十五）翻译权，即将作品从一种语言文字转换成另一种语言文字的权利。

Article 13　Where a work is created by adaptation, translation, annotation or arrangement of a pre-existing work, the copyright in the work thus created shall be enjoyed by the adapter, translator, annotator or arranger, provided that the copyright in the original work is not infringed upon.

第十三条　改编、翻译、注释、整理已有作品而产生的作品，其著作权由改编、翻译、注释、整理人享有，但行使著作权时不得侵犯原作品的著作权。

Article 17　The copyright of cinematographic works and TV play works in audiovisual works shall be enjoyed by producers, but screenwriters, directors, photographers, lyricists, composers, and other authors shall enjoy the right of signature and have the right to obtain remunerations as agreed upon in the contracts signed with producers.

The ownership of the copyright of an audiovisual work other than those specified in the preceding paragraph shall be agreed upon by the parties; and where there is no agreement or the agreement is unclear, the copyright shall be enjoyed by the producer, but the author shall have the

小语说语：Good Faith

The principle of good faith

诚信原则

Article 7 When conducting a civil activity, a person of the civil law shall, in compliance with **the principle of good faith**, uphold honesty and honor commitments.

第七条 民事主体从事民事活动，应当遵循诚信原则，秉持诚实，恪守承诺。

Article 142 Where an expression of intent is made to another person, the meaning of the expression shall be interpreted according to the words and sentences used, with reference to the relevant terms, the nature and purpose of the civil juristic act, the custom, and **the principle of good faith**.

第一百四十二条 有相对人的意思表示的解释，应当按照所使用的词句，结合相关条款、行为的性质和目的、习惯以及诚信原则，确定意思表示的含义。

Article 500 During the course of concluding a contract, the party that falls under any of the following circumstances and causes loss to the other party shall bear the liability for compensation:

…

(3) conducting any other acts contrary to the principle of good faith.

第五百条 当事人在订立合同过程中有下列情形之一，造成对方损失的，应当承担赔偿责任：

……

（三）有其他违背诚信原则的行为。

Article 509 The parties shall comply with **the principle of good faith**, and perform such obligations as sending notices, rendering assistances, and keeping confidentiality in accordance with the nature and purpose of the contract and the course of dealing.

第五百零九条 当事人应当遵循诚信原则，根据合同的性质、目的和交易习惯履行通知、协助、保密等义务。

Article 558 After the parties' claims and obligations are terminated, the parties shall, in compliance with **the principle of good faith** and the like, perform such obligations as sending notification, rendering assistance, keeping confidentiality, and retrieving the used items according to the course of dealing.

第五百五十八条　债权债务终止后，当事人应当遵循诚信等原则，根据交易习惯履行通知、协助、保密、旧物回收等义务。

later hid in the apartment building and waited for the women to return from an evening out. ②

When they returned, he **confronted** them. The three began arguing, and Chen chased the women to their apartment.

Liu entered first and locked the door behind her, leaving JG outside. Chen stabbed JG in the neck a dozen times before fleeing the scene.

JG died after arriving at a nearby hospital.

In 2017, a Tokyo court **found** Chen **guilty of** killing JG and **sentenced** him **to** 20 years in prison. Ms. Jiang was dissatisfied with the result, saying that Chen should have received the **death penalty**.

She also said that Liu shared some of the blame for her daughter's death because she had locked JG out of the apartment when she was attacked. She was also upset about some improper posts Liu had made about her daughter on the Sina Weibo micro-blogging platform.

Ms. Jiang **filed the lawsuit** in 2019, seeking more than 2 million yuan in compensation for her financial losses and mental anguish.

The court said on Monday that Liu was obviously at fault in the incident and should **bear the civil penalty** as she had not informed JG of the potential danger posed by Chen, who had **intimidated** her before the killing, nor had she **taken JG's safety into account** when she locked her outside the apartment. ③

It supported Ms. Jiang, who said she suffered mental anguish after losing her only daughter, and added that people who bring danger around them **have an obligation to** take necessary measures to prevent others from being harmed.

"JG deserves praise and the compensation, as she offered emergency aid to Liu," the court said. "But Liu, as JG's friend and the one who received the aid, did not express gratitude and comfort to the relatives of **the deceased**, but instead **aggravated** the pain of the mother with improper online posts, which should be **condemned**."

A number of people, including national lawmakers and political advisers, attended the announcement of the **verdict**.

(**Source**: https://english.court.gov.cn/2022-01/11/c_761843.htm)

Comprehension Check

Directions: *Tell whether each of the following statements is true or false according to the* *information from Passage 1.*

1. Liu must pay more than 696,000 yuan to Ms. Jiang within 10 days if neither party continues to appeal.

2. The case dates back to Nov 3. 2016, when JG, 24, was stabbed to death in her apartment in Tokyo by Chen.

3. Liu had posted some improper remarks about JG on the Sina Weibo micro-blogging platform after the incident.

4. The case suggested that when the parties are in danger, they do not have to be responsible for the safety of the people around them in order to protect themselves.

5. In addition to the judge and the parties, political advisers also attended the announcement of the verdict.

Background Information

（一）案例速览

扶危济困是中华民族的传统美德，诚信友善是社会主义核心价值观的重要内容。司法裁判应当守护社会道德底线，弘扬美德义行，引导全社会崇德向善。基于民法诚实信用基本原则和权利义务相一致原则：在社会交往中，引入侵害危险、维持危险状态的人，负有采取必要合理措施以防止他人受到损害的安全保障义务；在形成救助关系的情况下，施救者对被救助者具有合理的信赖，被救助者对于施救者负有更高的诚实告知和善意提醒的注意义务。

在本案中，作为被救助者和侵害危险引入者的刘某某，对施救者 JG 并未充分尽到注意和安全保障义务，具有明显过错，理应承担法律责任。JG 作为一名在异国求学的女学生，对于身陷困境的同胞施以援手，给予了真诚的关心和帮助，并因此受到不法侵害而失去生命，其无私帮助他人的行为，体现了中华民族传统美德，与社会主义核心价值观和公序良俗相契合，应予褒扬，其受到不法侵害，理应得到法律救济。刘某某作为 JG 的好友和被救助者，在事发之后，非但没有心怀感恩并对逝者亲属给予体恤和安慰，反而以不当言语相激，进一步加重了他人的伤痛，其行为有违常理人情，应予谴责，应当承担民事赔偿责任并负担全部案件受理费。

（二）《中华人民共和国民法典》相关法条

Article 7 When conducting a civil activity, a person of the civil law shall, in compliance with the principle of good faith, uphold honesty and honor commitments.

第七条 民事主体从事民事活动，应当遵循诚信原则，秉持诚实，恪守承诺。

Article 8 When conducting a civil activity, no person of the civil law shall violate the law, or offend public order or good morals.

第八条 民事主体从事民事活动，不得违反法律，不得违背公序良俗。

Article 10 Civil disputes shall be resolved in accordance with law. Where the law does not specify, custom may be applied, provided that public order and good morals may not be offended.

第十条 处理民事纠纷，应当依照法律；法律没有规定的，可以适用习惯，但是不得违背公序良俗。

Article 1181 Where an infringed person dies, his close relatives have the right to request the tortfeasor to bear tort liability. Where an infringed person dies, the person who has paid for his medical expenses, funeral expenses, and other reasonable expenses has the right to request the tortfeasor to compensate the expenses, except for those expenses already paid by the tortfeasor

第一千一百八十一条 被侵权人死亡的，其近亲属有权请求侵权人承担侵权责任。被侵权人死亡的，支付被侵权人医疗费、丧葬费等合理费用的人有权请求侵权人赔偿费用，但是侵权人已经支付该费用的除外。

Vocabulary and Key Notes

1. **rule** *v.* to decide officially 裁决，裁定；判定；决定

2. **anguish** *n.* extreme unhappiness caused by physical or mental suffering（肉体或精神上的）极度痛苦，剧痛，悲痛

3. **confront** *v.* to face, meet, or deal with a difficult situation or person 面对，面临；遭遇；直面，正视

4. **find sb. guilty of** 判处某人犯……罪

5. **sentence** *v.* to decide and say officially what a punishment will be（法官）宣布判决，宣判

6. **penalty** *n.* ① a punishment, or the usual punishment, for doing something that is against a law 刑罚，惩罚，处罚；② a type of punishment, often involving paying money, that is given to you if you break an agreement or do not follow rules 罚金，罚款

7. **intimidate** *v.* to frighten or threaten someone, usually in order to persuade them to do something that you want them to do 恫吓，恐吓

8. **aggravate** *v.* to make a bad situation worse 使（局势等）更严重，加剧

9. **verdict** *n.* an opinion or decision made after judging the facts that are given, especially one made at the end of a trial（根据事实作出的）意见，决定；（尤指）判决，裁决

10. **the Chengyang District People's Court in Qingdao** 青岛市城阳区人民法院

11. **file the lawsuit** 提起诉讼

12. **bear the civil penalty** 承担民事处罚

13. **take sth. into account (also take account of sth.)** to consider or remember something when judging a situation 考虑到；顾及

14. **the deceased** a person who has recently died 新近去世的人；亡故者

Translation

Directions: *Translate the following sentences from Passage 2 into Chinese.*

1. The compensation included 496,000 yuan for Ms. Jiang's financial losses and 200, 000 yuan for her mental anguish over the death of her daughter, JG. It also covered some lawsuit-related expenses, according to the ruling by the Chengyang District People's Court in Qingdao, Shandong province.

2. Earlier on the day of the stabbing, Liu had quarreled with Chen. Armed with a knife, Chen later hid in the apartment building and waited for the women to return from an evening out.

3. The court said on Monday that Liu was obviously at fault in the incident and should bear the civil penalty as she had not informed JG of the potential danger posed by Chen, who had intimidated her before the killing, nor had she taken JG's safety into account when she locked her outside the apartment.

Supplementary Reading

"Blind Box" Sales

"盲盒"销售

The China Consumers Association has criticized K Corp., a leading chicken fast-food chain, for using a limited number of blind box sales to lure customers to over-purchase its food and cause food waste.

The association said on its website on Wednesday that such marketing can lead to impulsive and excessive consumption to obtain the limited edition blind boxes, which is "against public order and the spirit of the law".

The article was posted after K Corp. China collaborated with top domestic blind box toymaker Pop Mar to offer 260, 000 dolls with its 99 yuan ($15.60) family-sized chicken bucket from Jan 4. The doll set features seven models of Dim, a popular character created by Pop Mar, with six regular ones and one hidden model, meaning customers have to pay at least 594 yuan to collect a complete set.

The sale sparked a frenzy on the internet.

By Friday, more than 85 percent of the toys had been sold across the nation, with remaining sales delayed in cities affected by the COVID-19 pandemic, Pop Mar said.

On Xianyu, a popular secondhand goods exchange platform, a set of six regular models is priced at around 700 yuan. Many users have also offered eating services for those who cannot finish the whole bucket, with prices ranging from 79 to 699 yuan.

The association said that to collect the whole set, customers need to buy at least six chicken buckets and the probability of obtaining the hidden model is 1 in 72. Some people have paid 10, 494 yuan to buy 106 buckets and others have discarded the food they can't finish.

K's fast food has an expiry date and should be consumed in time and purchased on demand, the association said. The Anti-Food Waste Law adopted in April clearly stipulates that food operators should resist food waste, prompt customers to consume moderately and take measures to prevent waste rather than induce or mislead them to purchase excessively, it said.

The association also said that customers should consume "scientifically and rationally" and resist undesirable consumption behaviors.

Neither Pop Mar nor K China responded to requests for comment. K customer service said the dolls are still on sale and customers can consult local outlets for details.

(**Source**: https://global.chinadaily.com.cn/a/202201/13/WS61df8517a310cdd39bc80c61.html)

Further Discussion

Answer the following questions:

1. Have you ever experienced a conflict about square dance? How did you deal with it?

2. If you were Liu, how would you deal with the danger faced by yourself and the people around you ?

3. We can all play a part in reaching the national food waste reduction goal. What should we do today to reduce food waste, save money, and protect the environment?

小语说语：Public Order and Good Morals

The Principle of Public Order and Good Morals

公序良俗原则

- **原文**

The group of individuals participating in square dancing should **adhere to public rules and social customs** and never disturb others around them, according to the Shanghai Municipal Regulation on the Protection and Promotion of Public Cultural Services, which was approved by the city's legislature on Tuesday.

根据10月27日星期二上海市人大常委会通过的《上海市公共文化服务保障与促进条例》，跳广场舞的群众应当遵守相关规定和**公序良俗**，不得影响他人的正常工作和生活。

- **《中华人民共和国民法典》法条学习**

Article 8　When conducting a civil activity, no person of the civil law shall violate the law, or offend **public order or good morals**.

第八条　民事主体从事民事活动，不得违反法律，不得违背**公序良俗**。

Article 10　Civil disputes shall be resolved in accordance with law. Where the law does not specify, custom may be applied, provided that **public order and good morals** may not be offended.

第十条　处理民事纠纷，应当依照法律；法律没有规定的，可以适用习惯，但是不得违背**公序良俗**。

Article 143　A civil juristic act is valid if the following conditions are satisfied:

…

(3) the act does not violate any mandatory provisions of laws or administrative regulations, nor offend **public order or good morals**.

第一百四十三条　具备下列条件的民事法律行为有效：

……

（四）不违反法律、行政法规的强制性规定，不违背**公序良俗**。

Article 153　A civil juristic act that offends **the public order or good morals** is void.

第一百五十三条　违背**公序良俗**的民事法律行为无效。

Article 979　Where the management of another person's affairs is contrary to the true will of the beneficiary, the custodian does not have the right provided in the preceding paragraph, unless the true will of the beneficiary is in violation of law or against **the public order or good**

morals.

第九百七十九条　管理事务不符合受益人真实意思的，管理人不享有前款规定的权利；但是，受益人的真实意思违反法律或者违背**公序良俗**的除外。

Article 1012　A natural person enjoys the right to name, and is entitled to determine, use, change, or allow others to use his name in accordance with law, provided that public order and **good morals are not offended**.

第一千零一十二条　自然人享有姓名权，有权依法决定、使用、变更或者许可他人使用自己的姓名，但是不得违背**公序良俗**。

Article 1015　A natural person shall take the surname of either his father or mother, and may take a surname other than his father's or mother's in any of the following situations:

…

(3) taking a surname with other legitimate reasons that do not offend **public order and good morals.**

第一千零一十五条　自然人应当随父姓或者母姓，但是有下列情形之一的，可以在父姓和母姓之外选取姓氏：

……

（三）有不违背**公序良俗**的其他正当理由。

Article 1026 To determine whether an actor has fulfilled the obligation to reasonably verify the information as provided in Subparagraph 2 of the preceding Article, the following factors shall be considered:

…

(4) the relevance of the information with **public order and good morals**;

…

第一千零二十六条　认定行为人是否尽到前条第二项规定的合理核实义务，应当考虑下列因素：

……

（四）内容与**公序良俗**的关联性；

……

第十二章 绿色原则案例

导读

人类只有一个地球，建设美丽家园是人类的共同梦想。党的十八大以来，中国坚持绿水青山就是金山银山的理念，全面加强生态文明建设，交出了可圈可点的绿色答卷。然而本章节的经典案例也警示我们，只有把生态文明建设纳入制度化、法治化轨道，实行最严格的生态环境保护制度，才能为建设美丽中国筑牢根基。

案例阅读

Passage 1

Case of Environmental Pollution

污染环境案

In July 2002, defendant entity Part B (Zhejiang) Co., Ltd. (hereinafter referred to as "B Company") was formed with the business scope including production and sales of building hardware, high-strength precision fasteners for automobiles, and precision stamping molds. ① The **waste acid effluent** and **sludge** generated in the production of the Company were hazardous waste, which must be collected in categories and disposed of by an entrusted entity qualified for the disposal of **hazardous waste.** ② From 2008, defendant surnamed Huang assumed the post of vice-general manager of B Company and took charge of the routine operation and management of the Company. From April 2016, defendant surnamed Jiang directly took charge of the disposal of **acid pickling sludge** of B Company.

From July 2016 to May 2017, **in violation of** the state regulations on the management of hazardous waste, without **issuance of the hazardous waste transfer forms,** defendant entity B Company and defendants Huang and Jiang delivered the acid pickling sludge to defendants Li, Tu, and Liu having no qualification of hazardous waste disposal for **illegal disposal.** ③ By means of **forging** the official seals of the relevant state organs and companies and preparing false official documents and certificates, Li, Tu, and Liu illegally disposed of acid pickling sludge. The **aforesaid** defendants transported hazardous waste in an inter-provincial manner by automobile or ship and illegally **dumped** and disposed of acid pickling sludge, 1,071 tons in total, in Huai'an City, Yangzhou City, and Suzhou City of Jiangsu Province and Tongling City of Anhui Province. In particular, on May 22. 2017, Jiang, Li, and Tu, **in collusion with** defendants Wang, Wu, Zhu, Zha, and other persons, dumped 62.88 tons of acid pickling sludge to **the dam of the Yangtze River in the Economic and Technological Development Zone** of Tongling City, Anhui Province, which caused serious environmental pollution. After the case was exposed, it was found upon identification and appraisal that the aforesaid defendants illegally dumped and disposed of acid pickling sludge, causing the environmental damage of over CNY5.11 million and **giving rise to** the expenditures of emergency disposal, **ecological environment restoration**, and **identification and appraisal**, over CNY1.39 million in total. ④

In addition, from June to November 2017, having no qualification of disposal of hazardous waste, defendants Li, Tu, Liu, Wu, Zhu, and Zha illegally collected such toxic and hazardous substances as industrial sludge and waste bakelites from over ten enterprises in Jiangsu Province and Zhejiang Province, transported such toxic and hazardous substances in an inter-provincial manner to the river beach in Jiangbin Village, Tongling City, Anhui Province by ship, and dumped them there. In particular, 313 tons of waste bakelites and over 2,525 tons of industrial sludge were dumped and over 2,400 tons of industrial sludge were attempted to be dumped. ⑤

(**Source**: http://www.lawinfochina.com/SearchList.aspx)

Comprehension Check

Directions: *Use an appropriate word or phrase from the box with their proper form to complete each sentence. Each word or phrase can be used once only.*

precision	dispose	entrust	defendant	by means of
inter-provincial	organ	toxic	substance	aforesaid

1. This is an important task which the people have __________ to us.

2. The rules of court dictate that a __________ is entitled to all evidence which may help his case.

3. The Company will not force the employee to work __________ violence, intimidation or illegal restriction of personal freedom.

4. Twenty-seven provinces in China will first offer online bus ticket booking by the end of

this year, when their __________ online bus ticket booking system largely completes, according to the Ministry of Transport.

5. The river has been polluted with __________ waste from local factories.

6. Deputies to the People's Congresses have the right to address inquiries to state __________.

7. I further understand and agree the Bank is entitled the __________ rights at the Bank's discretion and without prior notice.

8. Give the right computer a massive database of faces, and it can process what it sees - then recognizes a face it's told to find — with remarkable speed and __________.

9. The __________ has been scheduled as a poison.

10. Medical supplies are __________ of hygienically.

Background Information

（一）案例速览

本案由安徽省芜湖市镜湖区人民检察院于 2018 年 7 月 16 日以被告单位 B 公司以及被告人黄某某、姜某某、李某某、涂某某等 12 人犯污染环境罪向安徽省芜湖市镜湖区人民法院提起公诉。2018 年 9 月 28 日，安徽省芜湖市镜湖区人民法院依法做出一审判决，认定被告单位 B 公司犯污染环境罪，判处罚金一千万元；被告人黄某某犯污染环境罪，判处有期徒刑六年，并处罚金二十万元；被告人姜某某犯污染环境罪，判处有期徒刑五年九个月，并处罚金二十万元；判处被告人李某某等 10 人犯污染环境罪，判处有期徒刑六年至拘役四个月不等，并处罚金。一审宣判后，被告单位 B 公司和被告人黄某某等人提出上诉。2018 年 12 月 5 日，安徽省芜湖市中级人民法院二审裁定驳回上诉，维持原判。判决已生效，该案例的实施在守护好长江母亲河的司法实践方面具有典型意义。

（二）《中华人民共和国民法典》相关法条速览

Article 9 When conducting a civil activity, a person of the civil law shall act in a manner that facilitates conservation of resources and protection of the ecological environment.

第九条 民事主体从事民事活动，应当有利于节约资源、保护生态环境。

Article 509 The parties shall avoid wasting the resources, polluting the environment, or damaging the ecology in the course of performance of the contract.

第五百零九条　当事人在履行合同过程中，应当避免浪费资源、污染环境和破坏生态。

Article 1229　A tortfeasor who has polluted the environment or harmed the ecological system and thus causes damage to others shall bear tort liability.

第一千二百二十九条　因污染环境、破坏生态造成他人损害的，侵权人应当承担侵权责任。

Article 1231　Where environmental pollution or ecological damage is caused by two or more tortfeasors, the extent of liability of each tortfeasor shall be determined according to the factors such as the type, concentration, and quantity of discharge of the pollutants, the way, scope, and degree of damage to the ecological system, and the impact of the act on the consequences of damage.

第一千二百三十一条　两个以上侵权人污染环境、破坏生态的，承担责任的大小，根据污染物的种类、浓度、排放量，破坏生态的方式、范围、程度，以及行为对损害后果所起的作用等因素确定。

Article 1235　Where ecological damage is caused in violation of the State regulations, the State authorized agencies or the organizations authorized by law have the right to request the tortfeasor to compensate the following losses and expenses:

(1) losses caused by loss of service function from the time the ecological environment is damaged to the time the restoration is completed;

(2) losses caused by permanent damage to the function of the ecological environment;

(3) expenses for investigation, appraisal, and assessment of the damage to the ecological environment;

(4) expenses for cleaning-up the pollution and restoring the ecological environment; and

(5) other reasonable expenses incurred to prevent the occurrence or aggravation of the damage.

第一千二百三十五条　违反国家规定造成生态环境损害的，国家规定的机关或者法律规定的组织有权请求侵权人赔偿下列损失和费用：

（一）生态环境受到损害至修复完成期间服务功能丧失导致的损失；

（二）生态环境功能永久性损害造成的损失；

（三）生态环境损害调查、鉴定评估等费用；

（四）清除污染、修复生态环境费用；

（五）防止损害的发生和扩大所支出的合理费用。

（三）《中华人民共和国刑法》相关法条速览

Crimes of Impairing the Protection of Environment and Resources

破坏环境资源保护罪

Article 338 Whoever, in violation of the regulation of the State, discharges, dumps or treats of radioactive wastes, wastes containing pathogens of infectious diseases, toxic substances or other hazardous waste on the land or in the water bodies or the atmosphere, thus causing a major environmental pollution accident which leads to the serious consequences of heavy losses of public or private property or human casualties, shall be sentenced to fixed-term imprisonment of not more than three years or criminal detention and shall also, or shall only, be fined; if the consequences are especially serious, he shall be sentenced to fixed-term imprisonment of not less than three years but not more than seven years and shall also be fined.

第三百三十八条 违反国家规定，向土地、水体、大气排放、倾倒或者处置有放射性的废物、含传染病病原体的废物、有毒物质或者其他危险废物，造成重大环境污染事故，致使公私财产遭受重大损失或者人身伤亡的严重后果的，处三年以下有期徒刑或者拘役，并处或者单处罚金；后果特别严重的，处三年以上七年以下有期徒刑，并处罚金。

Vocabulary and Key Notes

1. **waste acid effluent** 废酸液

2. **sludge** *n.* thick, soft, wet mud or a substance that looks like it; industrial or human waste that has been treated 污泥

3. **hazardous waste** 危险废物

4. **acid pickling sludge** 酸洗污泥

5. **in violation of** 违反

6. **issuance of the hazardous waste transfer forms** 开具危险废物转移联单

7. **illegal disposal** 非法处置

8. **forge** *v.* If someone forges something such as a banknote, a document, or a painting, they copy it or make it so that it looks genuine, in order to deceive people. 伪造

9. **aforesaid** *adj.* [only before noun] (formal or law) mentioned before, in an earlier sentence 前面提到的；上述的

10. **dump** *v.* If you dump something somewhere, you put it or unload it there quickly and carelessly. 倾倒；倾卸

11. **in collusion with** 串通；与……勾结

12. **Economic and Technological Development Zone** 经济技术开发区

13. **giving rise to** 产生
14. **ecological environment restoration** 生态恢复
15. **identification and appraisal** 鉴定和评估

Translation

Directions: *Translate the following sentences from Passage 1 into Chinese.*

1. In July 2002, defendant entity Part B (Zhejiang) Co., Ltd. (hereinafter referred to as "B Company") was formed with the business scope including production and sales of building hardware, high-strength precision fasteners for automobiles, and precision stamping molds.

2. The waste acid effluent and sludge generated in the production of the Company were hazardous waste, which must be collected in categories and disposed of by an entrusted entity qualified for the disposal of hazardous waste.

3. From July 2016 to May 2017, in violation of the state regulations on the management of hazardous waste, without issuance of the hazardous waste transfer forms, defendant entity B Company and defendants Huang and Jiang delivered the acid pickling sludge to defendants Li, Tu, and Liu having no qualification of hazardous waste disposal for illegal disposal.

4. After the case was exposed, it was found upon identification and appraisal that the aforesaid defendants illegally dumped and disposed of acid pickling sludge, causing the environmental damage of over CNY5.11 million and giving rise to the expenditures of emergency disposal, ecological environment restoration, and identification and appraisal, over CNY1.39 million in total.

5. In particular, 313 tons of waste bakelites and over 2,525 tons of industrial sludge were dumped and over 2,400 tons of industrial sludge were attempted to be dumped.

Passage 2

Criminal Case of Illegally Fishing Aquatic Products with an Incidental Civil Public Interest Action

非法捕捞水产品刑事附带民事公益诉讼案

From January 2018 to April 2019, defendant Li, though being fully aware that the Jia River Basin of the Yangtze River in the Jiangdu District of Yangzhou City was closed for fishing and that electrofishing was a prohibited, sailed a speedboat to illegally fish aquatic products in the Jia River waters for more than 60 times by using electrofishing with an electrofishing tool composed of an electromagnetic wave high-frequency **inverter**, **a dip net** with wires, and other components, catching more than 900 jin (a Chinese unit of mass, about 480 kg) of **silver carp**, **bream**, and other wild fish, and made a profit of 9,000 yuan. ① **The Fishery Supervision Unit** of the Jiangdu District of Yangzhou City determined that the electrofishing tool used by Li was a fishing instrumentality prohibited by **the Fisheries Law of the People's Republic of China**. The Announcement No. 6 [2017] of the former Ministry of Agriculture of the People's Republic of China — Announcement on Releasing the List of Protection Areas First Comprehensively Prohibiting the Fishing of Aquatic Life in the Yangtze River Basin and the Collection of Materials on National Aquatic Germplasm Resources Protection Areas specifically and comprehensively prohibited fishing in the national aquatic **germplasm** resource protection zones for four major types of domesticated fish in the Yangzhou section of **the Yangtze River**, and the Jia River Basin of the Yangtze River in the Jiangdu District of Yangzhou City was within the above **closed fishing area.** ② **The** Jiangdu District **People's Procuratorate** of Yangzhou City, Jiangsu Province brought a criminal case with an incidental **civil public interest action in accordance with** the law.

During the trial, the Jiangdu District People's **Procuratorate** of Yangzhou City, Jiangsu Province and Li **reached a settlement agreement** on ecological and environmental **remediation**: (1) that Li should publicly apologize on a provincial media outlet within ten days from the date of signing the settlement agreement; (2) that Li should reintroduce **fish fry** worth 25,000 yuan within ten days from the date of signing this settlement agreement (already preformed); and (3) that Li should further reintroduce fish fry worth 22,500 yuan within two years from the date of signing this settlement agreement. The Rugao City People's Court of Jiangsu Province held at the first instance that Li had violated regulations on the protection of aquatic resources, fished aquatic products by using a prohibited method in **the closed fishing zone**, fell under serious circumstances, and was guilty of the crime of illegally fishing aquatic products. ③ **In view of** the fact that after the case arose, Li voluntarily appeared, and sincerely **confessed** his crime, which constituted **voluntary surrender** and that he had **disgorged illegal income** and made reintroductions for ecological and environmental remediation, a lighter punishment may be imposed. ④ The court of first instance sentenced Li to imprisonment of one year and **confiscation** of 9,000 yuan of illegal income, for the crime of illegally fishing aquatic products.

(**Source**: http://www.lawinfochina.com/SearchList.aspx)

Comprehension Check

Directions: *Use an appropriate word or phrase from the box with their proper forms to complete each sentence. Each word or phrase can be used once only.*

confiscate	domesticate	disgorge	in view of	confess
remediate	in accordance with	aquatic	incident	settlement

1. This analysis work was complemented with other preparatory activities, ________ drafting the policy documents.

2. Forest ecosystem has special peculiarities and functions which can be used to ________ the radionuclide contaminated soils.

3. It is illegal for anyone to give lighted cigars to dogs, cats, and other ________ animal kept as pets.

4. But the problem as a result of historical bequeath, the latent capacity of ________ product market and action did not get sufficient play.

5. After hours of questioning, the suspect ________.

6. The new laws allow the ________ of assets purchased with proceeds of the drugs trade.

7. Any kind of travel tends to rack up several ________ costs-taxi fares, Internet access fees, phone calls, tips, laundry charges.

8. They were made to ________ all the profits made from the record.

9. The terms of the ________ agreement are "confidential" and the matter requires that they be "confidential".

10. We calculate the minimum monthly repayment ________ our usual practice.

Background Information

（一）案件速览

This is a criminal case with an incidental civil public interest action arising from the illegal fishing of aquatic products. The place where the present case arose was the Yangzhou section of the Yangtze River Basin in national aquatic germplasm resource protection zones for four major types of domesticated fish, an important migration channel for fish, and the best place for fish to fatten, lay eggs, and overwinter. As Li's electrofishing was highly lethal to aquatic life in the natural waters, and posed a serious threat to the ecological resources and water environment, the people's court sentenced him to fixed-term imprisonment, in addition to confiscation of his illegal income, for the crime of illegal fishing. In the meantime, Li had to assume the liability for ecological remediation by reintroduction to ensure the timely and effective remediation of the ecology and environment of the Yangtze River Basin.

本案系非法捕捞水产品引发的刑事附带民事公益诉讼案件。本案中，案发地位于四大家鱼种质资源区的长江流域扬州段，是鱼类的重要洄游通道，也是鱼类育肥产卵和越冬的最佳场所。李某某电鱼的行为对自然水域的水生生物产生极大杀伤力，严重威胁生态资源和水环境，故人民法院依法以非法捕捞罪判处其有期徒刑并没收违法所得。同时，李某某仍需承担增殖放流的生态修复责任，确保长江流域生态环境得到及时有效修复。

（二）Significance 典型意义

The ten-year ban on fishing in the Yangtze River is an important measure to implement the spirit of General Secretary Xi Jinping's important instructions "to jointly provide great protection and refrain from large-scale development," protect the Yangtze River, also referred to as the Mother River, and strengthen the construction of ecological civilization and an significant decision by taking into account the big picture in favor of future generations, which is a contribution for the time being and benefits the future generations. In December 2020, the Supreme People's Court, the Supreme People's Procuratorate, the Ministry of Public Security, and the Ministry of Agriculture and Rural Affairs jointly formulated the Opinions on Punishing Illegal Fishing and Other Illegal and Criminal Activities in the Yangtze River Basin to explicitly crack down on illegal fishing in the Yangtze River Basin and other types of violations and crimes that endanger aquatic life resources, ensuring the smooth implementation of the fishing ban in the Yangtze River Basin.

长江十年禁捕是贯彻习近平总书记关于“共抓大保护、不搞大开发”的重要指示精神，保护长江母亲河和加强生态文明建设的重要举措，是为全局计、为子孙谋，功在当代、利在千秋的重要决策。2020 年 12 月，最高人民法院、最高人民检察院、公安部、农业农村部联合制定了《依法惩治长江流域非法捕捞等违法犯罪的意见》，明确对长江流域非法捕捞等危害水生生物资源的各类违法犯罪进行严厉打击，确保长江流域禁捕工作顺利实施。

(**Source:** http://www.lawinfochina.com/SearchList.aspx)

（三）Civil public interest litigation 民事公益诉讼

民事公益诉讼指的是国家公诉机关（即人民检察院）以国家或公共利益代表的身份就社会中的某些民事违法行为向审判机关提起民事诉讼的活动，也称为民事检察诉讼或公益诉讼。

（四）Environmental public interest litigation 环境公益诉讼

环境公益诉讼是指社会成员，包括公民、企事业单位、社会团体依据法律的特别规定，在环境受到或可能受到污染和破坏的情形下，为维护环境公共利益不受损害，针对有关民事主体或行政机关而向法院提起诉讼的制度。

Environmental Public Interest Litigation in China permits qualified environmental non-governmental organizations to file litigation to protect the public interest in safeguarding the environment and natural resources from pollution and ecological destruction.

中国的环境公益诉讼允许有资质的非政府环境保护组织提起诉讼，以保护环境和自然资源等公共利益免受污染和生态破坏。

Environmental Public Interest Litigation by non-governmental organizations emerged in China over the last decade amidst the growing focus on environmental issues and the increasing political need to bring greater public participation to the area.

在过去十年中，环境问题日益变成人们关注的焦点，公众参与环境保护的政治需求也日益增长，在这种背景下，中国政府设立了环境公益诉讼制度，而这一诉讼主要由非政府组织提起。

(**Source:** https://mp.weixin.qq.com/s/keBoHS6tuFDTGtoPQj8egw)

Vocabulary and Key Notes

1. **fishing aquatic products** 捕捞水产品
2. **an electromagnetic wave high-frequency inverter** 电磁波高频逆变器
3. **a dip net** 抄网
4. **silver carp** 鲢鱼
5. **bream** 鳊鱼
6. **The Fishery Supervision Unit** 渔政监督大队
7. **the Fisheries Law of the People's Republic of China** 《中华人民共和国渔业法》
8. **germplasm** *n.* germ cells and their precursors serving as the bearers of heredity and being fundamentally independent of other cells [胚][遗] 种质（经生殖细胞传递的遗传物质）；胚质；生殖质（决定性细胞分化的卵质成分）
9. **The People's Procuratorate** 人民检察院
10. **civil public interest action** 民事公益诉讼

11. **in accordance with** 依照；按照；与……一致

12. **reached a settlement agreement on** 达成和解协议

13. **remediation** *n.* correcting an error or fault 纠正错误

14. **fish fry** 鱼苗

15. **the closed fishing zone** 禁渔区

16. **in view of** 鉴于；考虑到

17. **confess ~ (to sth./to doing sth.)** *v.* to admit, especially formally or to the police, that you have done sth. wrong or illegal 供认，坦白，承认（错误或罪行）

coerced confession 逼供

direct confession 直接供认

judicial confession 当庭供认

plenary confession 完全供认；彻底坦白

threshold confession 当即供认（指逮捕后未审问便作的供认）

confession of judgment 债务认决（书）

（指债务人就债款到期不付同意接受未经通知或未经听审的偿债判决）

18. **constituted voluntary surrender** 构成自首

19. **disgorge** *v.* give up illegally gained profits under pressure 被迫放弃不法所得

disgorge illegal income 退缴违法所得

20. **confiscation** *n.* seizure of private property for public use without compensation 没收；充公

Translation

Directions: *Translate the following sentences from Passage 1 into Chinese.*

1. From January 2018 to April 2019, defendant Li, though being fully aware that the Jia River Basin of the Yangtze River in the Jiangdu District of Yangzhou City was closed for fishing and that electrofishing was a prohibited, sailed a speedboat to illegally fish aquatic products in the Jia River waters for more than 60 times by using electrofishing with an electrofishing tool composed of an electromagnetic wave high-frequency inverter, a dip net with wires, and other components, catching more than 900 Jin (a Chinese unit of mass, about 480 kg) of silver carp, bream, and other wild fish, and made a profit of 9,000 yuan.

2. The Announcement No. 6 [2017] of the former Ministry of Agriculture of the People's Republic of China – Announcement on Releasing the List of Protection Areas First

Comprehensively Prohibiting the Fishing of Aquatic Life in the Yangtze River Basin and the Collection of Materials on National Aquatic Germplasm Resources Protection Areas specifically and comprehensively prohibited fishing in the national aquatic germplasm resource protection zones for four major types of domesticated fish in the Yangzhou section of the Yangtze River, and the Jia River Basin of the Yangtze River in the Jiangdu District of Yangzhou City was within the above closed fishing area.

3. The Rugao City People's Court of Jiangsu Province held at the first instance that Li had violated regulations on the protection of aquatic resources, fished aquatic products by using a prohibited method in the closed fishing zone, fell under serious circumstances, and was guilty of the crime of illegally fishing aquatic products.

4. In view of the fact that after the case arose, Li voluntarily appeared, and sincerely confessed his crime, which constituted voluntary surrender and that he had disgorged illegal income and made reintroductions for ecological and environmental remediation, a lighter punishment may be imposed.

Supplementary Reading

Counties in Yellow River Basin Have been Told to Rectify Environmental Violations

黄河流域各县整顿环境违法行为

Two counties in the Yellow River Basin have been told to rectify violations that jeopardize the waterway's environment as inspectors continue their one-month mission to four provincial regions.

High-profile central environmental inspection teams arrived in Ningxia Hui autonomous region and Heilongjiang, Guizhou and Shanxi provinces early this month. Environmental violations reported in Luoping county, Ningxia, and Hancheng county, Shanxi, were among eight such cases discovered by inspectors.

Many companies based in Fine Chemical Industrial Park in Luoping, an area with a water shortage, took water illegally from the Yellow River for an extended period of time. In addition, a large amount of waste water from the park was not adequately disposed of, according to a media release from the Ministry of Ecology and Environment.

Of the 81 companies based at the park, which is only 5 kilometers from river, only one had a water consumption permit. The park's water supplier took more than 21 million cubic meters of water from the river without official approval since May 2017, the release said.

During an inspection in 2018, inspectors found that waste water from the park was not properly dealt with before being discharged, the release added. Despite the introduction of a new sewage disposal plant in 2019, it had operated abnormally and work there was stopped in late March.

Although local authorities ordered companies to transport their waste water to a plant 50 km away for disposal, some companies continued to illegally discharge sewage. From February to June, the park's managing authority even used more than 70 million cubic meters of sewage to control dust at a landfill.

Inspectors failed to ascertain the location of a large amount of undisposed sewage. From January to November, the park consumed 5.95 million metric tons of water, while 310,000 tons of sewage was disposed of during this time.

"The Luoping government has failed to bring the park under effective regulation," the release stated.

According to a separate release, nearly 1.3 million cu.m. of solid waste was disposed of illegally in some 25 hectares of the Yellow River in Hancheng for years. From 2013 to 2018, central government bodies issued 10 documents demanding that mining and construction waste be removed. However, the problem has yet to be addressed, the release said.

Piles of waste "with complex components" have hindered nearby wetlands in playing their role in the local ecosystem. The waste also poses significant environmental hazards to the Yellow River, according to the release.

Having failed to get a firm grasp of the nature of China's new development principles, the Hancheng government "breached its duties" and the problem was prolonged, the release added.

(**Source**: http://ex.chinadaily.com.cn/exchange/partners/45/rss/channel/www/columns/2n8e04/stories/WS61ccee97a310cdd39bc7e2ff.html)

Further Discussion

Answer the following questions:

1. Could you give more examples of environmental pollution?
2. What shall be done in order to improve urban and rural living environment?

小语说语：The Green Principle

The Green Principle: Conservation of resources and protection of the ecological environment

绿色原则：即节约资源、保护生态环境原则

Article 9 When conducting a civil activity, a person of the civil law shall act in a manner that facilitates **conservation of resources and protection of the ecological environment.**

第九条 民事主体从事民事活动，应当有利于**节约资源、保护生态环境**。

Article 286 The unit owners shall abide by laws, regulations, and the stipulations on management, and their relevant acts shall meet the requirements of **conserving resources and protecting the ecological environment.**

第二百八十六条 业主应当遵守法律、法规以及管理规约，相关行为应当符合**节约资源、保护生态环境**的要求。

Article 346 The right to use a lot of land for construction purposes shall be created in conformity with the requirements for **conservation of resources and protection of the ecological environment,** and in compliance with the provisions of laws and administrative regulations on the planned use of the lot, and may not impair the rights to usufruct already created thereon.

第三百四十六条 设立建设用地使用权，应当符合**节约资源、保护生态环境**的要求，遵守法律、行政法规关于土地用途的规定，不得损害已经设立的用益物权。

Article 509 The parties shall **avoid wasting the resources, polluting the environment, or damaging the ecology** in the course of performance of the contract.

第五百零九条 当事人在履行合同过程中，应当**避免浪费资源、污染环境和破坏生态**。

Article 619 A seller shall deliver the subject matter in compliance with the packaging method as agreed in the contract. Where there is no agreement between the parties on the packaging method or the agreement is unclear, if the packing method cannot be determined according to the provisions of Article 510 of this Code, the subject matter shall be packed in a general way, or, in the absence of a general way, in a manner sufficient to protect the subject matter and conducive to **saving resources and protecting the ecological environment.**

第六百一十九条 出卖人应当按照约定的包装方式交付标的物。对包装方式没有约定或者约定不明确，依据本法第五百一十条的规定仍不能确定的，应当按照通用的方式包装；没有通用方式的，应当采取足以保护标的物且有利于**节约资源、保护生态环境**的包装方式。

第三篇

法律英语实践

一、背景知识引入

根据《中华人民共和国立法法》第六十一条规定，“法律根据内容需要，可以分**编、章、节、条、款、项、目**。编、章、节、条的序号用中文数字依次表述，款不编序号，项的序号用中文数字加括号依次表述，目的序号用阿拉伯数字依次表述。法律标题的题注应当载明制定机关、通过日期。经过修改的法律，应当依次载明修改机关、修改日期。”

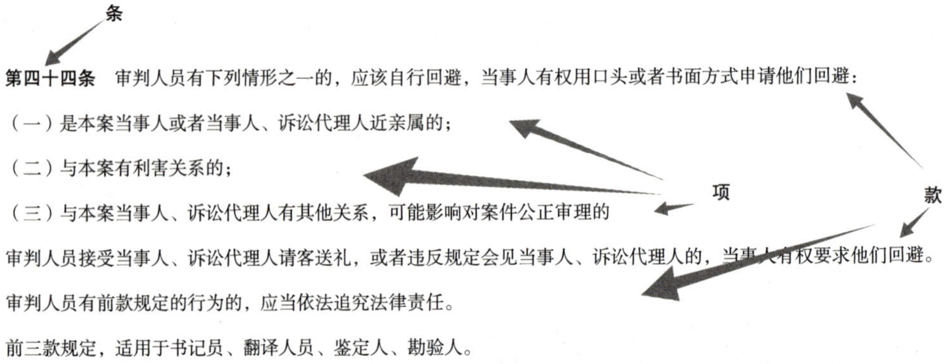

第四十四条 审判人员有下列情形之一的，应该自行回避，当事人有权用口头或者书面方式申请他们回避：

（一）是本案当事人或者当事人、诉讼代理人近亲属的；

（二）与本案有利害关系的；

（三）与本案当事人、诉讼代理人有其他关系，可能影响对案件公正审理的

审判人员接受当事人、诉讼代理人请客送礼，或者违反规定会见当事人、诉讼代理人的，当事人有权要求他们回避。

审判人员有前款规定的行为的，应当依法追究法律责任。

前三款规定，适用于书记员、翻译人员、鉴定人、勘验人。

弄懂法律规范中条、款、项、目的含义，在执法活动中正确使用法律规范的条、款、项、目，对于规范执法行为，提高执法质量是大有益处的。

二、翻译实践

除项、款、目没有专门术语对应翻译外（直接翻译内容即可），编、章、节、条均有术语对应翻译。

典：Code

例：《民法典》

The Civil Code

总则：General Provisions

例：总则

General Provisions

附则：Supplementary Provisions

例：附则

Supplementary Provisions

编：Part

例：第一编　总则

Book One General Part

章：Chapter

例：第一章　基本规定

Chapter I　General Provisions

节：Section

例：第一节　民事权利能力和民事行为能力

Section 1　Capacity for Enjoying Civil-law Rights and Capacity for Performing Civil Juristic Acts

条：Article

例：第十三条　自然人从出生时起到死亡时止，具有民事权利能力，依法享有民事权利，承担民事义务。

Article 13　A natural person shall, from the time of birth until the time of death, have the capacity for enjoying civil-law rights, and may enjoy civil-law rights and assume civil-law duties in accordance with law.

款：paragraph

例：《中华人民共和国宪法》第 34 条第一款

The first paragraph of Article 34 of *the Constitution of the People's Republic of China*

项：item

例：第二十一条　税法第六条第一款第四项、第六项所说的每次收入，是指：

Article 21.　For the purposes of items (4) and (6) of the first paragraph of Article 6 of the Tax Law, the term "each payment" shall mean:

目：sub-item

例：第五十四条　法律根据内容需要，可以分编、章、节、条、款、项、目。

Article 54.　Where necessary as required by its content, a law may adopt a structure consisting of Parts, Chapters, Sections, Articles, Paragraphs, Items, and Sub-items.

XX 条例：regulations

例：《中华人民共和国财产保险合同条例》

Regulations of the PRC on Contracts of Property Insurance

XX 通知：circular

例：国务院办公厅关于在外留学人员有关问题的通知

Circular of the General Office of the State Council Concerning Matters Relating to Students Studying Abroad

XX 意见：suggestions

例：《关于加强个体私营经济税收征管强化查帐征收工作的意见》

Suggestions on Strengthening the work of Tax Collection Administration of Self-employed Private Economy and Intensifying Tax Collection on Audit of Accounts

XX 决定：decision(s)

例：《关于严惩严重破坏经济的罪犯的决定》

the Decision of the Standing Committee of the National People's Congress Regarding the Severe Punishment of Criminals Who Seriously Undermine the Economy

法案：bill

例：香港特别行政区立法会通过的法案，须经行政长官签署、公布，方能生效。

A bill passed by the Legislative Council of the Hong Kong Special Administrative Region may take effect only after it is signed and promulgated by the Chief Executive.

条约：Treaty

例：《引渡条约》

Extradition Treaty

协定：Agreement(s)

例：《多边贸易协定》

Multilateral Trade Agreements

公约：convention

例：《生物多样性公约》

the Convention on Biological Diversity

解释：Interpretations

规则：Rules

简则：Basic Rules

暂行通则：Interim General Rules

通则：General Rules

通告：Announcement

批复：Official Reply

办法：Measures

暂行办法：Interim Measures

实施办法：Measures for the implementation of...

暂行条例：Interim Regulations

实施条例：Regulations for the Implementations of...

规定：Provisions

暂行规定：Interim Provisions

施行（实施）细则：Rules for the implementation of...

令（命令）：Decree

通令：Circular Decree

案例汇编：Reporter

卷宗号：Citation

第十四章 法条学译——定义法条

一、法条原文

第五十七条　法人是具有民事权利能力和民事行为能力，依法独立享有民事权利和承担民事义务的组织。

二、法条译文

Article 57　A legal person is an organization that has the capacity for enjoying civil-law rights and the capacity for performing civil juristic acts, and that independently enjoys civil-law rights and assumes civil-law obligations in accordance with law.

三、翻译解析三步骤

（一）首先挑出句子主干

法人是组织。

法律条文中用于表“是”的词汇，主要是：is/refers to/means

所以翻译成：A legal person is/refers to/means an organization.

类似法条，如：

例 1：第一百八十条　不可抗力是不能预见、不能避免且不能克服的客观情况。

Article 180 “Force majeure” means objective conditions which are unforeseeable, unavoidable, and insurmountable.

例 2：第四百六十九条　书面形式是合同书、信件、电报、电传、传真等可以有形地表现所载内容的形式。

Article 469　A writing refers to any form that renders the content contained therein capable of being represented in a tangible form, such as a written agreement, letter, telegram, telex, or facsimile.

（二）确定其他成分在句中的作用，采用定语从句

法人是（具有……的）组织，和（享有……的）组织。

A legal person is an organization (that...) and (that...).

（三）在确定基本的句子结构后，分析具体的选词和固定表达

1. 有……能力 has the capacity for; have the ability to; be able to; be capable of

2. 具有民事权利能力 enjoy civil-law rights

3. 具有民事行为能力 perform civil juristic acts

4. 承担民事义务 assume civil-law obligations；承担民事责任 bear civil liability

5. 依法 in accordance with law

四、课后练习

Directions: *Translate the following sentences into English.*

1. 第九百九十条　人格权是民事主体享有的生命权、身体权、健康权、姓名权、名称权、肖像权、名誉权、荣誉权、隐私权等权利。

2. 第四百九十六条　格式条款是当事人为了重复使用而预先拟定，并在订立合同时未与对方协商的条款。

3. 第一千一百二十二条　遗产是自然人死亡时遗留的个人合法财产。

4. 第四百七十三条　要约邀请是希望他人向自己发出要约的表示。

5. 第八十七条　为公益目的或者其他非营利目的成立，不向出资人、设立人或者会员分配所取得利润的法人，为非营利法人。

第十五章 法条学译——授权性规范

授权性规范是规定人们可以作出一定行为或者可以要求别人作出一定行为的法律规范。授权性规范的立法语言表达式为“可以……”“有权……”“享有……权利”等。

一、法条原文

第一千一百六十七条　侵权行为危及他人人身、财产安全的，被侵权人有权请求侵权人承担停止侵害、排除妨碍、消除危险等侵权责任。

二、法条译文

Article 1167　Where a tortious act endangers another person's personal or property safety, the infringed person has the right to request the tortfeasor to bear tort liability such as cessation of the infringement, removal of the nuisance, or elimination of the danger.

三、翻译解析三步骤

（一）首先挑出句子主干

本句是以“的”结尾的偏正复句。

以“的”结尾的条件句一般传递次要信息，而主句传递主要信息，可根据主从句的逻辑关系用合适的英语连接词将从句和主句连接在一起。即由 if, when, where, in case 等词引导的 **SVO 结构的条件句（……的 / 时 / 的情况下）+ 主句。**

主句为：被侵权人有权干某事。

法律条文中表示“有权”“享有……的权利”的表达，主要是：

have/enjoy the right to; be entitled to; may

所以主句可以翻译成：the infringed person has the right to...

故该句可以翻译成：Where a tortious act endangers..., the infringed person has the right to...

类似法条，如：

例 1：第四十四条　人民法院变更财产代管人的，变更后的财产代管人有权请求原财产代管人及时移交有关财产并报告财产代管情况。

Article 44　Where the people's court appoints a new custodian, the new custodian is entitled to request the former custodian to deliver the relevant property and a property management report in a timely manner.

例 2：第一百四十七条　基于重大误解实施的民事法律行为，行为人有权请求人民法院或者仲裁机构予以撤销。

Article 147 Where a civil juristic act is performed based on serious misunderstanding, the person who performs the act has the right to request the people's court or an arbitration institution to revoke the act.

例 3：第七十五条 设立人为设立法人以自己的名义从事民事活动产生的民事责任，第三人有权选择请求法人或者设立人承担。

Article 75 Where an incorporator engages in civil activities in his own name for the purpose of establishing a legal person and thus incurs civil liability, a third person creditor may elect to request either the legal person or the incorporator to bear the liability.

（二）词的转换

法律英语语体较为严谨正式，因此在翻译汉语法律文件时，通常将汉语动词转换为英语名词。此外还有名词转换为动词、动词转换为形容词、副词转换为形容词等其他转换方法。在该条法规中，应将“停止侵害、排除妨碍、消除危险”译成“cessation of the infringement, removal of the nuisance, or elimination of the danger”。

（三）在确定基本的句子结构后，分析具体的选词和固定表达

1. 被侵权人 the infringed person
2. 享有……权 have a right to; enjoy the rights; enjoy the right to/be entitled to
3. 有权 have the right to; may; reserve the right to; have the power (authority) to
4. 侵权人 tortfeasor
5. 停止侵害 cessation of the infringement
6. 排除妨碍 removal of the nuisance
7. 消除危险 elimination of the danger
8. 承担侵权责任 bear tort liability

四、课后练习

Directions: *Translate the following sentences into English.*

1. 第一千二百五十条 因第三人的过错致使动物造成他人损害的，被侵权人可以向动物饲养人或者管理人请求赔偿，也可以向第三人请求赔偿。动物饲养人或者管理人赔偿后，有权向第三人追偿。

2. 第一百二十条 民事权益受到侵害的，被侵权人有权请求侵权人承担侵权责任。

3. 第一百二十二条 因他人没有法律根据，取得不当利益，受损失的人有权请求其返还不当利益。

4. 第五十三条 被撤销死亡宣告的人有权请求依照本法第六编取得其财产的民事主体返还财产；无法返还的，应当给予适当补偿。

第十六章 法条学译——命令性规范

命令性规范是指规定人们的积极义务，即规定主体应当或者必须作出一定积极行为的规范。命令性规范的立法语言表达式为“应当……”“必须……”“有……义务”等。

一、法条原文

第一千一百五十九条　分割遗产，应当清偿被继承人依法应当缴纳的税款和债务；但是，应当为缺乏劳动能力又没有生活来源的继承人保留必要的遗产。

二、法条译文

Article 1159　Upon partitioning an estate, the taxes and debts payable or owed by the decedent in accordance with law shall be paid out of the estate, provided that a necessary portion of the estate is preserved for any successor who has neither the ability to work nor the source of income.

三、翻译解析三步骤

（一）转换语态

“……应当清偿……；……应当为……保留”该句为典型的无主句，即没有明确的主语，因此可以将汉语句子中的宾语转换为英语句子中的主语，使用被动语态。即：

... shall be paid...; ... is preserved...

（二）“但”字句的翻译

一般来说，“但是”通常可以用 but 或 however 翻译，但考虑到法律文本的严谨性，provided that 更符合法律文本的风格。

类似法条，如：

例 1：第十条　处理民事纠纷，应当依照法律；法律没有规定的，可以适用习惯，但是不得违背公序良俗。

Article 10　Civil disputes shall be resolved in accordance with law. Where the law does not specify, custom may be applied, provided that public order and good morals may not be offended.

例 2：第三百七十七条　地役权期限由当事人约定；但是，不得超过土地承包经营权、建设用地使用权等用益物权的剩余期限。

Article 377　The duration of an easement shall be agreed upon by the parties, provided that it may not exceed the remaining term of the right to usufruct, such as the right to contractual management of land or the right to use a lot of land for construction purposes.

（三）在确定基本的句子结构后，分析具体的选词和固定表达

1. 应当：shall

2. 必须：have to; must

3. 有……义务：be obliged to; have the obligation to; have duties to; be liable for/to

4. 履行义务：perform/fulfill one's obligation/duty (of)

5. 承担义务：assume/bear the obligation (of)

6. 继承人：successor

7. 遗产：an estate

四、课后练习

Directions: *Translate the following sentences into English.*

1. 第二百八十八条　不动产的相邻权利人应当按照有利生产、方便生活、团结互助、公平合理的原则，正确处理相邻关系。

2. 第二百九十一条　不动产权利人对相邻权利人因通行等必须利用其土地的，应当提供必要的便利。

3. 第一千零五条　自然人的生命权、身体权、健康权受到侵害或者处于其他危难情形的，负有法定救助义务的组织或者个人应当及时施救。

4. 第一千一百四十三条　遗嘱必须表示遗嘱人的真实意思，受欺诈、胁迫所立的遗嘱无效。

5. 第三百零三条　共有人约定不得分割共有的不动产或者动产，以维持共有关系的，应当按照约定，但是共有人有重大理由需要分割的，可以请求分割。

6. 第四百六十条　不动产或者动产被占有人占有的，权利人可以请求返还原物及其孳息；但是，应当支付善意占有人因维护该不动产或者动产支出的必要费用。

第十七章 法条学译——禁止性规范

禁止性规范是指规定人们的消极义务（不作为义务），即禁止人们作出一定行为的规范。禁止性规范的立法语言表达式为“不得……”“禁止……”等。

一、法条原文

第八百一十条　从事公共运输的承运人不得拒绝旅客、托运人通常、合理的运输要求。

二、法条译文

Article 810　A carrier engaging in public transport may not reject an ordinary and reasonable transport request made by a passenger or consignor.

三、翻译解析三步骤

（一）首先挑出句子的主干

承运人不得拒绝要求。

法律条文中用于表示“不得、禁止”的词汇，主要有：free from; 否定性主语 +shall/may; may not; shall no; be prohibited by

所以翻译成：A carrier may not reject an request.

类似法条，如：

例 1：第三条　民事主体的人身权利、财产权利以及其他合法权益受法律保护，任何组织或者个人不得侵犯。

Article 3　The personal rights, proprietary rights, and other lawful rights and interests of the persons of the civil law are protected by law and free from infringement by any organization or individual.

例 2：第一百三十二条　民事主体不得滥用民事权利损害国家利益、社会公共利益或者他人合法权益。

Article 132　No person of the civil law shall abuse his civil-law rights and harm the interests of the state, the public interests, or the lawful rights and interests of others.

（二）翻译带“的”定语

1. 用分词短语后置作为定语；

2. 简单的形容词依照句意转换为英语前置定语；

3. 用介词短语翻译汉语的定语；

4. 用不定式短语翻译汉语的定语；

5. 用从句翻译汉语的定语。

（从事……的）承运人不得拒绝（某人/单位）（……的）要求。

A carrier (engaging in...) may not reject (...) request (made by...).

（三）在确定基本的句子结构后，分析具体的选词和固定表达

1. 承运人 carrier

2. 托运人 consignor

四、课后练习

Directions: *Translate the following sentences into English.*

1. 第八百九十五条　保管人不得使用或者许可第三人使用保管物，但是当事人另有约定的除外。

2. 第一百三十二条　民事主体不得滥用民事权利损害国家利益、社会公共利益或者他人合法权益。

3. 第一百六十条　民事法律行为可以附期限，但是根据其性质不得附期限的除外。

4. 第一百九十三条　人民法院不得主动适用诉讼时效的规定。

5. 第五百九十七条　法律、行政法规禁止或者限制转让的标的物，依照其规定。

6. 第二百零七条　国家、集体、私人的物权和其他权利人的物权受法律平等保护，任何组织或者个人不得侵犯。

第十八章 普法海报习作专栏

法律英语作为一门实践性较强的课程，教师可在期末专门设计“法律语言训练营”，要求学生通过本课程学习，以小组形式制作相关主题的法律视频 / 法律海报展示学习成果并进行相关知识点答辩。目的是通过学生的“说法普法”教学环节，重在对知识创造性输出，帮助学生在学习法律语言知识的同时，增加法律思辨能力和合作学习能力，培养正确的职业伦理和职业素养。

设计主题：安全防范，构建安全校园，安全人生

情景设计：校园安全是公安机关和教育部门共同的责任，直接关系到千万个家庭的安宁幸福、亿万青少年的安全健康成长。为了增强同学们面对各种安全隐患本能存在的一种安全防范认识，** 大学邀请国际商法英语班级制作相关普法视频 / 海报，介绍对商务活动中的风险防御、减少损失的策略及建议，旨在提升同学们的法治意识、防骗识诈能力和法律英语语言综合运用能力。

成绩指标：

成绩（100%）= 微视频 / 海报（70%）+ 答辩（30%）

微视频 / 海报成绩（100%）= 教师评价（80%）+ 学生互评（20%）

答辩成绩（100%）= 教师评价（80%）+ 学生互评（20%）

学生互评采用问卷星投票选出的第 1 名小组为 20 分，第 2—3 名为 18 分，第 4—5 名为 15 分，其余为 13 分。由于组长在整个活动中的统筹安排和担当，每人给予 5 分平时分奖励。

微视频 / 海报评价指标：

视频 / 海报内容（40%）+ 语言（20%）+ 编辑制作（30%）+ 创新性（10%）=100 分

1）内容（40%）：紧扣主题，立意鲜明，内容编排架构合理，能条理完整地表达本主题知识点；

2）语言（20%）：法律英语语言标准，表达流畅，声音洪亮，语速适中，富有感染力；

3）编辑制作（30%）：版面设计合理生动，效果自然，构图美观，配乐得当，字幕规范，字幕与语音同步，字体适合阅读学习，色彩协调，视觉互动效果好；片头有组员名单，片尾有文献出处；

4）创新性（10%）：脚本撰写，图片，音乐，编辑制作等方面具有新颖的角度和表现手法。

答辩评价指标：

内容（30%）+ 语言表达（30%）+ 团队合作（30%）+ 反应敏捷（10%）=100 分

附上学生普法海报作品：

内容涵盖网络欺诈、个人信息泄露、网贷、信用卡诈骗、校园欺凌。

Cyberspace Fraud
网络欺诈

一、Definition 什么是网络诈骗?

Cyberspace fraud usually refers to the fraudulent means of deceiving property from others in various forms on the Internet in order to achieve a certain purpose.

网络诈骗通常是指为达到某种目的在网络上以各种形式向他人骗取财物的诈骗手段。

The main act or link of network fraud occurs on the Internet. The criminal defrauds a large amount of public or private property by making up facts or concealing the truth.

网络诈骗的主要行为、环节发生在互联网上，诈骗分子利用虚构事实或者隐瞒真相的方法，骗取金额较大的公私财物。

There are many kinds of cyberspace fraud, mainly including fake lottery frauds, impersonating relatives and friends frauds, marriage frauds, online shopping frauds, employment and recruitment frauds,

网络欺诈主要有虚假中奖诈骗、冒充亲友诈骗、征婚交友诈骗、网络购物诈骗、就业招聘诈骗、

and online game equipment frauds, lottery prediction frauds, stock speculation frauds, private equity frauds, phishing frauds and other means.Among them, three cyberspace frauds are widely spread among college students.

彩票预测诈骗、炒股暴富诈骗、私募基金诈骗、网络钓鱼诈骗等手段。

二、Cases in 案例分析

1 A boy from The College of Arts was cheated 4000 yuan by strangers who personated to be T-mall customer service staff.

文学院发生一起被冒充天猫客服诈骗4000元。

2 A boy from The Civil Engineering College was frauded 5000 yuan by a so-called bank customer service officer.

土木学院一学生被冒充银行客服诈骗5000元。

3 In a naked chat case, the victim was extorted more than 10,000 yuan.

在一起裸聊案件中，受害者被骗1万元。

4 Tempted to do click farming, a freshman was frauded 5000 yuan in one hour.

一起刷单案中，一名大一学生一个小时就被骗5000元。

三、Legal Consequences 法律后果

According to the 266th provision of Criminal Law

依照《刑法》第二百六十六条

Whoever defrauds public or private property, if the amount involved is relatively large, shall be sentenced to fixed-term imprisonment of no more than three years, criminal detention or public surveillance, and shall also be fined or only fine;

诈骗公私财物，数额较大的，处三年以下有期徒刑、拘役或者管制，并处或者单处罚金；

If the amount involved is huge, or if there are other serious circumstances, he shall be sentenced to fixed-term imprisonment of no less than three years but not more than ten years, and shall also be fined;

数额巨大或者有其他严重情节的，处三年以上十年以下有期徒刑，并处罚金；

If the amount involved is especially huge, or is there are other especially serious circumstances, he shall be sentenced to fixed-term imprisonment of no less than ten years or life imprisonment and shall also be fined or be sentenced to confiscation of property.

数额特别巨大或者有其他特别严重情节的，处十年以上有期徒刑或者无期徒刑，并处罚金或者没收财产。

四、Preventive Measures 预防措施

1.It's important to build awareness of cyberspace security. As the saying goes, there is no such thing as a free lunch. Don't be greedy for cheap. 树立网络安全意识很重要。俗话说的好，天下没有免费的午餐。不要贪图小便宜。

2. Buy from big, well-known online retailers or reputable sellers.

从大型，知名的在线零售商或信誉良好的卖家那里购买。

3. Check that the payment website is secure before you enter your credit card information.

在输入信用卡信息之前，请检查支付网站是否安全。

4. Look out for a padlock symbol in the bottom right of the browser window and a Web address beginning with "https://". Also watch out for warnings, like those about expired certificates.

注意浏览器窗口右下角的挂锁符号和以"https://"开头的网址，同时也要注意一些警告，比如说那些关于过期证书的警告。

5. Be wary of emails or messages which might be attempts to get your personal information. Try to find out why they need it, how they are going to store it, how long they are storing it for, where are they storing it.

提防那些可能试图获取你的个人信息的电子邮件或信息。试图弄清楚对方为什么需要你的个人信息，以及对方将如何储存它、储存多久、储存于哪里。

钓鱼网站
骗局
网络诈骗
6. Never share your PIN numbers, passwords or other personal information with strangers or which link to a page that asks you for this kind of information.
永远不要将你的密码或其他个人信息告知陌生人或其他要求你提供这类信息的链接页面。
7. Keep your computer protected via updated patches, anti-virus and firewall software regularly.
定期更新电脑补丁、防病毒和防火墙软件来保护你的电脑。
8. Avoid using public or free (unsecured) WiFi networks to do any online transacting that involves entry of personal details.
避免使用公共的或免费的(不安全的)无线网络进行任何涉及个人信息输入的在线交易。
9. If you have responded to a scam, then you should STOP all communication with them and ignore any new messages or attempts to contact you. You can also block their number or email address on your device.
如果你已经陷入了一个骗局，那么你应该停止与对方的所有沟通交流，并忽视任何企图联系你的新消息。你也可以在电子设备上拉黑他们的电话号码或电子邮件地址。
10. If you have given them your banking details, call your bank immediately (on a number you know to be real) or go into a branch. If you have given the scammers your personal information, change the passwords for all your accounts immediately.
如果你已经向对方提供了你的银行账户信息，请立即(用一个你已知是可靠的电话号码)打电话给银行工作人员或者直接去分行。如果你已经向骗子提供了你的个人信息，请立刻更改你所有账户的密码。
我们竭诚为您服务!
虚假网
广西大学国际商法英语阅读课程语言训练营
成员:罗婧 黄惠琪 朱芳芳 梁冕
指导教师:梁卿
2021年6月
This message is brought to you by :

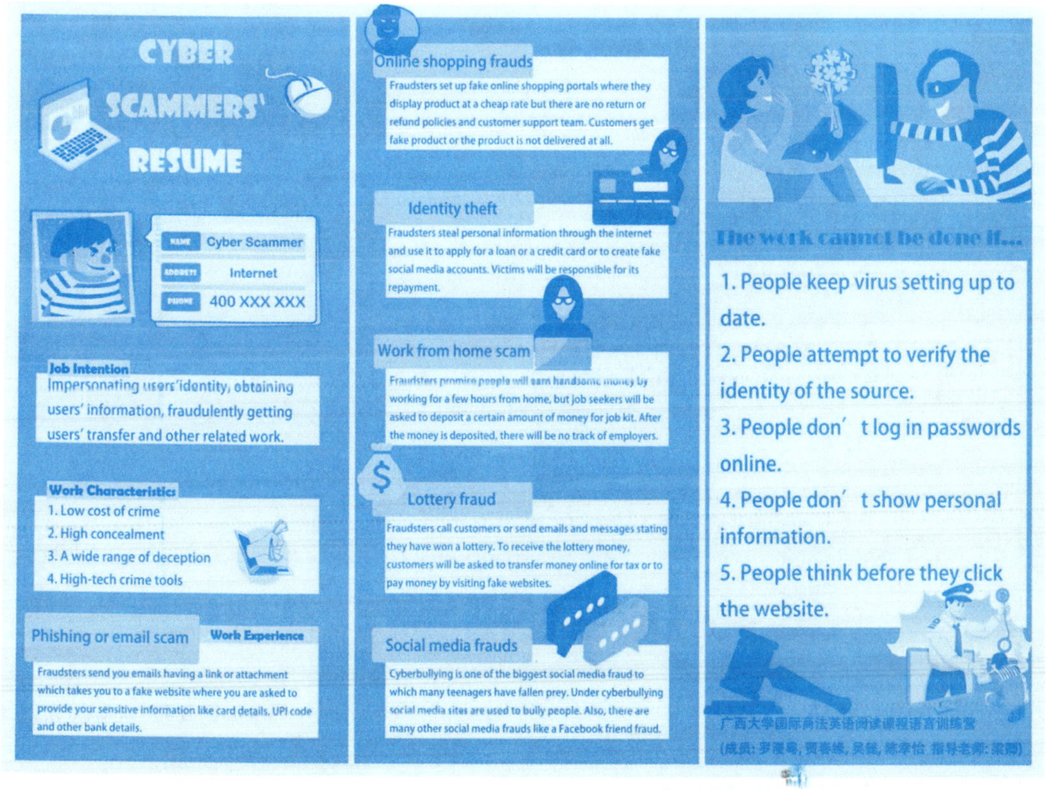
CYBER SCAMMERS' RESUME
NAME Cyber Scammer
ADDRESS Internet
PHONE 400 XXX XXX
Job Intention
Impersonating users'identity, obtaining users' information, fraudulently getting users' transfer and other related work.
Work Characteristics
1. Low cost of crime
2. High concealment
3. A wide range of deception
4. High-tech crime tools
Work Experience
Phishing or email scam
Fraudsters send you emails having a link or attachment which takes you to a fake website where you are asked to provide your sensitive information like card details, UPI code and other bank details.
Online shopping frauds
Fraudsters set up fake online shopping portals where they display product at a cheap rate but there are no return or refund policies and customer support team. Customers get fake product or the product is not delivered at all.
Identity theft
Fraudsters steal personal information through the internet and use it to apply for a loan or a credit card or to create fake social media accounts. Victims will be responsible for its repayment.
Work from home scam
Fraudsters promise people will earn handsome money by working for a few hours from home, but job seekers will be asked to deposit a certain amount of money for job kit. After the money is deposited, there will be no track of employers.
Lottery fraud
Fraudsters call customers or send emails and messages stating they have won a lottery. To receive the lottery money, customers will be asked to transfer money online for tax or to pay money by visiting fake websites.
Social media frauds
Cyberbullying is one of the biggest social media fraud to which many teenagers have fallen prey. Under cyberbullying social media sites are used to bully people. Also, there are many other social media frauds like a Facebook friend fraud.
The work cannot be done if...
1. People keep virus setting up to date.
2. People attempt to verify the identity of the source.
3. People don′t log in passwords online.
4. People don′t show personal information.
5. People think before they click the website.
广西大学国际商法英语阅读课程语言训练营

网络骗子的简历
名字 网络骗子
地址 网络
电话 400 XXX XXX
求职意向
从事身份冒充，套取用户信息，骗取用户转账等相关工作。
工作特点
1. 犯罪成本低
2. 隐蔽性高
3. 多样化欺诈方式
4. 高科技化工具
工作经历
网络钓鱼或电子邮件诈骗
诈骗者会发送含有链接或附件的电子邮件。这些链接或附件会把你带到一个要求你提供银行卡信息、UPI密码和其他银行详细资料等敏感信息的假网站。
网络购物诈骗
这种情况下，诈骗者会建立虚假的网上购物网站，网站上会有低价产品，但没有退货或退款政策和客户支持团队。客户付款后，网站会发假货甚至不发货。
身份盗窃
在身份盗窃里，骗子通过互联网窃取受害者的个人信息，用于申请贷款、信用卡或创建虚假社交媒体账户。受害者将负责还款。
在家工作骗局
在这种情况下，诈骗者承诺人们只要在家工作几个小时就能赚到可观的钱。报名参加该计划的求职者须存入一定数额的钱以购买工作资料。钱存入银行后，就不会有雇主的踪迹了。
彩票欺诈
在彩票欺诈中，诈骗者会打电话给客户或发送电子邮件和短信，声称他们中了彩票。为了获得彩票奖金，顾客将被要求在网上转账纳税或通过访问虚假网站付款。
社交媒体欺诈
网络欺凌是许多青少年沦为牺牲品的最大社交媒体欺诈之一。在网络欺凌中，社交媒体网站被用来欺凌他人。此外还有许多其他社交媒体诈骗，比如说，Facebook好友诈骗。
如果……这些工作就无法完成
1. 人们不断更新病毒设置。
2. 人们核实消息来源。
3. 人们不在网络上保存密码。
4. 人们不暴露个人信息。
5. 人们三思而后点
广西大学国际商法英语阅读课程语言训练营

防止信息泄露！！！

这些你中招了吗

个人信息勿泄露，
安全意识存心头

To fill in real personal information when registering on small or unknown websites.

To click the false links such as phishing websites attached, to induce users to fill in account password, mobile phone number, verification code and other information.

To connect unknown Wi-Fi in public places, especially unencrypted Wi-Fi hotspots.

To publish daily news on social platforms, such as posting tickets and passports, or location information by using the function of "location".

Business Law

以下信息由广西大学国际商法英语视读课程语言训练营所提供。
指导教师：梁卿
成员：李婉菱 冯瑞静 李倩杏
时间：2021年6月
信息来源链接：https://www.chuangkit.com/design?d=44d36909-53d0-4193-9fea-7a40ebd47f30

Disclosure of personal information by various documents.

个人信息勿泄露，
安全意识存心头

The logistics form on the package contains the online shopper's name, telephone number, address and other information, which may be leaked if netizens inadvertently throw away the delivery form after receiving the goods.

Tickets, printed the name of the ticket buyers, ID number and other information, are easily discarded. Once they are found, personal information will be stolen.

Information such as name, bank card number and consumption record are recorded on the paper statement of shopping by swiping a card. Disposing it carelessly will also cause disclosure of private information.

预防小课堂

- Don't fill in real personal information when registering on small or unknown websites.
- Don't throw away the delivery form randomly, including the online shopper's name, telephone number, after receiving the goods.
- Don't connect unknown Wi-Fi in public places, especially unencrypted Wi-Fi hotspots.
- Don't disclose personal information when chatting with strangers.
- Don't be greedy for the cheapness of the street.

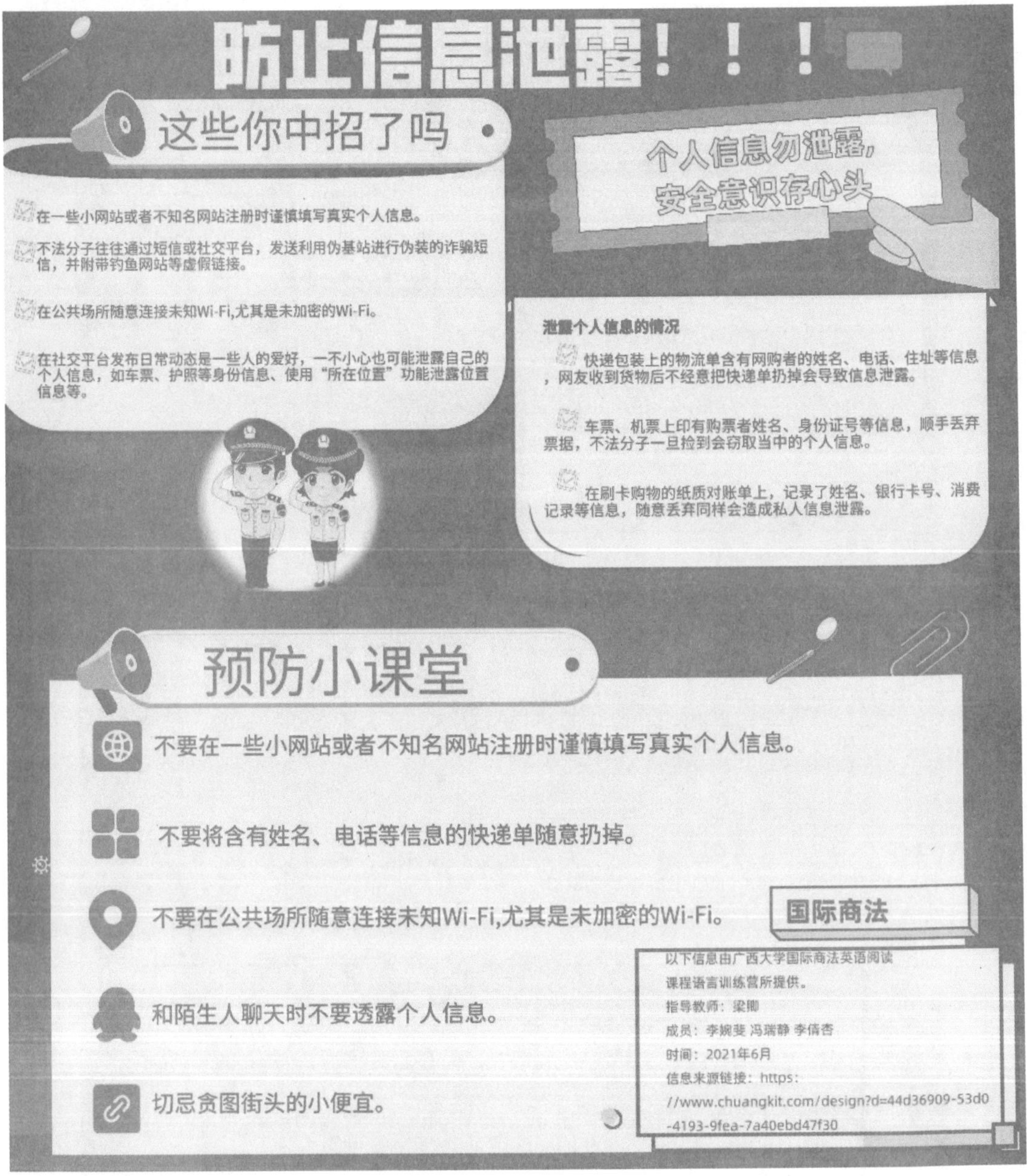
防止信息泄露！！！
这些你中招了吗
在一些小网站或者不知名网站注册时谨慎填写真实个人信息。
不法分子往往通过短信或社交平台，发送利用伪基站进行伪装的诈骗短信，并附带钓鱼网站等虚假链接。
在公共场所随意连接未知Wi-Fi,尤其是未加密的Wi-Fi。
在社交平台发布日常动态是一些人的爱好，一不小心也可能泄露自己的个人信息，如车票、护照等身份信息、使用“所在位置”功能泄露位置信息等。
个人信息勿泄露，
安全意识存心头
泄露个人信息的情况
快递包装上的物流单含有网购者的姓名、电话、住址等信息，网友收到货物后不经意把快递单扔掉会导致信息泄露。
车票、机票上印有购票者姓名、身份证号等信息，顺手丢弃票据，不法分子一旦捡到会窃取当中的个人信息。
在刷卡购物的纸质对账单上，记录了姓名、银行卡号、消费记录等信息，随意丢弃同样会造成私人信息泄露。
预防小课堂
不要在一些小网站或者不知名网站注册时谨慎填写真实个人信息。
不要将含有姓名、电话等信息的快递单随意扔掉。
不要在公共场所随意连接未知Wi-Fi,尤其是未加密的Wi-Fi。
和陌生人聊天时不要透露个人信息。
切忌贪图街头的小便宜。
国际商法
以下信息由广西大学国际商法英语阅读
课程语言训练营所提供。
指导教师：梁卿
成员：李婉斐 冯瑞静 李倩杏
时间：2021年6月
信息来源链接：https:
//www.chuangkit.com/design?d=44d36909-53d0
-4193-9fea-7a40ebd47f30

SAY NO TO INTERNET LOAN

对网络贷款坚决说"NO"

Learn about Internet loan and try to refuse it.

让我们一起了解网贷，远离非法贷款!

ESTABLISH A CORRET CONCEPT OF CONSUMPTION

以下信息是由广西大学国际商法英语阅读课程语言训练营所提供

成员:谭雅楠 蒋东晓　　指导老师: 梁卿

时间:2021 年6 月

随着互联网的普及，互联网正在逐步渗透到人们日常生活的各个方面。网上贷款也正在成为一种趋势，借助互联网的优势，可以足不出户的完成贷款申请的各项步骤。

With the popularity of the Internet, the Internet is gradually infiltrating into all aspects of people's daily lives. Online loans are also becoming a trend. With the advantage of the Internet, you can complete the steps of loan application without leaving home.

CURRENT SITUATION

现状

(1) In recent years, it is still difficult for SMEs to borrow under the conditions of the loosening of the credit market.
近年，中小企业借贷在国家放宽信贷市场的条件下仍然比较困难。

(2)Nowadays, young people are spending more and more money, but don't have the income to match it, so they are borrowing more and more online.
现代年轻人花销越来越高，却没有与之匹配的收入，所以在网上借贷的情况也越来越多。

(3) Illegal operation of online lending platforms.
网贷平台违法违规经营。

Reasons
原因

(1) The lack of regulatory system and the imperfection of relevant laws.
监管制度的缺失，以及相关法律的不完善。

(2) Nowadays, young people have a high consumption and a large number of overdraft consumption. Their income cannot support their consumption, so they can only choose online loan.当代年轻人消费较高，大量的透支消费，其收入无法支持他的消费，所以只能选择网贷。

(3) Borrowing money from friends will affect the relationship and give away personal privacy.
向朋友借钱会影响双方关系和泄露个人隐私。

(4) Online lending is relatively free, and the process is simple and fast.
网络借贷比较自由，流程简单、快捷。

Examples
事例

Female college students have been asked to borrow money through online lending platform Jiedaibao using nude photos of their ID cards as collateral. If they fail to repay the loans, they are threatened with publishing the photos to their family and friends.
校园贷曝出"裸条"借贷，女大学生通过网络借贷平台借贷宝，被要求"裸持"（以手持身份证的裸照为抵押）进行借款，逾期无法还款则被威胁公布裸照给家人朋友。

Zheng, a freshman, borrowed 10,000 yuan through a loan advertisement on campus, but the loan company asked him to repay 42,000 yuan six days late. When the loan failed, he swallowed two bottles of medicine in despair.
大一新生郑某通过校园内的借贷广告，借了一万块钱，结果晚还6天，借贷公司让其还4.2万元。还不上贷，他绝望之下吞下两瓶药。

Impact
影响

（1）It is easy to breed bad habit of borrowing and develop bad habit of high consumption. Carrying a heavy repayment burden, while violent dunning threatens personal safety.
易滋生借款恶习，养成高消费的不良习惯。身背沉重的还款负担，同时暴力催款威胁人身安全。

（2）Criminals use "usury loans" to carry out other criminal activities.
不法分子利用"高利贷"进行其它犯罪活动。

（3）Involving family members, once the borrower is unable to repay, the remaining debt is borne by his family.
连累家人，一旦借款人无力还款，剩余的债务就由其家人承担。

（4） Affect the interpersonal relationship of the borrower.
影响借款人的人际交往。

Recommendations
建议

（1）Choose a formal lending platform and a lending product from a formal financial institution in the country.
选择正规的借贷平台和国家正规金融机构的借贷产品。

（2）Pay attention to protecting personal privacy and personal information. Criminals will use the leaked information for telephone fraud and use various means to allow students to borrow.
注意保护个人隐私，个人信息。不法分子会利用泄露的信息进行电话诈骗，以各种手段让学生借贷。

（3）College students should establish a correct concept of consumption, not vanity, not comparison. If the living expenses are not enough, ask the parents for help in time.
大学生要树立正确的消费观，不虚荣不攀比。如果生活费不够，及时向家长求助。

（4）Strengthen the education of college students' basic financial knowledge, improve students' risk awareness, and cultivate students' "financial business". Only by mastering basic financial knowledge and eliminating ignorant borrowing psychology can college students borrow rationally and not be overwhelmed by temporary enjoyment.
加强对大学生基础金融知识的教育，提高学生风险意识，培养学生的"财商"。大学生只有掌握基本的金融知识、消除懵懂的借贷心理，才能理性借贷，不被一时的享乐冲昏头脑。

ATTENTION
THE INFORMATION
PRIVACY LEAKAGE
IS
KILLING
YOU

BACKGROUND 背景

The Civil Code has taken effect on January 1st, 2021.
Article 1032 of Chapter 6 of the Civil Code, "Privacy and Protection of Personal Information", "a natural person enjoys the right of privacy. No organization or individual could infringe upon other's right to privacy by means of spying, intrusion, disclosure, publishing or any other means."

2021年01月01日施行的民法典 ——：根据民法典第六章“隐私权和个人信息保护”的第一千零三十二条所述：“自然人享有隐私权。任何组织或者个人不得以刺探，侵扰，泄露，公开等方式侵害他人的隐私权。”

RISK OF PRIVACY LEAKAGE | 隐私泄露危害

1 Disorder in personal daily life 个人的日常生活受影响

① Spamming text messages or advertising emails keep swarming upon you;

② Receiving continuous harassing phone calls, being promoted products or even being cheated.

2 Personal financial loss 个人在经济层面上的损失

① Credit card fraud: without your knowledge or permission to transact a number of credit cards;

② Malicious overdraft consumption causes considerable financial losses;

3 Damage to private reputation 个人在名誉方面的受损

Being involved in certain illegal cases even crimes for no reason. For example, tax evasion of companies, traffic safety accidents and illegal online loans.

Legal Provisions:
法律条款
According to Article 1,033 of Chapter VI of the Civil Code, any organization or individual shall not carry out the following acts of privacy infringement unless otherwise provided by law or expressly agreed by the right holder: (1) Invading the tranquility of the private life of any other by phone calls, SMS, instant messaging tools, emails, leaflets, or any other means, etc.; And (6) Infringing upon the right of privacy of any other by other means.
根据民法典第六章的第一千零三十三条规定，隐私侵权行为，除法律另有规定或权利人明确同意外任何组织或者个人不得实施下列行为：第一点，以电话短信、即时通讯工具、电子邮箱、传单等方式侵扰他人的私人生活安宁，以及第六点，以其他方式侵害他人的隐私权。
Why will privacy infringement will occur?
1)Objective Factors: Criminals' variable means of fraud
2)Subjective Factors: Victims' s weakness of network security and a defensive psychology.

Tips for Protecting Private Information
保护隐私信息的技巧
1
Don‘t disclose personal information on social media apps.
在各类社交APP中切勿透露个人信息。
2
Be careful when shopping online.
网络购物要当心。
3
The purpose should be clearly stated on the copy of the ID card.
身份证复印件上要写明用途。
4
If you encounter criminals who leak privacy information, report the offence at once. 如果遇到不法分子泄露隐私信息请立刻举报。
5
If you encounter misfortune, please call the police in time, dial 110 or 12321 to report fraud. 若遭遇不幸，请及时报警，拨打报警电话110或拨打12321 诈进行骗举报。

Thank You for your attention
www
The Link to Image Source:
① 金山海报/创客贴:
wps.chuangkit.com/templatecenter
② Fotor 懒设计：www.fotor.com.cn/design/all-designs/
③ 搜狐网站:
m.sohu.com/a/460680900_120386998?strategyid=00014&qq-pf-to=pcqq.group
④百度：/image.baidu.com
⑤PicsArt Photo Studio Application 美易
（Android Version 安卓版）
制作单位：广西大学国际商法英语阅读课程语言训练营
指导老师：梁卿
小组成员：蒋佳镁 黄怡虹
甘美莎 李淼
2021年6月

What is Credit Card Fraud?

什么是信用卡诈骗？

Credit card fraud is the illegal possession for the purpose of using credit card to swindle people for large amount of property and belongings under circumstance of violating the credit card regulations.

Main Forms of Credit Card Fraud

信用卡诈骗的主要表现形式

1. Using forged credit card or obtaining a credit card by deception with a fake ID card. 使用伪造或骗领的信用卡的
2. Using canceled credit cards. 使用作废信用卡的
3. Illegal using other's credit cards as their own. 冒用他人信用卡的
4. Malicious overdraft. 恶意透支的

Common Schemes of Credit Card Fraud

常见套路

1. acting as a credit card agent 代办信用卡

2. increasing credit limit 信用卡提额

3. overdue credit card 信用卡逾期

Real case one

真实案例 1

On July 23,2019, living in Qingdao of Shandong province, Mr. Cheng reported to the police that: mobile phone received one text message, which shows that the credit card record is good to raise the amount. According to the other side of the operation, Mr. Cheng entered the website provided by the other side, filling in the personal name, ID card, card number, password, and verification code. Subsequently, the mobile phone received the bank card consumption information. Mr. Cheng dialed the construction bank customer service telephone consultation, the bank staff told the credit card had been stolen to brush, Mr. Cheng just knew to be cheated 9800 yuan.

- 广西大学国际商法英语阅读课程语言训练营
- 成员：刘雅淇（作者）
  庄张红（组长）
  王梅兰（组员）
  黄敏　（组员）
- 指导老师：梁卿
  2021 年 6 月

Real case one

真实案例 1

2019 年 6 月 23 日，家住山东青岛的程先生报警称：手机收到一条短信，上面显示信用卡记录良好可以提额，程某正有此意提高额度，就按照对方提示进行操作，进入对方提供的网址，填写个人姓名、身份证，卡号，密码，及验证码等。随后，手机收到银行卡消费信息，程某就拨打建行客服电话咨询，银行工作人员告知信用卡被盗刷了，程某才知道被骗了 9800 元。

How to Prevent

如何防范

1. We should apply for credit cards through regular channels. For example, it can be handled through the official channel of the bank branch or the online application channel authorized by the bank.
2. Cardholders should be alert to unfamiliar customer service calls and websites. Never give out your credit card password, ID card verification code and other key payment information to anyone.
3. Keep personal credit cards safe and don't give credit cards to others.

1. 通过正规渠道办理信用卡，可通过银行网点、官方渠道、银行授权的网申渠道办理。
2. 持卡人应对陌生客服来电，陌生网址链接保持警惕。切勿向任何人泄露自己的信用卡密码，身份验证码等关键支付信息。
3. 妥善保管信用卡，切勿将卡交给他人使用。

A REMINDER FROM GUANGXI UNIVERSITY
学校
校园欺凌
SAY NO TO SCHOOL BULLYING
制作单位：广西大学国际商法英语阅读课程语言训练营
成员：周广洪 韦新苗 许维银 周敏怡
指导老师：梁卿
时间：2021年6月

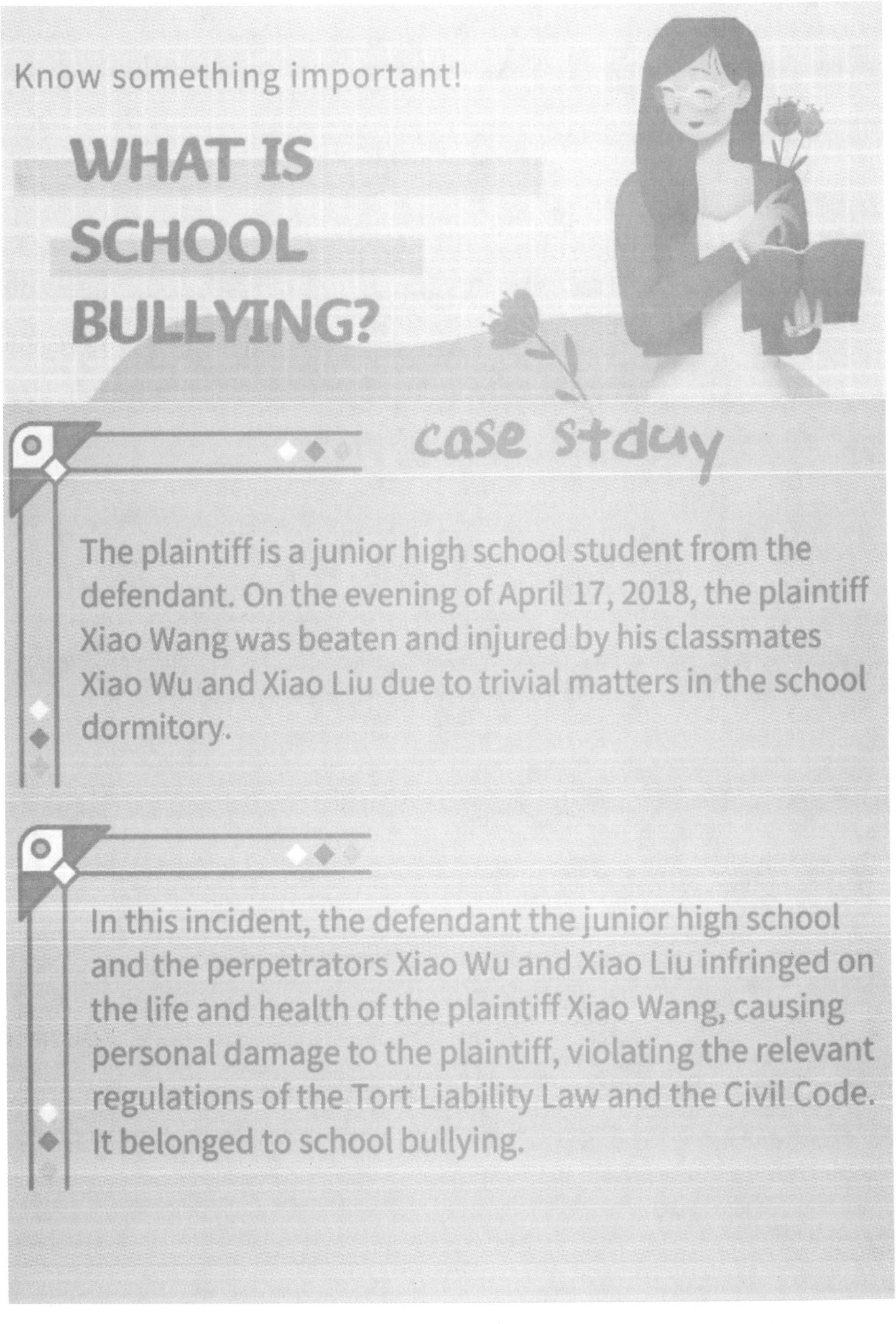
Know something important!
WHAT IS
SCHOOL
BULLYING?
case stduy
The plaintiff is a junior high school student from the defendant. On the evening of April 17, 2018, the plaintiff Xiao Wang was beaten and injured by his classmates Xiao Wu and Xiao Liu due to trivial matters in the school dormitory.
In this incident, the defendant the junior high school and the perpetrators Xiao Wu and Xiao Liu infringed on the life and health of the plaintiff Xiao Wang, causing personal damage to the plaintiff, violating the relevant regulations of the Tort Liability Law and the Civil Code. It belonged to school bullying.

Now let's learn something significant about school bullying.

Definition

In 2020, China's revised Law on the Protection of Minors held that student bullying occurs between students. one party intentionally or maliciously conducts bullying, insult through body, language and Internet, causing personal injury, property damage, or mental damage to the other party

Types

- Direct bullying: direct physical bullying, direct verbal bullying, etc
- Indirect bullying: relationship bullying, cyberbullying, etc

Key Elements

1 Subjective Will: Malicious, aggressive

2 Power Gap: Bullies > Victims

3 Bullying Nature: long-term, repetitive

School bullying and school violence

ESSENTIAL DIFFERENCES

Types / Differences	School Bullying	School Violence
Relation	One of the most common school violence	Including school bullying
Participant	Only campus personnel	Campus personnel and off-campus personnel
Victim	Students	Students or Teachers
Behavioral Nature	Continuity and recurrent	Occasional infringement

Reasons

Learn it and stop it

WHY DOES IT EXIST?

- The students lack of empathy and would like to bully the weak. This is often related to the family's excessive indulgence.
- The bullies' family members believe that violence can solve problems, which brought a very bad demonstration effect.
- Some schools do not pay enough attention to moral education and legal education.
- Some bad social habits have caused students to blindly follow.

HOW TO DRIVE AWAY SCHOOL BULLIES?

Government

First, local education departments should carry out work around the working mechanism, publicity and guidance, education and punishment, student bullying prevention and control and other aspects. For example, the Ministry of Education of the CPC Central Committee, the Ministry of Public Security and other ministries and commissions have issued many regulations on maintaining campus safety, such as the Office for Handling Student Injury Accidents, and the government has also strengthened the provisions on campus safety in the Compulsory Education Law and the Law on the Protection of Minors.

Second, local education departments should, in accordance with relevant policies and regulations and student campus safety education requirements, guide schools to further improve school rules and discipline, and improve the working mechanism of education and punishment.

Third, the state should standardize the bullying reporting system. Once all the teachers and staff of the school should take the initiative to stop the bullying, they should stop the students and report to the school in time.

Fourth, to improve students' awareness of protecting themselves with the law, local education departments and schools should strengthen the newly revised Law of the People's Republic of China on the Protection of Minors, the Law of the People' s Republic of China on Prevention of Juvenile Delinquency and other laws.

school

First, the schools should carry out special educational lectures with the theme of bullying management, and invite public security, justice and other relevant departments to the school to carry out legal education.

Second, the school should establish rules and regulations, formulate and improve the prevention and treatment systems and measures for school bullying, establish emergency response plans for school bullying, and clarify the responsibilities of teachers and staff in relevant posts to prevent and deal with school bullying.

Third, the school should establish a sound accountability system to accountable and educate students and teachers who intentionally conceal or turn a blind eye to school bullying, so as to create a good atmosphere for the whole school to supervise school bullying.

Fourth, the school should make full use of the psychological counseling room to carry out students' mental health counseling and counseling work, publish the telephone number of student assistance or school bullying treatment, and clarify the person in charge.

HOW TO DRIVE AWAY SCHOOL BULLIES?

Family

- **First,** if the parents find that the child's behavior has problems or clothes and bags are abnormal residual, to ask in time, do not turn a blind eye.
- **Second**, although violence is wrong to fight violence, parents must ensure that children are not bullied and let them establish confidence (according to the survey, 80% of the children bullied are weak and do not love to talk). The way to help children build confidence is to accompany their children to exercise and enhance the relationship between families. If the conditions allow, let the child participate in self - defense training, though physical role may not be small, but the psychological role is certainly not small.
- **Third,** parents need to communicate more with their teachers. Parents and teachers often communicate can not only to reduce or avoid bullying, but also understand their children's learning conditions and school performance.

Self-help

- **First,** do not tease the bully and strong companions, in the school does not take the initiative to conflict with the students, once the timely to find the teacher to solve.
- **Second,** study and activities with friends as soon as possible. When you go out alone to play with your friends, do not go to a quiet place with few people. Remember to go home on time
- **Third**, take the initiative to participate in self - defense training. For this we can greatly improve our self - dignity and reduce the possibility of him becoming a bully.
- **Fourth,** you can first loudly warn the bullies if you encounter school bullying. By doing so, the teachers and students around can pay attention to the behaviors of the offender. The offenders mostly know that their behavior is wrong, guilty. If the other side continues bullying, we should have appropriate self - defense, rather than endure being beaten.

参考答案

第一篇◎域外安全案例

第一章 社区安全案例

Passage 1

I.

1-3 C A B

II.

1.

① There is reasonable belief by law enforcement that an abduction has occurred.

② The law enforcement agency believes that the child is in imminent danger of serious bodily injury or death.

③ There is enough descriptive information about the victim and the abduction for law enforcement to issue an AMBER Alert to assist in the recovery of the child.

④ The abduction is of a child aged 17 years or younger.

⑤ The child's name and other critical data elements, including the Child Abduction flag, have been entered into the National Crime Information Center (NCIC) system.

2.

① Read it carefully.

② Keep an eye out for the abducted child, the suspect, or the suspect vehicle.

③ Call the police immediately if you see or hear anything relevant.

Translation

1. 奥尔顿警方联系了周围的执法机构，就孩子的失踪发布了安珀警报。

2. 一旦执法部门确定一名儿童被绑架，并且绑架案件符合安珀警报标准，执法部门就会通知广播公司和州交通官员。

3. 2003年通过的《保护法案》在司法部内确立了安珀警报协调员的角色，要求司法部发布各州可自愿采用的安珀警报最低标准或指导方针。

Passage 2

I.

1-5 T F F T T

II.

1. possessing; consuming; trafficking
2. 1.27 cm (0.5 inches); 1.2 m (3.9 feet)
3. singular punitive measure; jail sentence
4. male; 18~50 years old; in good health; not in death row
5. 24

Translation

1. Yuen 在保释期间因持有、吸食和贩卖毒品罪再次被捕。

2. 在17岁前往新加坡之前，Yuen 曾因涉嫌伪造驾驶证诈骗惹上麻烦。据报道，为了购买烟酒，他销售伪造驾驶证给其他学生。

3. 新加坡以最严格的执法和最严厉的刑罚全方位解决毒品问题，保护人民福祉和我们在一个安全绿色的国家中生活和养育下一代的共同心愿。

第二章　校园安全案例

Passage 1

Comprehension Check

1-5 F F F T F

6-10 F T F F F

Translation

1. 为进一步促进学生的学习与发展，促进大学的学术使命，斯坦福大学培养了一个注重个人和集体责任、崇尚谦恭的公民归属感的环境。

2. 本政策适用于斯坦福大学的所有校园和场所进行的活动，包括大学在校外批准或资助的所有项目和活动。

3. 根据加州法律和大学政策，21岁以下的任何人，在校园内任何公共或私人空间购买、持有或消费酒精都是违法的。

4. 该政策适用于任何本科生参加的学生团体或居住的住所。

Passage 2

Comprehension Check

1. sentenced
2. trail
3. unconditionally
4. defendant
5. impose
6. attorney
7. condemn
8. reassure
9. penalty
10. tremendously

Translation

1. 陪审团在死刑问题上未能达成一致的裁决，所以法官判了无期徒刑。

2. 她的失踪在中国引发了广泛关注，即时通信应用微信上建立了一些微信群，转发有关她案件的信息。

第三章　食品安全案例

Passage 1

Comprehension Check

1-5 T T F F T

Translation

1. DNA 遗传指纹是指利用全基因组测序技术（WGS）对从病人身上分离出来的沙门氏菌进行遗传指纹鉴定，该方法比其他任何分型方法都能提供更详细的 DNA 指纹图谱。

2. 有关当局正在对受影响的农场采取生物安全措施和其他监管行动。

3. 重要的是，并不是所有的鸡蛋都受到了影响，但如果您购买了被召回的鸡蛋，我们建议您将产品退回购买地点以获得全额退款，或者将鸡蛋扔进垃圾桶里，而不是直接丢弃到花园里。

Passage 2

Comprehension Check

1. compliance

2. consistent

3. randomly

4. transmitted

5. approach

6. supply chain

7. volume

8. inspection

9. premises

10. rectify

Translation

1. 这包括了食品供应过程中的控制措施，例如对高风险食品（如肉类、鸡蛋等）的海外来源进行认证、本地食品机构的许可、检查和测试。

2. 在检查过程中，我们会收集样本以确保食物符合我们的监管标准，其中包括微生物、杀虫剂、药物残留、防腐剂、污染物和添加剂的检测和监察。

3. 虽然病原体可以通过食物传播，但诸如诺如病毒等病毒也可以在人与人之间传播，或通过环境表面传播，特别是由于发生不当的个人卫生行为时。

第四章　旅行安全案例

Passage 1

Comprehension Check

1-5 T T T F T

Translation

1. 反诈骗行动机构，即（英国）国家欺诈和网络犯罪报告中心，在 2020–2021 财政年度收到假日和旅行相关欺诈报告 1907 起，与上一年度相比，下降 70% 以上。

2. 在最近政府宣布恢复国际旅行后，2021 年 5 月 17 日星期一，反诈骗行动机构发起全国性宣传活动，提醒公众预订假期时，在汇款和提供个人信息前要三思而后行。

3. 在骗取无辜人员理所应得的假期和血汗钱方面，犯罪分子会不择手段。

4. 犯罪分子诈骗手段越来越复杂，这就是为什么在预订假期和安排旅行时我们要尽力调查的原因。

5. 7% 的受害者报告他们成为嫌疑人的受害者。这些嫌疑人冒充合法旅游公司，其行为包括克隆比较网站、航空公司网站和度假住宿网站。

Passage 2

Comprehension Check

1-5 T T T T F

Translation

1. 如果在最后一刻取消，您可能会损失为该旅行支付的费用。购买旅行保险可以弥补这一点和其他意料之外的可能性，并帮助您挽回部分或全部损失。

2. 您必须告知保险公司投保前已存在的健康状况，否则，在后续的某些索赔中很难得到保险公司理赔。

3. 另一方面，如果您计划滑雪或爬山，请确保您的保单涵盖高危险运动，保费包括医疗运送计划，包括必要的航空运费。

4. 某些保单在您出发时间前开始生效。这样的保单可确保您不因原旅行计划改变受到损失。

5. 通常情况下，此类保单为每次旅行提供最多 90 天的保险，在保险期间不限制您的旅行次数。

第五章　网络安全案例

Passage 1

Comprehension Check

1-5 F F F T T

Translation

1. 面对联邦贸易委员会的指控，一款在线填色书应用的运营商将被要求告知现有的未成年用户的家长，并且给现有的未成年用户退款。该运营商在没有告知儿童用户的父母并征得他们同意的情况下，收集并披露了儿童用户的个人信息，此举违反了儿童隐私法。

2. 根据和解协议，若非得到父母的同意，上述公司须删除其收集的 13 岁以下的儿童用户的个人信息，且须给注册 Recolor 应用程序时年龄在 18 岁以下的现有付费用户退款。

Passage 2

Comprehension Check

1-5

1. **YES**. According to the bullying checklist, it meets the necessary criteria to be considered bullying (cyberbullying is bullying).

Application of the TxSSC's bullying checklist for schools:

- Multiple incidents of texting and social media posts make this a pattern of acts.
- The acts are between Taylor and Devin, making it from one student directed at another. These actions have created a situation where Taylor is stunned by other students at school, making it more than one individual directed at another. Since Devin comes from a wealthy family who hold high positions in the community, and Taylor does not, there is a difference in socioeconomic status. This exploits an imbalance of power. There also could be other imbalances of power that are not immediately apparent.
- Social media and texting are considered electronic means.
- These acts are creating an intimidating and abusive environment. Since other students are starting to shun Taylor at schools, it is disrupting the educational process and school operations.
- Social media and texting were used as electronic communication devices.
- These incidents are happening off of school property and outside of a school sponsored event or school-related activity.
- Since Taylor no longer wants to attend school, and both Taylor and Devin have to be separated at school, it is both interfering with Taylor's educational opportunities and disrupting orderly operations.

2. **NO**. According to the bullying checklist, it does not meet all the necessary criteria to be considered bullying. Specifically, it lacks exploiting an imbalance of power.

Application of the TxSSC's bullying checklist for schools:

- The trading of verbal taunts is a pattern of acts.
- Since both are exchanging verbal taunts, both are directing behavior toward each other.
- Jordan and Dakota are the same age, from the same neighborhood, and are both members of the baseball team. From this description, there does not appear to be an exploitation of an imbalance of power (even though there may be other imbalances of power unknown). Based on this information, the actions do not meet the legal definition of bullying.

3. **YES**. According to thc bullying checklist, it meets the necessary criteria to be considered bullying.

Application of the TxSSC's bullying checklist for schools:

- The behavior on the bus by Logan has occurred for several weeks, making it a pattern of acts.
- The behavior on the bus from Logan and the other students is directed at Cameron, making it from one or more students directed at another student. The fact that Cameron is shy and does not have many friends, and Logan is well-known and has many friends creates an imbalance of power. The number of students involved also creates an imbalance of power.
- The actions occurring on the bus, including throwing paper airplanes and making fun of Cameron represents both physical contact and verbal expression.
- These actions are physically harming Cameron and have created fear of harm at school. The actions are also persistent, which has created an intimidating, threatening, and abusive educational environment that disrupts the educational process (by missing several days at school).
- The actions occur on a bus used to transport students.

4. **NO**. While it does meet most of the criteria for being bullying, the action appeared to happen only once. Further, it did not happen on school grounds or at a school-sponsored activity. For actions to be considered bullying and under the school district's authority, cyberbullying is the only type of bullying that can happen off-campus where the school is required to intervene.

Application of the TxSSC's bullying checklist for schools:

- The action happened one time. As far as we know, this was an isolated incident and was not a pattern of acts.
- The action happened from Parker to Morgan, making it from one student directed at another. Parker is bigger than Morgan, which creates and imbalance of power.
- Parker pushed and dumped out Morgan's bag, making it a physical expression. Parker also teased Morgan, which could be considered verbal expression.
- The action of pushing Morgan down physically harmed her and could have reasonably put her in fear.
- It occurred off of school property and outside of a school sponsored event or related activity.

5. **YES**. According to the bullying checklist, it meets the necessary criteria to be considered bullying.

Application of the TxSSC's bullying checklist for schools:

- Stealing the basketball, and then posting on social media is a pattern of acts. The fact that is was shared over 50 times could also be considered when determining this as a pattern of acts.
- Incidents are between Jayden and Avery (one student directed at another). The action also turns into multiple students directed at one student following the sharing of the video by other classmates. Differences in classification and age between Jayden and Avery leads to exploiting an imbalance of power.
- Using Twitter to post the video is considered electronic means.
- These acts are creating an intimidating, threatening, and abusive environment. It is infringing on Avery's rights as a student. Since other students are starting to laugh at Avery in the halls, it is disrupting the educational process and school operations.
- Social media was used as an electronic communication device.
- These incidents are happening off of school property and outside of a school sponsored event or school-related activity.
- Since Avery has not been able to focus in class because of the laughing, it is both interfering with Avery's educational opportunities and disrupting orderly operations.

Translation

1. 离开学校以后，德文开始向瑞安发送有损泰勒形象的照片，并且在社交媒体上发帖"抨击"泰勒。

2. 尽管他们之间没有发生肢体上的冲突，但他们双方都用和其他朋友结盟的方式来"对着干"。

3. 那天晚上，艾弗里在推特上看到杰登发了一条艾弗里投篮没中的短视频，还写着"这就是打球太烂的样子"。

第六章　交易安全案例

Passage 1

Comprehension Check

1-5 T F F F T

Translation

1. 在一场前所未有的全球大流行期间，新冠疫情为骗子们变本加厉地坑骗消费者提供了契机。

2. 更重要的是，罗梅罗并没有通知客户有关发货延迟、取消订单或给予退款等信息。

3. 本案属于联邦贸易委员会努力处理“网上购物”欺诈的一部分，而这类诈骗极力地利用人们对个人防护用品及其他与疫情相关产品的高度需求。

Passage 2

Comprehension Check

Part I

1-5 F F T T T

Part II

1. facilitate

2. imposed

3. filed

4. violating

5. barred

6. bilked

7. concealed

8. suspended

Translation

1. 弗雷尔及其公司于 2019 年对联邦刑事指控认罪，且在 2020 年 11 月与联邦贸易委员会达成和解协议。

2. 据状词中所说，格林尼及其公司提交了一项支付处理申请，该项申请隐瞒了弗雷尔的欺诈行为；同时格林尼及其公司还否认弗雷尔及其公司向消费者提供被禁的债务减免服务，且无视对弗雷尔有关欺骗消费者和违反电话营销规则的犯罪行为的反复警告和直接证据。

3. 拟议的终审裁定还对格林尼及其公司施加 2860 万美元的罚款，这项裁定由于无法全额支付，在实现 20493 美元的赔付后，将会部分暂停执行。

第二篇◎民法典案例

第七章　平等原则案例

Passage 1

Short Answer Questions

1. Any signs, including words, graphs, letters, numerals, three-dimensional symbols, color combinations, sound or any combination thereof.

2. A trademark submitted for registration shall bear noticeable characteristics and be readily distinguishable, and it may not conflict with the legitimate rights obtained by others earlier.

3. A natural person enjoys the right to name and is entitled to determine, use, change, or allow others to use his name in accordance with law, provided that public order and good morals are not offended.

No organization or individual may infringe upon other's rights to name or rights to entity name by means such as interference, misappropriation, impersonation, or the like.

Translation

1. 任何能够将自然人、法人或者其他组织的商品与他人的商品区别开的标志，包括文字、图形、字母、数字、三维标志、颜色组合和声音等，以及上述要素的组合，均可以作为商标申请注册。

2. 该行为利用他人声誉谋取私利，不仅损害了奥运健儿的权益，而且给社会带来了负面影响。

3. 据称，国家知识产权局将加强打击恶意抢注商标的行为，保护良好的营商环境；另外，使用不当手段申请商标注册的申请人或机构将受到依法惩处。

4. 自然人享有姓名权，有权依法决定、使用、变更或者许可他人使用自己的姓名，但是不得违背公序良俗。

5. 任何组织或者个人不得以干涉、盗用、假冒等方式侵害他人的姓名权或者名称权。

Passage 2

T or F

1-5 T F T F T

Translation

1. 周日，中国网络安全审查办公室表示，检测到网约车巨头“嘟嘟出行”App 涉嫌非法收集用户个人信息，已通知各应用商店下架该软件。

2. 嘟嘟回应称，已暂停新用户注册，并将按规定下架整改，切实保障用户权益。

3. 该公司补充说，它将提高技术能力，以保护用户的个人信息和数据，保护用户免受互联网安全风险，并继续提供安全、方便的服务。

4. 嘟嘟在其 IPO 招股说明书中标明了中国相关法律法规，并表示："我们严格遵守数据安全和隐私政策，严格按程序进行用户数据的收集、传输、存储和使用。"

5. 嘟嘟出行中国版上的一则公告显示，该软件已于 6 月 29 日，即上市前一天更新了用户信息和数据隐私政策。嘟嘟在其代驾业务的应用程序上增加了两项新服务，并在给路透社的声明中称，此举是"定期更新"。

第八章　自愿原则案例

Passage 1

1. fainted
2. allay
3. violation
4. adage
5. has hailed
6. deed
7. ruled
8. pulse (get your finger on the pulse 紧跟潮流)
9. netizen
10. stipulated

Translation

1. 沈阳市中级人民法院最近裁定，对于好心的药店老板给老人做心肺复苏术时意外致使老人肋骨骨折一案，药店老板不须承担责任。

2. 这一及时的行动救了齐女士的命，但却压断了 12 根肋骨。为此，她将孙某告上了法庭，要求孙某赔偿她的医疗费。

3. 对孙某的诉讼让许多人认为，俗话说得好，善举难免受罚。难怪许多人不愿帮助那些陷入困境的人，因为害怕这会给自己招致麻烦。

4. 在咨询了医学专家后，法院裁定药店老板的做法没有违反医疗规则，他不需承担任何责任。

5. 2017 年 3 月 15 日，中国最高立法机关全国人民代表大会通过的《民法通则》第一百八十四条规定，因自愿实施紧急救助行为造成受助人损害的，救助人不承担民事责任。

Passage 2

T or F

1-5 F T T F F

Translation

1. 据一家报纸报道，中国东部的一名离婚妇女花了六年时间反对法院判决，该判决称她有责任偿还前夫在婚姻期间所借的超过 2000 万元（310 万美元）的债务。

2. 据《江强晚报》报道，这对夫妇于 2012 年离婚，但她收到了浙江杭州法院的传票，此前她和她的前夫被五个不同的团体起诉，声称前夫欠他们钱。

3. 在杭州，包括这位女士在内的大约 100 名离婚妇女，她们在社交媒体应用微信上组建了聊天群，以发泄她们在偿还前夫所欠债务时的沮丧感。

4. 最高人民法院在一月份发布规定，婚姻中的一方无须偿还另一方在婚姻存续期间所借的债务，但债权人能够证明该债务用于夫妻共同生活、共同生产经营或者基于夫妻双方共同意思表示的除外。

5. 据该报报道，杭州的另一名离婚妇女成功上诉，法院裁定她的前夫对他们婚姻存续期间所借的 100 万元人民币承担全部责任。

第九章　公平原则案例

Passage 1

Comprehension Check

1. discarding

2. hygiene

3. Municipal

4. complaints

5. infringe

6. speculation

7. smuggle

8. overturn

9. pending

10. verdict

Translation

1. 华东政法大学一名大三学生小王说她在进入园区之前被保安告知，需将背包中携带的零食丢弃或吃掉，这些零食共计 46.30 元。

2. 据报道，自 2017 年 11 月以来，上海 Dey 度假区已禁止外带超过 600 毫升的户外食品、酒精和非酒精饮料。

3. 自 1 月下旬参观公园以来，小王同学一直在向市政府公共热线和监察机构投诉。

4. 她要求取消公园的禁令，并要求公园赔偿46.30元的损失。此案于4月23日开庭审理，目前在等待判决。

5. 尽管上海 Dey 声称食品禁令是出于卫生原因，但这并没有阻止中国网民猜测 Dey 在亚洲实施双重标准，迫使游客购买他们的食品。

Passage 2

T or F

1-5 F T T F T

Translation

1. 据《上海法治报》报道，学生组队将 A 公司告上法庭。此案在北京互联网法院电子诉讼平台审理。学生们指控，他们无法像 A 公司网站上所宣传的那样为 Phone 12 和 12 Pro Max 手机充电，并且其产品连接电源适配器一侧，始终是 USB–A 接口，与市场上大多数第三方充电器不兼容。

2. 此案呈递于本月一场公益诉讼比赛当中。

3. 张律师说，消费者可以直接与 A 公司谈判，或通过消费者协会进行调查和调解，或起诉申请退货。

4. 一些人说，他们在升级到 Phone 12 时被迫购买新的充电器和适配器，但其他人担心，如果要求 A 公司免费提供适配器，A 公司会将成本转嫁给消费者。

5. 欧盟提议，通过立法要求 USB–C 成为所有智能手机的标准充电端口，以减少浪费，保护消费者利益。A 公司警告称，此举可能会扼杀创新。

第十章　诚信原则案例

Passage 1

Comprehension Check

1. clarify

2. enormously

3. plaintiff's

4. market order

5. constitute

6. held

7. norms

8. benign

9. compensate

10. disrupt

Translation

1. 本案明确：利用网络爬虫技术盗用大数据资源用于经营同类业务的，构成不正当竞争。

2. G 公司将 Y 公司及相关责任人诉至法院，称其上述行为违背了商业道德和诚实信用原则，构成不正当竞争。

3. 法院在本案中认定，原告 G 公司权利人经过收集、分析、编辑、整合所合法拥有的、具有商业价值的大数据资源，应当受到相关法律保护。

4. 被告 Y 公司具有破坏他人市场竞争优势、谋取竞争优势的主观故意，属于严重破坏市场秩序的行为，构成不正当竞争。

5. 深圳市中级人民法院于 2018 年 5 月 23 日做出民事判决，判令被告 Y 公司向原告 G 公司赔偿经济损失及合理维权费用 50 万元。

Passage 2

T or F

1-5 T F F T T

Translation

1. 梁某某是一家提供中文字幕盗版电影网站的创始人。周一，上海第三中级人民法院以侵犯著作权罪判处被告人梁某某有期徒刑三年六个月，并处罚人民币一百五十万元人民币（合计 23.5 万美元）。

2. 法院还追缴违法所得，并没收了其用于犯罪行为的资金和工具。

3. 这些影视作品未经授权和传播许可便上传至公司网站及客户端，供客户在线观看和下载。

4. 法院审理认为，被告人梁某某行为属于特别严重情节，已构成侵犯著作权罪，但因其如实供述罪行并予以配合，故从轻处罚。

5. 保护知识产权将有助于鼓励更多新创造和新发明，而且社会也应该通过合法和适当的方式促进智力创造的传播。

6. 郑某是上海 Y 律师事务所专门从事知识产权保护的律师。他表示同意法院的判决，因为通过从网上分享未经授权的电影来牟利的行为是非法的，这类似于 21 世纪初销售盗版数字影碟的犯罪行为。

第十一章　守法和公序良俗原则案例

Passage 1

Comprehension Check

1. unveil
2. spark
3. adhere to
4. approved
5. Venue
6. assume
7. regulations
8. stipulates

Translation

1. 根据周二上海市人大常委会通过的《上海市公共文化服务保障与促进条例》，跳广场舞的群众应当遵守相关规定和公序良俗，不得影响他人的正常工作和生活。

2. 条例自明年初起正式实施，其中要求，活动举办地所在乡镇人民政府、街道办事处以及公共场所管理单位应加强组织协调，保障活动有序开展。

Passage 2

Comprehension Check

1-5 T F T F T

Translation

1. 根据山东省青岛市城阳区人民法院的裁决，被告需赔偿原告江女士各项经济损失 49.6 万元及失去爱女 JG 的精神损害抚慰金 20 万元，并承担案件相关费用。

2. 案发当天早些时候，刘与陈发生过争吵。随后，陈某某带着一把刀埋伏于公寓楼里，等待着刘某某与 JG 晚上回到公寓。

3. 本周一，法院审理表示，被告刘某某没有告知舍友 JG 陈某某的潜在危险性，而陈

参考文献

［1］Bryan A. Garner. Black's Law Dictionary [M]. New York: Thomson Reuters,2019.

［2］姜栋，王雪梅．英文法律报刊文章选读 [M]．北京：中国人民大学出版社，2009．

［3］全国人大常委会法制工作委员会. 中华人民共和国民法典: 汉英双语版 [M]. 北京: 法律出版社，2021．

［4］周雅荣．美国法律辞典：汉英双解 [M]．上海：文汇出版社，2016．